The
Reference Shelf®

Aging in America

The Reference Shelf
Volume 86 • Number 1
H. W. Wilson
A Division of EBSCO Information Services
Ipswich, Massachusetts
2014

GREY HOUSE PUBLISHING

The Reference Shelf

The books in this series contain reprints of articles, excerpts from books, addresses on current issues, and studies of social trends in the United States and other countries. There are six separately bound numbers in each volume, all of which are usually published in the same calendar year. Numbers one through five are each devoted to a single subject, providing background information and discussion from various points of view and concluding with an index and comprehensive bibliography that lists books, pamphlets, and articles on the subject. The final number of each volume is a collection of recent speeches. Books in the series may be purchased individually or on subscription.

Library of Congress Cataloging-in-Publication Data

Aging in America / [compiled by H. W. Wilson].
  pages : illustrations ; cm. -- (The reference shelf ; volume 86, number 1)
  Includes bibliographical references and index.
  ISBN: 978-1-61925-432-9 (v. 86, no. 1)
  1. Older people--United States. 2. Older people--Care--United States. 3. Older people--Care--Economic aspects--United States. 4. Aging--Social aspects--United States. 5. Aging--Economic aspects--United States. 6. Baby boom generation--United States. I. H.W. Wilson Company. II. Series: Reference shelf ; v. 86, no. 1.
HQ1064.U5 A63399 2014
305.26/0973

Cover: © Ulrich Baumgarten/Getty Images

The Reference Shelf, 2014, published by Grey House Publishing, Inc., Amenia, NY, under exclusive license from EBSCO Information Services, Inc.

Printed in the United States of America

Contents

3

Caring for Elder Parents

4

Redefining the Senior Years

5

How Living Longer Is Advancing Medicine and Health Care

6

An Aging World Population

Preface

Aging in America

In the past several decades, sociologists, medical professionals, and economists in the United States have been warning of a coming "age crisis," because the number and proportion of older Americans in the population will soon reach unprecedented levels. This demographic shift is the result of both the fact that Americans are living longer thanks to improvements in medical care, nutrition, and technology, and the fact that the baby boomers—one of the largest demographic groups of the American population—have begun reaching retirement age. The effects of this shift might not seem readily apparent, but aging in America has the potential to dramatically alter American society and poses serious economic and social problems for the country as a whole.

The Baby Boomer Generation

The baby boom refers to the massive increase in births that followed the end of World War II and continued for more than twenty years; the baby boom generation is the subset of the global population that resulted from this proliferative period. In the years surrounding the Great Depression and World War II, birth rates decreased around the world as young people delayed marriage and married couples delayed having children, responding to the potential uncertainty of the future. In 1946, after the end of World War II, the economic environment in America improved drastically and many Americans felt they were returning to an age of prosperity and potential. This and other factors converged to create a generation of family-oriented Americans that was unprecedented in history.

Within a year of the war, the birth rate increased by more than 20 percent and remained high until the mid-1960s. Demographers estimate that there were between 77 and 79 million Americans born during this period, constituting the largest swell of the American population in history. Over subsequent decades, the sheer size of the baby boomer generation translated into massive economic and social changes across the nation. For instance, when the baby boomers were still babies (in the 1940s and 1950s), the baby food and diaper industries expanded by more than 70 percent; when they were school-age children (in the 1950s and 1960s) new schools, day care centers, and colleges sprung up across the country. As the baby boomers reached adulthood in the 1970s and 1980s, suburban expansion accelerated and the demand for housing and homes led to one of the biggest housing booms in recent history.

In 2011, the first wave of the baby boomers began reaching age sixty-five, the retirement age in many states. According to the Pew Research Center, each day for the next twenty years, approximately ten thousand Americans will reach retirement age; by 2030 more than 72 million Americans, roughly 20 percent of the population, will be sixty-five or older. Some journalists have referred to this demographic phenomenon as the "silver tsunami," referring to the way that the population bump of the baby boomer generation has moved through American history.

Health Care and Extended Care

On average, Americans are now living longer due to better nutrition, major advances in preventative health care, and an overall shift in health orientation within the population. The average life expectancy has increased from sixty-three to sixty-five years in 1940, to seventy-eight years in 2010, and experts believe life expectancies will continue to increase.

The aging population of the twenty-first century is far different than it was in past eras. Older Americans are more active and productive, remaining in the work-force longer and wanting to remain independent and socially active into their later years. As the baby boomers move into their retirement years, the needs of the elderly are likely to become a much more visible issue in many areas of American life.

While the older population is healthier than in times past, the elderly still suffer from higher levels of acute and chronic illnesses, such as Alzheimer's disease and osteoporosis, and other health issues. In a 1996 article in *JAMA*, researchers found that the cost of health carefor a person older than sixty-five is, on average, three to five times higher than for someone under sixty-five. By the year 2030, America will experience at least a 25 percent increase in health care spending as a result of caring for the increasing elderly population. Just as the baby boomer generation strained the nation's available child care facilities in the 1940s and school system in the 1950s and 1960s, in the coming decades the age wave will strain available extended care facilities, retirement living facilities, and the geriatric medical care industry as a whole.

The cost of caring for a larger elderly population will fall on elderly individuals and their families, but there is also significant concern that increasing demand could destabilize state and federal medical assistance programs. The Kaiser Foundation estimates that, in the worst-case scenario, spending on programs like Medicare will increase from over $550 billion in 2011 to more than $900 billion over the period from 2014 to 2023. Several different studies indicated that the hospital coverage portion of the Medicare allotment would be exhausted by 2024, and projections like this have become a major political issue with Democrats and Republicans debating the pros and cons of cuts to Medicare benefits. Changes to the Medicare system, including the Medicare Advantage program, contributed to a reduction in medical costs in 2012 and 2013, and further legislation within the federal government is intended to address this issue further in coming years.

A related set of problems results from baby boomers having fewer children and being more likely to get divorced than the previous generation. This means that elderly baby boomers are more likely to live alone and have fewer children to help provide extended care. Organizations like the American Association for Retired Persons (AARP) argue that family caregivers have always been the core of the extended care network of American society, and some studies have shown that it would cost more than $380 to 400 billion to replace the care given by family members with paid alternatives. Individuals who choose to devote time and resources to caring for parents and family members often suffer from reduced income and productivity, and this makes it difficult to balance caring for one's parents with the need to meet present financial burdens while simultaneously providing for one's own eventual retirement. The AARP is lobbying for increased federal and state benefits for family caregivers and also encourages corporations to begin recognizing the need to provide flexible schedules and other benefits to employees who provide care for the elderly.

Social Security and Economic Growth

One of the key threats of the age crisis is that mass waves of retirement may cause economic stagnation and reduced growth, and could translate into major problems within key industries. In a 2013 article in *Governing,* journalist Mike Maciag discussed how the retirement boom could have a devastating effect on key government industries. Increased education and other factors have reduced general interest in government employment across the board, which includes the US Postal Service, correctional institutions, and many other essential service industries. As a result, public employees are older, on average, than employees in the private sector and this means that public services will experience the threat of the retirement boom before many other industries. To give one example, in June 2013, more than 40 percent of correctional officers for the Connecticut Department of Corrections were eligible for retirement, while recruitment in this industry has reached an all-time low.

As the post-retirement-age population continues to grow, the retirement crisis will begin to hit other industries as well. Companies that may have experienced one to three retirements per year may stand to lose double this amount in the same period of time. Many companies will likely have difficulty attracting sufficient new employees to compensate and some estimates indicate that economic growth in many industries may be reduced by 5–10 percent or more.

The problem of providing employer- and state-sponsored pension benefits and Social Security benefits to the baby boomer generation poses another significant threat to the American economy. Some economists have predicted that the Social Security system will collapse under the strain as the proportion of individuals paying taxes into the system decreases and the proportion of individuals drawing Social Security benefits increases. Similar problems may result from the fact that larger numbers of retirees will put a strain on federally sponsored and private pensions programs. As demand increases, government agencies are debating potential and often-controversial programs to cut Social Security benefits, while an increasing number of employers have been discontinuing or restructuring pension plans, often to the detriment of retirees. Given that most retired persons live on annual incomes of less than $30,000, any reduction in benefits could be devastating to the well-being of America's retired population. In addition, the strain of providing for the baby boomer wave might, according to some sources, drastically reduce available benefits for the next generation reaching retirement.

The increased health and longevity of retired persons poses additional economic and sociological challenges. Individuals, for example, will be drawing on retirement benefits for a longer period, thus extending the burden on both taxpayers and on personal retirement savings. An increasing number of older individuals are choosing to remain in the workforce for longer periods, in the hopes of saving additional money for retirement or postponing the need to draw on retirement benefits. Mandatory retirement policies in many industries will increasingly come under scrutiny because the healthier and more active retirees of the future may increasingly object to being forced to retire when they might still be able to be productive. This applies mainly to older individuals and couples that might have difficulty living on Social Security and pension benefits.

Industries are being forced to adjust to conditions where a larger proportion of their employees may begin reaching an age where they require specific aids and services to remain productive. Older employees sometimes require assistance in adjusting to technological advances, and providing training programs and technology assistance is an increasingly pressing issue in many industries. In other situations, corporations may find that older employees need to schedule their work in different ways or to work during different hours than younger employees.

In a similar way that the baby boomer generation stimulated growth in the baby care, housing, and education markets, the American economy will also grow in new ways as the baby boomers come into retirement. There will likely be increasing demands for products, services, and facilities geared toward the needs of older individuals; therefore, industries previously focused on younger consumers may find that their target audience is becoming older. Just as the aging population causes economic strain and stagnation in some areas, economic growth is also typically a factor in demographic shifts, and the broader implications of this facet of American development are only beginning to be understood.

Addressing a Complex Issue

The aging crisis in America presents a host of complex issues that require innovative strategies and solutions. America is not the only nation dealing with the issue, however; China, Australia, and the United Kingdom are also experiencing similar demographic trends. Ultimately, a combination of efforts will be needed, drawing upon innovation from the private sector and socially conscious policies from the public sector to address these issues, both for the good of the aging population and the next generation that follows in their wake.

1

Health and Aging by the Numbers

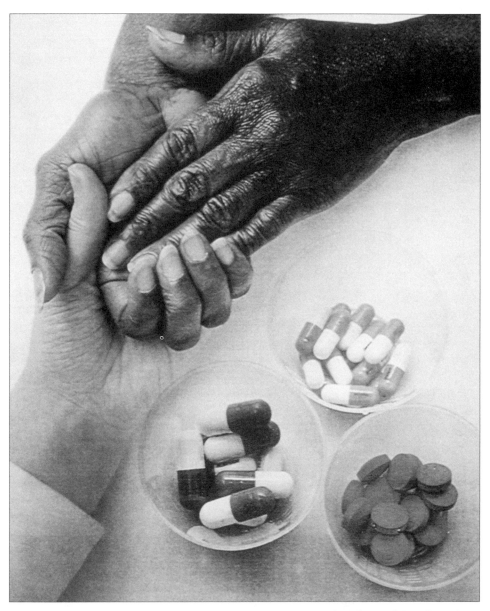

Statistics, Costs, and Outlooks

The baby boomer generation is the nickname given to the large number of Americans born between 1946 and 1964. As the oldest baby boomers reached age sixty-five in 2011, health professionals and policy makers expressed concern as to whether the United States was prepared to handle the largest population of older individuals in its history.

In 2010, about 13 percent of the US population (forty million people) was sixty-five years old and over. But by 2030, when the last of the baby boomers reaches age sixty-five, nearly 20 percent of the population (seventy-two million people) will be age sixty-five and over. Additionally, the US Census Bureau predicts that the number of people eighty-five and older could grow from 5.5 million in 2010 to as high as 19 million by 2050, approximately one-fifth of the total population.

This demographic shift presents many challenges, as an increasing number of older Americans face health and economic concerns with fewer younger Americans to provide care and support. Increased life expectancy may lead to more people living longer with chronic health conditions and functional limitations; therefore, the lack of available caregivers and the financial burden on the Medicare system must be addressed. Americans should also adopt healthy diets, engage in physical activity, and seek preventative care to preserve their good health.

Life Expectancy and Chronic Health Conditions

Average life expectancy has increased significantly over the past few generations. An individual who reached age sixty-five in 1960 could expect to live another 14 years; by contrast, someone who reached sixty-five in 2009 could expect to live another 19.2 years. Increased longevity may, however, bring more chronic health conditions such as heart disease, diabetes, and respiratory problems. Medical advancements also mean that people are living longer with these conditions, which increase treatment costs and raise issues such as quality of life.

The rate of particular chronic health conditions varies by gender, race, and ethnicity. In general, women reported more asthma, arthritis, and hypertension than men. Men reported more heart disease, cancer, and diabetes than women. Overall, the rate of diabetes increased for all races, genders, and ethnicities, from 13 percent in 1997–98 to almost 21 percent in 2009–10. Non-Hispanic African Americans reported higher levels of hypertension and diabetes than non-Hispanic whites (69 percent versus 54 percent for hypertension, and 32 percent versus 18 percent for diabetes), while Hispanics reported higher levels of diabetes than non-Hispanic whites (33 percent versus 18 percent), but lower levels of arthritis (44 percent versus 53 percent). These differences demonstrate that there is no single solution to the chronic health issues facing the aging population. The changing gender, racial, and ethnic composition of the US population may impact age-related health care in the coming years, and must be taken into consideration.

Functional Limitations

Functional limitations describe how individuals struggle with basic household tasks, and as people enter old age they become more likely to have one or more functional limitations. In 2009, for example, about 41 percent of older people enrolled in Medicare reported some functional limitation. About 12 percent reported at least one instrumental activities of daily living (IADL) limitation, which include using the telephone, light or heavy housework, meal preparation, shopping, or managing money. About 25 percent reported limitations with at least one activities of daily living (ADL) limitation, which include bathing, dressing, eating, getting into or out of a chair, walking, or using the toilet.

Functional limitations are physically and emotionally challenging, and they can be expensive to work around. Home care assistance might allow individuals to continue living independently within their communities, and the cost may be covered by Medicare. About 4 percent of older Americans live in long-term care facilities due to functional limitations, and Medicare does not cover the cost of this service.

Overall, the percentage of individuals reporting functional limitations decreased from 49 percent in 1992 to 41 percent in 2009. However, because the actual number of older Americans is expected to increase so dramatically over the next two decades, health care experts still worry there could be a lack of trained personnel to provide the necessary assistance. This concern grows as the baby boomers' children grow older and struggle with limitations of their own.

Many older Americans also experience hearing and vision problems. For example, 46 percent of older men and 31 percent of older women reported trouble hearing, while about 11 percent of women and 18 percent of men reported having worn a hearing aid. Vision problems affected about 13 percent of men and 15 percent of women. These problems can decrease quality of life, and while they are often correctable, assistive devices such as hearing aids can be prohibitively expensive for many people.

Health Insurance and Medicare

Most Americans age sixty-five and older have health insurance through the federal government's Medicare program. These plans operate similarly to private insurance policies: the beneficiary pays a premium, and in return the policy covers services such as hospital stays and physician visits. Most Medicare plans require beneficiaries to pay up to half of the cost themselves. Medicare generally does not cover long-term nursing home care or dental care, and mostly did not cover prescription drugs until the Medicare Part D program began in January 2006.

Many Medicare beneficiaries require supplemental insurance to pay for services that are not covered. Some have used policies provided by a former employer, while others purchase insurance themselves on the private market, but around 9 percent do not have supplemental insurance at all. Low-income individuals, including about 12 percent of older Americans, receive supplemental coverage through the federal government's Medicaid program.

The reliance of so many Americans on health care funded by the federal government presents a significant issue of its own—the available care is dependent upon the available funds. The number of home health care visits has varied significantly during the past twenty years due to policy changes. Between 1992 and 1996, for example, they increased from 3,822 to 8,376 per 1,000 enrollees, following an expansion of coverage for this benefit. However, visits declined to 2,295 by 2001, due to the Balanced Budget Act of 1997. As the baby boomer population joins the Medicare system, the large number of new beneficiaries may place additional burdens on a system that is already strained.

Health Care Costs and Out of Pocket Expenses

The average annual health care costs for older Americans on Medicare increased from $9,850 in 1992 to $15,709 in 2008. These costs varied by race, ethnicity, and income, and were significantly higher for those with chronic health conditions or residing in long-term care facilities. Average prescription drug costs also skyrocketed during this period, from $700 to $2,834 annually. Those without a chronic illness, however, paid an annual average of $1,230 for prescription drugs, whereas those with five or more chronic conditions paid an average of $5,300.

Since Medicare only pays part of the costs, older Americans must find a way to cover the shortfall. Even with supplemental insurance coverage, most pay at least some out-of-pocket expenses. Access to timely health care is important to manage chronic health conditions, and affordability is important to maintain the health of the aging population. Since 1997, the percentage of older Americans who reported delaying health care due to cost has remained at approximately 5 percent, while around 2–3 percent reported difficulty obtaining care.

Unfortunately, older Americans continue to spend more and more of their household income on health care services. Medicare paid for about 60 percent of health care costs for its enrollees age sixty-five and older in 2008, but enrollees paid about 18 percent of their costs out-of-pocket (not including supplemental insurance premiums, which can be significant). Medicaid covered approximately 7 percent, and other payers (mostly private insurance policies) covered approximately 15 percent. If out-of-pocket costs continue to grow, the increased financial burden could lead more people to delay the care they need to manage chronic conditions, which in turn could require more invasive and expensive interventions later on.

The potential need for long-term care presents another significant financial problem. The majority of older Americans rely on Medicare as their primary insurance, but Medicare does not cover the largest part of long-term nursing home care. As a result, in 2009, about 41 percent of these costs were paid out-of-pocket, while 52 percent were covered by Medicaid. The average nursing home costs upwards of $6,000 per month, and the average stay is around two and a half years. As more people require residential care for longer periods of time, the significant cost burden will either fall on the individual or the federal Medicaid program. Given the enormous cost of such care, neither option seems sustainable in the long term.

Preventative Care

To control costs and preserve good health as long as possible, health care professionals encourage older Americans to pursue preventative care and healthy lifestyles. For example, flu and pneumonia are among the leading causes of hospitalization and death for Americans aged sixty-five and over. For this reason, physicians recommend vaccinations. In 2010, 63 percent of older Americans reported receiving a flu shot within the past twelve months, while 60 percent reported receiving a pneumonia shot.

Preventative screenings such as mammograms are also on the rise. The percentage of women aged sixty-five and over who had a mammogram within the preceding two years nearly tripled between 1987 and 2010, from 23 percent to 64 percent. However, significant differences in preventative care still exist based on socioeconomic status. In 2010, for example, about 51 percent of older women living below the poverty line reported having a mammogram within the previous two years, compared with 75 percent of older women with incomes above 400 percent of the poverty threshold. This suggests that those who are least able to afford proper treatment are also least likely to catch such an illness at its early stages.

Healthy Lifestyles

Obesity is a growing public health issue in the United States. The connection between obesity and chronic health problems such as type 2 diabetes, osteoarthritis, and hypertension raises concern about the potential impact on health care costs. The percentage of obese Americans aged sixty-five and over increased from 22 percent in 1988–94 to 38 percent in 2009–10, with individuals age sixty-five to seventy-four more likely to be obese than those age seventy-five and over. There is a gender difference as well: women were slightly more likely to be obese than men. Between 1999 and 2010, however, there was a significant increase in obesity percentage for men, but not for women.

Studies also suggest that poor diet may cause or exacerbate chronic conditions such as cardiovascular disease, hypertension, type 2 diabetes, osteoporosis, and some types of cancer. In 2005, the US Department of Agriculture (USDA) and the US Department of Health and Human Services (HHS) developed the *Dietary Guidelines for Americans* to establish standards for a healthy diet. In 2007, the average older American fared well for whole fruit, total grains, meat, and beans, but fell short in other categories such as total fruit and whole grains. Under the USDA standards, older Americans also tended to consume too much sodium, as well as too many calories from solid fats, alcoholic beverages, and added sugars. Adopting better dietary habits could reduce the frequency and severity of some chronic conditions, thus reducing health care costs and improving quality of life.

Additionally, physical activity plays an important role in maintaining good health. Studies suggest that even a moderate amount of regular physical activity can reduce the risks of some chronic illnesses, relieve symptoms of depression, and reduce functional limitations, thereby helping older individuals maintain independent living. The US Department of Health and Human Services establishes guidelines for aerobic and muscle-strengthening activities for Americans. In 2010, about 11 percent of individuals aged sixty-five and over reported engaging in activities that met these guidelines, an increase of 6 percent from 1998. Men were more likely to meet the guidelines (14 percent) than women (8 percent), and non-Hispanic whites were more likely to meet the guidelines (12 percent) than non-Hispanic blacks (5 percent). This suggests that older Americans—particularly women and non-Hispanic African Americans, who are also more likely to experience functional limitations— might need more encouragement and education on how to safely engage in the optimal amount of physical activity necessary to maintain good health.

Studies have also connected some conditions such as cancer, cardiovascular disease, and lower respiratory disease to cigarette smoking. The percentage of older male smokers declined dramatically from 29 percent in 1965 to 10 percent in 2010, but women remained relatively constant at about 10 percent. About 53 percent of men and 29 percent of women aged sixty-five and over reported that they were former smokers. As of 2010, there was no significant difference in cigarette smoking rates by ethnicity.

Future Health Outlook

The United States will soon have its highest ever population of people age sixty-five and older. People are, however, living longer and healthier lives than previous generations, and have much to look forward to in their retirement years. But potential pitfalls, including chronic health conditions and the economic effects of an aging population, must be addressed. Additionally, the AARP Public Policy Institute notes that the number of available caregivers for individuals aged eighty and older will decline sharply in the next several decades, from more than seven caregivers per person in 2010, to less than three per person by 2050. The United States must prepare now for the coming population changes in order to ensure the best possible experience for everyone.

Baby Boomers: Public Health's Biggest Challenges

By Susan Blumenthal and Katherine Warren
The Huffington Post, April 1, 2011

"Grow old along with me/the best is yet to be." Never has there been a time in human history when the words from the famous English poet Robert Browning have rung more true. More than a century ago, when Browning penned these words, the average life expectancy for Americans was 48 years.

Thanks to the triumph of public health and medical interventions, today we live in a world very different from Browning's, where 20-somethings are the new adolescents and 50 year olds are in the infancy of their second adulthoods.

Americans can now expect to live nearly twice as long than they did in the early nineteenth century, to an average age of 78, extending "the best" of years far beyond what Browning might ever have imagined.

No one knows this better than the baby boomers. New Year's Day marked the 65th birthday of this generation. Each day after January 1, 2011, another 10,000 "boomers" will turn 65. As the 79 million baby boomers born between 1946 and 1964 march towards their 65th birthdays, our nation must face the challenges of how an already strained federal budget will provide Social Security and Medicare benefits for future retirees.

An increasing incidence of chronic disease in this population, growing financial burdens on these federal programs, the declining number of primary care physicians and geriatric specialists in America, and the disappearance of pensions for many as a result of the economic crisis threaten this generation's "golden" years.

Against this backdrop, the American population is aging rapidly. In 2008, people aged 65 years or older represented 12.8 percent of the US population, about one in every eight people. By 2030, one in five Americans will be over the age of 65. According to recent data from the US Census Bureau, there are currently 79,000 people who have lived to be centenarians, older than 100 years, in the US today, a statistic that will reach more than 200,000 people by 2030.

While these demographic shifts are a testament to socioeconomic development and public health improvements, with them comes the challenge of a concurrent chronic disease pandemic. There is an urgent need to effectively address the increasing prevalence of age-related illnesses including heart disease, cancer, diabetes and neurodegenerative diseases such as Alzheimer's and Parkinson's.

Today, more than 75 percent of health care costs in the United States stem from chronic diseases, many of which are preventable. Over a million Americans die prematurely each year due to unhealthy lifestyle habits, including tobacco use, obesity, lack of exercise, and alcohol abuse. Although some of the secrets of longevity lie in our genes and biology, behavior is linked to as much as 50 percent of the cause of death worldwide. In fact, an important study of 3,000 Danish twins estimated that the heritability of human longevity was about 25 percent, with 75 percent of life expectancy attributable to lifestyle and environmental factors.

Despite these trends, current government and private sector support for prevention and public health programs accounts for only 3 to 5 percent of the $2.6 trillion of US health expenditures. The good news is that the recent health care reform legislation, the Patient Protection and Affordable Care Act, provides preventive care for older Americans, as Medicare recipients will no longer pay anything out of pocket for covered preventive services including yearly routine physical examinations; specific screening tests for heart disease, diabetes, some types of cancer, and bone density; as well as smoking cessation programs.

In the first two months of 2011, more than 150,000 seniors and other Medicare beneficiaries have received an annual wellness visit. These new benefits represent a critical step forward in making chronic disease prevention a reality for this population.

But a real revolution in chronic disease care must include new models for management of these illnesses as well, including the delivery of innovative services through Medicare and private sector plans. Transformative changes are particularly critical for the baby boomer generation, of which nearly two-thirds (35 million people) have at least one chronic health condition.

When first established, Medicare was a hospital-based care system. Since then, outpatient services and medication benefits have been added. But this patchwork model requires modernization. Furthermore, the need for home-based and long-term care of the aging population must be addressed.

The Patient Protection and Affordable Care Act established the Center for Medicare and Medicaid Innovation (CMMI), which will support new models to update Medicare's service delivery system. The law will also foster changes to payment and service delivery programs that increase access to health care, promote efficiency and effectiveness, as well as boost patient satisfaction. The new center will support pilot projects that if proven effective can be scaled up in communities across the country.

One of the most promising chronic disease management models is the patient-centered medical home, with its focus on strengthening the primary care physician-patient relationship and coordinating care across all components of the health care system. Pilot projects are also evaluating new models of long-term care that foster clinical collaboration across multiple specialists with the increased use of health information technology.

The economic downturn that began in 2007 has hit the baby boomers particularly hard as many have lost their jobs and employer-sponsored health benefits.

Access to health care is critical to promote healthy aging. Yet in 2009, about 8.6 million adults, ages 50 to 64 were uninsured, an increase of 1.1 million from 2008, as a result of record unemployment among this age group. Additionally, 9.7 million insured baby boomers have such high out-of-pocket costs relative to income that they are effectively uninsured.

Through the Patient Protection and Affordable Care Act, 17 percent of the 32 million uninsured people projected to gain coverage by 2019 will be ages 50 to 64. Those living in 16 states with high-uninsured rates, mostly in the South and West, will see the most gains from the legislation. With stronger consumer protections, the new health legislation will provide affordable coverage and also help protect baby boomers from loss of insurance due to economic hardship. This will provide them with access to both preventive and treatment services.

Another innovation available to improve health for baby boomers is the use of new media, tools that can bring important scientific knowledge to help consumers make informed health decisions. With more than 5 billion mobile phone users, 2.6 billion people on the internet worldwide, and 2.5 billion text messages sent every day in the US alone, today's information revolution connects people to knowledge about healthy aging as well as to information about the prevention and management of diseases like never before.

Patient tools such as the CDC's "I Move U" for Twitter and Facebook-based sites including "PatientsLikeMe," where people can share information about ill-nesses and treatments, are important resources. Other sites provide information about medications and their side effects as well as with an interactive electronic medical record. There is an estimated 17-year science to service gap between the time of a new discovery in the lab to its widespread use in clinical settings. In to-day's information age, why shouldn't this dissemination of scientific information take a nanosecond?

In addition to promoting prevention and chronic disease management, both the public and private sectors must make enhanced investments in research medicine's field of dreams. Research is the foundation for all medical and public health in-terventions to promote healthy aging and to find cures for the diseases that affect the baby boomer generation. Aging is, after all, the major risk factor for all chronic diseases.

Age-related diseases, such as Alzheimer's or Parkinson's, rob people of their health and place a burden on families, the health care system, and our nation's economy. In the example of Alzheimer's, if a discovery was made from research to delay the onset of the disease by just five years, it could save an estimated $50 billion per year and reduce the number of people with the illness by more than 50 percent after 50 years. But research doesn't just happen. It requires sustained investments in science and in the career development of researchers here in the United States and around the world.

The aging of the baby boom generation represents the newest challenge for med-icine and governments but also provides opportunities for rejuvenation and respon-sibility. Promoting healthy aging requires both personal and social responsibility, mobilizing all sectors of society. There is a recipe for healthy aging—don't smoke, maintain a healthy weight, eat smart, be physically and mentally active, obtain life-saving screening exams, enjoy strong connections to friends and family, and be an advocate for increased investments in research and establishing new health service delivery models.

The aging of the world's population challenges America as well as other countries and their governments to create twenty-first century health care systems and policies that address the needs of seniors. The wave of aging worldwide with its tsunami of chronic diseases underscores why actions are needed now to provide hope for a healthier and more prosperous future for today's baby boomers and for future generations—in a world where hopefully "the best is yet to be."

References

Alliance for Health Reform (2011). "Boomers Come of Age: Covering Early Retirees and Other 50–64 Year-Olds". Retrieved January 26, 2011.

The Alzheimer's Association (1994). "Alzheimer's Care Costs US a Trillion Dollars According to Report." Accessed January 18, 2011. www.alz.org

American Academy of Family Physicians, American College of Physicians, and American Osteopathic Association (2007). "Joint Principles of the Patient-Centered Medical Home." Accessed February 1, 2011.

Bernhardt, J (2010). "Healthy Aging 2.0: The Power of Digital Health and Wellness." Healthy Aging Globally: A Life Style Approach, Global Health Forum 2010.

Brookmeyer, R, Gray, S, and Kawas, C (1998). "Projections of Alzheimer's Disease in the United States and the Public Health Impact of Delaying Disease Onset." *American Journal of Public Health*. Accessed February 1, 2011.

Center for the Study of Presidency and Congress Commission of US Federal Leadership in Health and Medicine: Charting Future Directions. "A 21st Century Roadmap for Advancing America's Health: The Path from Peril to Progress." Washington, DC: 2010.

Cohn, D and Taylor, P (2010). "Baby Boomers Approach Age 65 - Glumly. Pew Research Center." Retrieved January 5, 2011.

Collins, SR, Doty, MM, and Garber, T (2010). "Millions of Baby Boomers Will Gain Coverage under Health Reform, Especially Those in Southern and Western States." The Commonwealth Fund. Accessed January 5, 2011.

Collins, SR, Doty, MM, and Garber, T (2010). "Realizing Health Reform's Potential: Adults Ages 50-64 and the Affordable Care Act." The Commonwealth Fund. Accessed January 5, 2011.

De Cabo, R. "The Science of Aging and Longevity." Healthy Aging Globally: A Life Style Approach, Global Health Forum 2010.

Department of Health and Human Services (2010). "Affordable Care Act prevention benefits increasing access, lowering costs for people with Medicare." Accessed March 17, 2011. Available at: www.HealthCare.gov/center/reports/prevention03162011a.pdf

Garaci, E (2010). "Healthy Aging Globally: A Life Style Approach." Global Health Forum 2010. Oct. 12, 2010.

Henig, RM (2010). "What Is It About 20-Somethings?" *The New York Times*. Retrieved January 3, 2011.

H.R. 3590—111th Congress: Patient Protection and Affordable Care Act. (2009). In GovTrack.us (database of federal legislation). Retrieved March 11, 2011.

Mechanic, R and Altman, S (2010). "Medicare's Opportunity to Encourage Innovation in Health Care Delivery." *New England Journal of Medicine*. Accessed Jan. 18, 2011.

Nielsen Online (2010). "The World in 2010: Facts and Figures." International Telecommunications Union. Accessed February 15, 2011.

US Department of Health and Human Services (2010). Center for Medicare and Medicaid Innovation. Accessed Jan. 18, 2011.

Senior Health Care Crisis Looms

By Michelle Healy
USA Today, May 28, 2013

Analysis of key population indicators illustrates strengths, challenges for senior health on national and state levels

An aging nation that's living longer but with growing rates of obesity, diabetes and other chronic diseases points to an emerging health care crisis, says a report out Tuesday that analyzes seniors' health status state-by-state.

Just two years ago, the first Baby Boomers turned 65, setting into motion a "tremendous demographic shift in the US population," said physician Rhonda Randall, a senior adviser to the not-for-profit United Health Foundation, which released America's Health Rankings Senior Report Tuesday.

The report focuses on 34 measures of senior health, including physical inactivity, obesity, self-reported health status, poverty, drug coverage, hospital re-admission rates and flu vaccinations. The data analyzed is from more than a dozen government agencies and private research groups.

As generations move into retirement, they become greater consumers of health care, Randall said. But those turning 65 today "are more likely to live longer than their parents and grandparents, and much more likely to live sicker for a longer period of time," she said.

Among signs of impending challenges the report cites:

- 1 in 8 Americans (13 percent or 40.3 million) are 65 or older, and that is projected to grow to 1 in 5 (19.3 percent, or 72.1) in 2030, the year all members of the Baby Boomer generation will have turned 65, according to Census data. By 2050, seniors will make up 25 percent of the population. Those 85 and older are projected to increase from 5.8 million in 2010 to 8.7 million in 2030.

- Nearly 8 in 10 seniors are living with at least one chronic health condition; 50 percent have two or more, the Centers for Disease Control and Prevention estimates. About 25 percent of older Americans are obese; 20 percent have been diagnosed with diabetes; more than 70 percent have heart disease; nearly 60 percent have arthritis, a leading cause of disability.

- Adults 65 and older spend nearly twice as much as those 45 to 64 on health care each year; they spend three to five times more than all adults younger than 65, according to CDC.

If not addressed, the increased burden of chronic disease will not only have severe economic consequences but affect older adults' overall well-being, Randall said. "This is a really important time in our nation's history for us to take a look at this demographic change and the health and behavior outcomes for this population. If we don't measure it, we won't know what to do about it."

The report offers "an important set of messages . . . for personal focus, family and community focus, and a heads-up to the providers, and a real heads-up to policy makers," said Jennie Chin Hansen, CEO of the American Geriatrics Society and author of one of several commentaries in the report.

Some of the trends are "very cautionary," Hansen added. They highlight "that we really do have to be thoughtful, strategic and intentional if we are going to insure that people's health and well-being is going to be made better. There's stuff we know, but now there's stuff we have to do. "

Overall, Minnesota tops the list in senior health, followed by Vermont (2), New Hampshire (3), Massachusetts (4) and Iowa (5).

At the bottom: Mississippi (50), Oklahoma (49), Louisiana (48), West Virginia (47) and Arkansas (46).

Minnesota's top ranking reflects a combination of factors, including a large number of seniors who report being in very good or excellent health, high rates of creditable drug coverage, relatively high availability of home health care workers, as well as a low rate of seniors at risk of going hungry and a low rate of hospitalization for hip fractures, according to the study.

But it notes challenges for Minnesota, as well, including a high percentage of chronic drinking, a low percentage of senior residents with a dedicated health care provider, and low per-person expenditures by the state to assist older adults in poverty.

In bottom-ranked Mississippi, a high percentage of seniors live in poverty and are at risk of going hungry; there is a high rate of premature death; a low percentage of seniors report very good or excellent health and a low rate report annual dental visits. But Mississippi scored well for a low prevalence of chronic drinking and a high rate of flu vaccination.

The senior population in Mississippi is predicted to grow 46 percent between 2015 and 2030. In Minnesota, the population is expected to grow 54 percent. Arizona tops that category with an expected increase of 101 percent, followed by Nevada (89 percent), Florida (88 percent), Alaska (70 percent) and Texas (67 percent).

Among other trends noted in the report:

- Alaska (21 percent) has the lowest percentage of seniors with multiple chronic health conditions, followed by Wyoming (22 percent) and Montana (23 percent). The highest percentages are in Florida (44 percent), New Jersey (43 percent) and Delaware (40 percent).

- Nationally, 30 percent of seniors in fair or better health report doing no physical activity or exercise other than their regular job in the last 30 days. Inactivity levels range from a low of 20.5 percent of seniors who report being inactive in Colorado and 21.3 percent in California to highs of 41.2 percent in West Virginia and 41.3 percent in Tennessee.

- Obesity rates among those ages 50 to 64 increased 8 percent from 1995 to 2010, suggesting that the next generation of seniors will experience higher rates of obesity compared with current seniors. Overall, 25 percent of adults ages 65 and older are considered obese. The prevalence varies from a low of 17 percent in Hawaii and 18 percent in Nevada to highs of 29 percent in Alaska and 30 percent in Michigan.

- An average of 9 percent of adults ages 65 and older live at or below recognized poverty thresholds, which is also associated with higher rates of chronic diseases and shorter life expectancy. Rates range from a low of 5 percent in Alaska and 6 percent in Utah to 12 percent in New Mexico and 14 percent in Mississippi.

How all 50 states ranked:

1.	Minnesota	27.	New Jersey
2.	Vermont	28.	Ohio
3.	New Hampshire	29.	North Carolina
4.	Massachusetts	30.	Florida
5.	Iowa	31.	Rhode Island
6.	Hawaii	32.	Indiana
7.	Connecticut	33.	Missouri
8.	Colorado	34.	Wyoming
9.	Utah	35.	Montana
10.	Maryland	36.	South Carolina
11.	North Dakota	37.	Illinois
12.	Delaware	38.	New Mexico
13.	Maine	39.	Texas
14.	Nebraska	40.	Alaska
15.	Oregon	41.	Tennessee
16.	Washington	42.	Nevada
17.	Pennsylvania	43.	Georgia
18.	Kansas	44.	Alabama
19.	South Dakota	45.	Kentucky
20.	Wisconsin	46.	Arkansas
21.	Virginia	47.	West Virginia
22.	Arizona	48.	Louisiana
23.	New York	49.	Oklahoma
24.	Idaho	50.	Mississippi
25.	California		
26.	Michigan		

Source: United Health Foundation

The Status of Baby Boomers' Health in the United States: The Healthiest Generation?

By Dana E. King, Eric Matheson, Svetlana Chirina,
and Jordan Broman-Fulks
JAMA Internal Medicine, March 11, 2013

From 1946 through 1964, 78 million children ("baby boomers") were born in the United States. In 2010, baby boomers made up 26.1 percent of the US population.[1] Medicine has improved significantly during baby boomers' lifetimes. Although these advantages have led to a progressively increasing life expectancy,[2] previous studies have shown mixed results regarding whether baby boomers are healthier than prior generations.[3,4] The present study examined the health status of aging baby boomers relative to the previous generation to provide a vitally important context for healthy workforce and policy planning in the coming years.

Methods: We analyzed data from the National Health and Nutrition Examination Survey (NHANES), including NHANES III (1988–1994) (for previous generation) and the NHANES for 2007 to 2010 (for baby boomers), focusing on respondents who were aged 46 to 64 years during either period. The 2 cohorts were compared with regard to health status, functional and work disability, healthy lifestyle characteristics, and presence of chronic disease.

Results: The demographic characteristics of the cohorts were very similar except for the proportions in each racial/ethnic group, with greater proportions of non-Hispanic blacks (11.3 percent vs 9.4 percent) and Hispanics (9.8 percent vs 3.7 percent) in the 2007–2010 group compared with the 1988-1994 group (P=.001). The mean (SD) ages were 54.1 (0.03) years in the 2007–2010 group and 54.5 (0.03) years in the 1988–1994 group; there was no difference in sex between the 2 cohorts (49.1 percent male [2007–2010 group] vs 47.5 percent male [1988-1994 group]). Overall health status was lower in baby boomers, with 13.2 percent reporting "excellent" health compared with 32 percent of individuals in the previous generation (P=.001). Of the sampled baby boomers, compared with the previous generation, 6.9 percent vs 3.3 percent used a walking assist device (P=.001), 13.8 percent vs 10.1 percent were limited in work (P=.003), and 13.5 percent vs 8.8 percent had a functional limitation (P=.001).

With regard to healthy lifestyle factors, obesity was more common among baby boomers (38.7 percent obese vs 29.4 percent [previous generation]; P=.001), and regular exercise was significantly less frequent (35.0 percent vs 49.9 percent exercise 12 times per month; $P=.001$); more than half of baby boomers reported no regular physical activity (52.2 percent vs 17.4 percent; $P=.001$). Moderate drinking was higher in the baby boomer cohort compared with the previous generation (67.3 percent vs 37.2 percent; $P=.001$). There were fewer current smokers in the baby boomer cohort than in the previous generation (21.3 percent vs 27.6 percent; $P=.001$).

The percentage of individuals with hypertension was more common among baby boomers than among individuals from the previous generation (43 percent vs 36.4 percent; $P=.001$), as was the percentage of individuals who take medication for hypertension (35.4 percent vs 23.2 percent; $P=.001$). Among baby boomers, hypercholesterolemia was more common (73.5 percent vs 33.8 percent; $P=.001$, and medication use for hypercholesterolemia was more than 10 times greater (25.9 percent vs 1.5 percent; $P=.001$). Baby boomers were also more likely to have diabetes (15.5 percent vs 12.0 percent; $P=.003$) and take medication for diabetes (11.3 percent vs 6.2 percent; $P=.001$). The slight trend toward higher prevalence of cancer in baby boomers vs the previous generation was not significant (10.6 percent vs 9.5 percent; $P=.25$). The frequency of emphysema decreased in the baby boomer generation (2.3 percent) relative to the previous generation (3.5 percent) ($P=.03$). Baby boomers were also less likely to have had a myocardial infarction (3.6 percent) compared with the previous generation (5.3 percent) ($P=.004$).

A logistic regression was conducted to control for changes in demographic characteristics (age, sex, race, and socioeconomic status) of the population between 1988–1994 and 2007–2010. The results indicated, after adjustment, that baby boomers remained more likely than the previous generation to have diabetes (odds ratio [OR], 1.46; 95 percent CI, 1.16–1.83); hypertension (OR, 1.38; 95 percent CI, 1.14–1.67); and hypercholesterolemia (OR, 5.94; 95 percent CI, 4.94–7.14).

Comment: Despite their longer life expectancy over previous generations, US baby boomers have higher rates of chronic disease, more disability, and lower self-rated health than members of the previous generation at the same age. On a positive note, baby boomers are less likely to smoke cigarettes and experience lower rates of emphysema and myocardial infarction than the previous generation.

The findings from the present study documenting poorer health status and increased rates of obesity, hypertension, diabetes, and hypercholesterolemia support an increased likelihood for continued rising health care costs and a need for increased numbers of health professionals as baby boomers age.[5,6] Given the link between positive healthy lifestyles and subsequent health in this age group,[7] the present study demonstrates a clear need for policies that expand efforts at prevention and healthy lifestyle promotion in the baby boomer generation.

Author Affiliations: Departments of Family Medicine (Dr King) and Epidemiology (Dr Shankar), West Virginia University School of Medicine, Morgantown; and Department of Family Medicine, Medical University of South Carolina, Charleston (Drs Matheson and Ms Chirina). Mr Broman-Fulks is a medical student at Medical University of South Carolina.

Correspondence: Dr King, Department of Family Medicine, West Virginia University School of Medicine, Robert C. Byrd Health Sciences Center, 1 Medical Center Dr, PO Box 9152, Morgantown, WV 26506 (kingdana@wvuhealthcare. com).

Author Contributions: *Study concept and design:* King and Chirina. *Analysis and interpretation of data:* King, Matheson, Chirina, Shankar, and Broman-Fulks. *Drafting of the manuscript:* King, Matheson, Chirina, and Broman-Fulks. *Critical revision of the manuscript for important intellectual content:* Chirina and Shankar. *Statistical analysis:* Chirina. *Study supervision:* King and Matheson.

Conflict of Interest Disclosures: None reported.

Funding/Support: This study was supported in part by grants 1R01ES021825-01 and 5R03ES018888-02 from the National Institutes of Health.

Additional Contributions: Alexander Brown, MA, assisted in the preparation of the manuscript.

Online-Only Material: The eAppendix is available at http://www.jamainternalmed.com.

Notes

1. US Bureau of the Census. Selected characteristics of Baby Boomers 42–60 years old in 2006. http://www.census.gov/population/age/publications/files/2006babyboomers.pdf. Accessed August 1, 2012.

2. Martin LG, Freedman VA, Schoeni RF, Andreski PM. Health and functioning among baby boomers approaching 60. *J Gerontol B Psychol Sci Soc Sci.* 2009; 64 (3): 369–377.

3. Rice DP, Fineman N. Economic implications of increased longevity in the United States. *Annu Rev Public Health.* 2004; 25: 457–473.

4. Sturm R, Ringel JS, Andreyeva T. Increasing obesity rates and disability trends. *Health Aff (Millwood).* 2004; 23 (2):199–205.

5. Olshansky SJ, Goldman DP, Zheng Y, Rowe JW. Aging in America in the twenty-first century: demographic forecasts from the MacArthur Foundation Research Network on an Aging Society. *Milbank Q.* 2009; 87 (4): 842–862.

6. Ricketts TC. The health care workforce: will it be ready as the boomers age? a review of how we can know (or not know) the answer. *Annu Rev Public Health.* 2011; 32: 417–430.

7. King DE, Mainous AG III, Geesey ME. Turning back the clock: adopting a healthy lifestyle in middle age. *Am J Med.* 2007; 120(7): 598–603.

Boomers' Health Fails to Measure up to Parents

By Barbara Bronson Gray
US News, February 4, 2013

Study finds higher rates of chronic disease, disability and lower self-rated health

The baby boom is turning out to be a health bust.

Despite growing up at a time of great innovation in health care, the 78 million people born in the United States between 1946 and 1964 aren't looking all that healthy today, according to a new study.

Medical advances have led to the longest life expectancy ever, but US baby boomers have higher rates of chronic disease, more disability and lower self-rated health than did their parents at a comparable age.

The research may surprise many baby boomers, who have embraced activities such as running, fitness classes and backpacking in unprecedented numbers.

"There seems to be somewhat of a disconnect between the reputation of baby boomers for being healthy and what we see in increasing rates of diabetes, high blood pressure and obesity," said study author Dr. Dana King, a professor of family medicine at West Virginia University School of Medicine. "It's really discouraging that they're not the healthiest generation."

The study, published as a research letter Feb. 4 in *JAMA Internal Medicine*, compared data on people aged 46 to 64 in two time periods—from 1988 to 1994 for the older generation, and from 2007 to 2010 for the baby boomers.

While 32 percent of their parents' generation described their health as "excellent," only about 13 percent of baby boomers did so.

Obesity was more common among baby boomers than their parents (39 percent versus 29 percent). In addition, 52 percent of boomers said they had no regular physical activity, while only 17 percent in their parents' generation reported inactivity.

There was one area of good news, however. Boomers have lower rates of heart attack and emphysema, and are less likely to smoke cigarettes, the study reported. King noted that the reduction in smoking—from 28 percent of the population to 21 percent—shows the value of conducting a concerted public health campaign. He said the nation needs to focus the same amount of effort now on obesity to discover truly effective solutions.

The findings didn't surprise some experts.

"Obesity seems to be the underlying cause of many of the health issues baby boomers are facing," said Nancy Copperman, a registered dietitian and director of public health initiatives at North Shore-LIJ Health System, in Great Neck, N.Y. "I wasn't surprised to see the data because we've seen the obesity epidemic over the past two to three decades really increase, and with that heart disease, diabetes and high blood pressure."

The study tapped data from the US National Health and Nutrition Examination Survey. Factors used to compare the two generations included health status, functional and work disability, healthy lifestyle characteristics, and presence of chronic disease.

The baby boomer generation had a higher percentage of people with high blood pressure, high cholesterol, diabetes and obesity than did their parents' generation.

Disability was defined conservatively, said King. "To be considered disabled you had to be walking only with an assistance device, such as a cane, or only able to climb up 10 steps, have trouble stooping down, or walking a quarter of a mile," he explained. Again, boomers consistently had a higher level of disability than their parents' generation.

So what was the previous generation doing right? "There was a huge difference in their typical amount of exercise," said King. "Fifty percent were getting moderate physical activity 12 times a month, while just 35 percent of baby boomers got that much exercise."

The research also showed that medication use for high blood pressure was higher among baby boomers, and prescription drug use for high cholesterol was 10 times greater among the younger generation than among the previous generation. Of course, many of the medications boomers take were not widely available when their parents were of similar age.

Do boomers rely too much on medications to solve their health issues? "I'm concerned that has a great deal to do with the problem," said King. "The drugs are supposed to be used in addition to a healthy lifestyle, not instead of it."

Baby boomers are definitely moving less than their parents did, said Copperman. "Our parents didn't have the conveniences we have. Now, often both parents are working and spending less time doing manual labor. Instead of mowing the lawn or cleaning the house, they might hire someone to do it," she noted.

But King said it's still not too late for baby boomers to get healthier. He said his previous research showed that it is possible to "turn back the clock" even in one's 50s and 60s.

Must We Ration Health Care
for the Elderly?

By Daniel Callahan
Journal of Law, Medicine and Ethics, Spring 2012

For well over 20 years I have been arguing that someday we will have to ration health care for the elderly. I got started in the mid-1980s when I served on an Office of Technology Assessment panel to assess the likely impact on elderly health care costs of emergent, increasingly expensive medical technologies. They would, the panel concluded, raise some serious problems for the future of Medicare. The panel did not take up what might be done about those costs, but I decided to think about that question and wrote a book called, *Setting Limits: Medical Goals in an Aging Society*.[1]

I contended that we would be forced eventually to limit medical care for the elderly, and particularly high-technology procedures for those beyond the late 70s or early 80s. The combination of a sharply growing number of the elderly combined with more and more expensive technology would be financially overwhelming. I did not try to specify when in the future treatment limits should be set. My aim was not to propose immediate rationing but to get the public to anticipate its eventual likelihood and to open a discussion of the problem.

I did not get a warm reception. My 15 minutes of fame was of the infamous kind. The eminent late geriatrician Robert Butler yelled at me in a taxi after a TV program we had been together on that the very title of my book, *Setting Limits*, was harmful. "We are a rich country," he said, "and can afford whatever it takes to provide health care." I was picketed at some lectures, accused of ageism, of promoting social euthanasia of the burdensome elderly, of sexism (because women live longer than men and thus would suffer more than men from rationing), and of all-around hard-heartedness. "What is it like to live with a Nazi?" my wife was once asked.

Even most of my friends joined the chorus: yes, there will be a problem, but I had just gone too far. Anyway, I was told time and again, more medical research would find cures for the diseases of aging; greater efficiency and the elimination of waste would hold costs down; and some said that aging is itself a curable disease. The final punch in the jaw was for many critics to exclaim, rubbing their hands in anticipated glee, "Well, let's see what you say when you get old!" I was at that time a callow youth of 56.

I am now 81, and nothing at all since then has persuaded me that we can avoid rationing care for the elderly, not tomorrow perhaps, but sooner or later, and probably sooner.

The Future of Medicare: Should We Be Worried?

The trustees of the Medicare program have projected its insolvency in eight years, and in a decade our overall national health care costs will double.[2] Now is the time to act they have repeatedly said, but so far in vain. "Medicare," the former Secretary of Health and Human Services, Michael O. Leavitt said in 2008, "is drifting toward disaster."[3] Within the next decade the baby boomers will begin retiring in ever growing numbers. They will come by the hundreds of thousands, into a medical world of always more expensive technological means of keeping them alive, and with likely higher expectations of medical benefits than their parents or grandparents.

Not one of the most dominant diseases of aging has been cured, but more ways have been found to keep patients alive with them. As the Congressional Budget Office (CBO) has noted, "[E]xamples of new treatments for which long-term savings have been clearly demonstrated are few…improvement in medical care that decreases mortality…paradoxically increase overall spending on health care…patients live longer and therefore use health services for more years."[4]

The age creep of technological aggressiveness with the elderly continues apace. Open-heart surgery for those in their 90s and even 100s is on the rise.[5] Age per se is rarely considered an obstacle any longer to treating the elderly. As for getting rid of waste and inefficiency, that has not happened: a great idea but no one knows how to achieve it. And health care costs have not declined because of research. The opposite has happened: they have historically risen in lock-step with research expenditures.

Should one think I am too pessimistic about the cost problem, consider some basic statistics. As of 2008 there were 44,831,390 Medicare beneficiaries. Between 2010 and 2030 the number will grow from 46 million to 79 million, a 17.7 percent increase in just 20 years.[6] During that same period, the ratio of workers (who pay the taxes for Medicare) to retirees will decline from the present ratio of 3.7 to 2.9. The costs of the program will increase from $503 billion to $937 billion, a 93 percent rise.[7]

Here is a brief sample of some judgments of health economists and policy analysts that have not made their way out of professional journals into public consciousness. Recall the "disaster" judgment of Michael O. Leavitt above and then add to it the following:

- The Henry J. Kaiser Family Foundation has determined that "none of the usual policy options…is likely to significantly close the gap between the growth of health spending and [national] income."[8]
- The Congressional Budget Office (CBO) has determined that "projected increases in [Medicare] spending…would require tax increases of an unprecedented magnitude…under current policy, future generations will be worse off by higher taxation or lower benefits."[9]

- The distinguished Harvard economist David Cutler, reviewing a study of projected Medicare costs, has written that "dire predictions about Medicare are unavoidable…one would need to cut medical spending for the elderly more than half to balance medical spending with revenue forecasts. No one has a way to do that."[10]

- The CBO has also determined that raising Medicare eligibility to 70 "would reduce costs by only 9 percent"[11]; and even if cancer, diabetes, and heart disease were eliminated, the savings by 2020 would be only 10 percent in overall costs.[12]

I have taken those pessimistic judgments seriously. They have been persistent and insistent, based on carefully developed demographic, medical, and budget projections. Yet much more frequently I have heard the evasions or the rosy scenarios of what one writer has called the "silver lining specialists" for well over 25 years now. But nothing, absolutely nothing, has changed over that time—no cost savings, no breakthrough cures, and no decline in costs.

Costs continue to rise now, at a 6–7 percent annual pace, just as they have done for years, and often at an even higher rate. But there has been one change. The Medicare trustees have steadily reduced the projected years remaining before the program's insolvency, now at the historically low point of eight years and dropping every year. At the same time, as the reform debate has made painfully evident, most politicians on the right and the left have loudly rejected any discussion of cuts in Medicare benefits. It may be necessary to reduce Medicare payments to hospitals and doctors (not too much though), but not beneficiary coverage; and even the former is proving difficult. This paper was written before the passage of the reform legislation, which has a number of strategies for controlling the costs of Medicare. It is much too early to know whether they will work or, for that matter, whether a Republican dominated Congress will allow them to be put in place.

Why Rationing?

My conviction, then, is that Medicare is racing downhill into an acute financial crisis, from which there will be no painless escape. Nothing is left for us but to deal head-on with the unpleasant options available, the most important of which is a reduction of benefits, that is, rationing. I will put aside an increase in taxation, not only because of a perennial resistance to move in that direction, but also because even under more favorable circumstances that would be a short-term solution only; there would be no end to it. It would, moreover, be the young, declining in proportion, who would be the ones to pay through increased taxation the health care costs of their elders, increasing in proportion (that is, the changing dependency ratio).

We are left then to find ways to set benefit limits, however unsavory. The astute physician Eric Cassell once said to me that "we doctors take sick people and make them sicker in order to make them well." Rationing will make us all sicker for a time, but it is the necessary painful cure to make us financially healthy in the long run—and to keep Medicare as a financially sustainable and equitable program.

Rationing is a word that is open to many interpretations, too numerous to inventory here. I will simply stipulate what I mean by the term—consonant, I think, with common usage. Rationing is an organized effort by a public or private institution (e.g., Medicare or a private insurer) to equitably limit the availability of some desired or needed medical treatments in the name of preserving the economic sustainability of the institution as a whole or equitably distributing a scarce resource.

I distinguish three forms of rationing: direct, indirect, and covert. By direct rationing I mean an open denial or partial restriction to a patient or class of patients of some treatment(s) they need or desire. A treatment may be denied because it is simply too expensive in itself regardless of patient benefit, or because its health benefits are not commensurate with its costs. By indirect rationing I mean to encompass a class of financial tactics aiming to influence patient behavior, such as copayments and deductibles. They are ordinarily not thought of as rationing tools but, if they are made draconian enough (e.g., a 50 percent copayment), they can be a coercive force on patient behavior tantamount to direct rationing. We already know that high pharmaceutical copayments can discourage patients from filling prescriptions or lead them to cut the recommended dosage.

By covert rationing I mean the kind that was prevalent in the British National Health Services for some decades after World War II: an unwritten agreement among physicians that patients beyond the age of 55 should not be given expensive technologies (particularly dialysis and open heart surgery). Patients were simply, and untruthfully, told that nothing could be done for their heart disease or kidney failure.[13] That era passed, but more recently Rudolf Klein, an eminent UK policy analyst, noted another rationing variant: "The most pervasive form of rationing is the least explicit: rationing by dilution. Decisions at the cold face of health care delivery—not to order an expensive diagnostic test, not to make a specialist referral or to reduce ward staffing levels in order to balance the budget."[14] In some countries, notably Canada and the UK, long waiting lists for elective treatments have been common. They do hold costs down, but they seem more a function of physician shortages than a conscious form of cost control.

Modes of Rationing

There have been many efforts to devise methods of rationing that are rational and equitable. My comments are oriented to the Medicare program only, bearing solely on its power to determine program benefits. I begin with four procedural premises.

First, rationing should be done by policy, not by individual doctors and patients at the bedside. There would otherwise be too much variation in decision making, discrepancies between doctor and patient values, and the possibility of physician bias. Rationing must, that is, be removed from the ordinary doctor-patient relationship and shifted to the policy level. Second, policy must be set by democratic process (which could be accomplished by Congress delegating responsibility to a federal agency). Third, the policy must be carried out in a transparent way. Fourth, there should always be a provision for appeal.

As for the substantive content of rationing decisions, I am most drawn to the British National Institute for Clinical Excellence (NICE). It evaluates new technologies and makes recommendations to the National Health Services (NHS) for their inclusion in NHS patient coverage. Its recommendations that a technology be accepted by the NHS are binding on that institution, but that does not require that physicians accept them. If it makes a recommendation that the NHS not accept a technology, then the decision to do so is up to the NHS. It usually follows the recommendation, but when the NHS actually denies a technology based on the NICE recommendation, it opens itself to public and media attacks, and sometimes backs down.[15]

One of the main (though not exclusive) economic tools it employs is that of Quality-Adjusted Life Years (QALYs), a way of relating the estimated extended life years a technology will bring in relationship to the quality of life it will bring. It is a leading means of assessing the cost effectiveness of a treatment. Its use requires careful evidence-based research, which in the US could be provided by a federal agency. Instead of contending as I did in my book that an age would have to be specified for setting limits, I would now use QALYs to determine (but not solely) what they would be, thus using a methodological tool applicable to all age groups.

Cultural and Political Obstacles to Rationing

The most basic obstacle, I believe, is the deeply rooted American belief in unlimited medical progress. With modern science-driven medicine, we have a model of medical progress that of its nature envisions no final end point, no stage that permits us to say we have enough. But the human body still ages and dies, just later and more slowly. Medicine has been enormously successful in warding off, forestalling, and ameliorating the ravages of age. But it cannot overcome them indefinitely. In the end we lose. We have, I would contend, reached a point where the very quest to overcome our biological limits is destructive of health care systems. Every developed country in the world now has an economic problem with its health care system, regardless of how it is organized. Aging is the final frontier of health care costs: there is always more that can be done to extend life, but almost always now in more costly ways. Some 65 percent of our health care costs are incurred by 20 percent of our population, mainly the elderly, dying slowly of chronic illnesses.

Most of all we lack a vision, or at least a plausible concept, of the kind of community values necessary to make possible, and plausible, a health care system that sets and learns to live with limits. We have been seduced by the romance of progress to think we need not do so, that we can tinker with and better manage health care to make the unlimited model work. But it is not working, and, after at least 50 years of trying unsuccessfully to control costs, we are nowhere near succeeding. Plausible arguments from justice have been offered as one antidote, that is, to equitably allocate resources between the old and the young, to ration fairly. But the language of justice has never had much power in American health care, and no theory of justice

I know of has a theory about the management of endless medical progress. Norman Daniels's "accountability for reasonableness" offers a plausible procedural way to make rationing decisions, but it has little purchase in the face of a culture that thinks it patently wrong to make such decisions at all, and a medical research drive embraced by just about everyone as the great hope for the future. It is not.

My own choice for language is not that of justice, but of a common good or solidarity conception of our life together. It has well served European health care systems, never much drawn to a rights-based or justice-oriented approach. All of us are subject to the common threat of illness, aging, and death. That is a powerful bond to draw us together. The young and the old need each other to cope with, and mutually bear, the economic and social burden of our shared fate. The hazard that the elderly now pose for the young is that the elderly have gained a disproportionate share of health care, one that will gradually increase in the years ahead. The elderly need to be the first to acknowledge that fact, not forcing the young to force them to do so. My hope is that, as the financial crisis gets worse, we will all be led to recognize that the day of endless open frontiers of progress, always aiming for more and better, are over. I readily concede that what I hope for is a long shot, but no more than the panaceas offered over the years.

There are also three other obstacles to rationing worth a mention: the politics of rationing, the response of the medical community, and the public acceptance. Legislators and politicians are notoriously gun shy about even raising much less discussing, much less legislatively pushing for, a rationing policy. Congress has, since the enactment of the Medicare program, refused to allow the administrators of that program to use cost-effectiveness criteria for its benefit coverage.[16] Industry opposition and some medical groups have long opposed such a move. Two major federal efforts in recent decades to establish technology assessments research agencies were initiated by Congress but either killed or neutered after industry and physician groups came to resist them.[17]

The same demons were at work to concertedly undermine the $1.1 billion comparative effectiveness effort initiated by President Obama as part of his stimulus package. That effort was forbidden to use its findings to establish medical practice guidelines or even to make recommendations. The final health care reform bill contained the same restriction. Cleary, limitations of that kind would make a good use of scientific evidence for rationing all but impossible.

The obstacles erected by some groups of influential physicians are important also. What the AMA has, in newspaper advertisements, called the "sacred doctor-patient relationship," has been advanced as a way of arguing that government should not tell doctors how to treat patients, for which evidence-based practice guidelines could be used. Every patient is different, the argument goes, and could be harmed by treatment based on probabilistic evidence gathered from groups of patients. Physicians should be free to treat patients as they please, needing no help from a nanny government.

There are a number of cogent responses to the first two obstacles, which I cannot respond to here.[18] In any event, I believe that they would have less force in

Congress but for the strong support of the public, providing a solid base for their efforts. The fear of the elderly that their benefits will be cut is a potent consideration in fashioning a reform of Medicare, enough to make the toughest cost-cutting legislator cringe. President Obama was responding to that powerful sentiment when he assured them that there was nothing in his reform aspirations that would bring that about. He wisely did not say whether his commitment was, like the post office "forever" stamps, good forever or for the present moment.

What Can Be Done about Public Sentiment?

Various recent and even older public opinion surveys display a troubling consistency. On the one hand nearly 80 percent of those surveyed for at least four decades have believed that the US needs a major health reform. On the unfortunate other hand, rarely is the public willing to accept higher taxes or be open to a cut in benefits to effect reform. That latter combination does not leave much room for legislative maneuver, hardly any at all, and surely helps explain why legislators do not want to go near the topic. Again and again over the years I have heard a common refrain: "Yes, we need to control costs, but not if that will harm my wife, or child, or elderly parent." It is patently hard to devise any reasonable public policy in the face of the medical equivalent of not-in-my-backyard, that ultimate enemy of any kind of common good value.[19] How will it be possible to change public sentiment and in particular to persuade the elderly that they will in the future have to accept less than they now have? I do not know, but I believe they will need a rationale that goes beyond a purely economic calculus. We have seen of late how the economic recession has changed American savings habits, cut back on the use of credit cards, and scaled back discretionary spending. In that case, however, the public could see the immediate necessity of a change in spending habits for the sake of their own economic survival. Nothing quite so immediately potent in eliciting fear is likely to influence the elderly to give up what they now have. A few more years of cost escalation may change their minds.

My own approach has been to see if we can get a national discussion going on some basic issues of aging, illness, death, and the goals of medicine.[20] Should death be seen as the greatest human evil, a premise of medical research? How long do we need to live to have a full and satisfying life? As I look about at my age group and my own life, around 80 seems to me sufficient. How can we develop an agreement that the main task of medicine in the years ahead is not to lengthen average life expectancy but to improve its quality within a finite boundary? I have been called an "apologist" and a "mortalist"—legitimating and passively accepting death as our human fate—for holding such views. I am prepared to accept those labels.

I conclude those reflections with four convictions:

- It is the obligation of a good society to help the young to become old but not to help the old people become indefinitely older.

- The young and the old have reciprocal responsibilities: the young should support the old, and the old should not be an undue burden on the young.

- Unless one is prepared to say that the elderly should have an unlimited right to health care under Medicare regardless of cost and however marginal the benefits, then one has in principle opened the door for rationing.

- Finally, if we do not ration openly, it will be done indirectly by pushing up copayment and deductibles to a painful, threatening level, or covertly by quiet unwritten understandings among physicians and hospital administrators. Nothing, patients will be told, can be done for you. I choose openness.

Even if one agrees with my four propositions, I am left troubled by the obstacle of the "sacred doctor-patient relationship" note above. While I reject the slogan when used to oppose government rationing, that is not the end of the problem. The traditional ethic of the physician is that of the care of individual patients. At least in the United States that ethic has been understood since the 20th century to stand in the way of considering the cost of care in making diagnostic or treatment decisions. There has been considerable agreement also (at least among most of those who have written on the subject), that if there must be rationing, it should be done at the policy level, not case by case by the doctor at the bedside. There would be too much room for variable judgments, inequities, and conflicting values, to go that route.

Yet the policy level argument can leave the physician in an awkward, painful position. In the worst of cases he would have to tell a patient that, while the best available treatment is what the doctor would prescribe, the Medicare program will not pay for it. And that would be all the worse if he had to tell one patient that information, knowing the patient could not afford it, but knowing that another patient was affluent enough to pay for it out of pocket. A somewhat analogous situation could arise with high copayments and deductibles, with the physician knowing that some, but not all, of his patients could not afford them. There would, in other words, be a de facto two-tier system. Problems of that kind, of course, are already encountered with private insurers, free to decline payment for some procedures, and even Medicare sets some limits. For the most part now, or so I believe, the treatment denials are not all that common and those that are literally life or death matters fairly rare. But they could, with serious rationing, become ubiquitous, creating a most unpleasant practice for many physicians (even allowing for negotiations and exemptions).

I can think of no happy way out of situations of that kind. Physicians are never going to be comfortable denying what they believe to be beneficial care in the name of saving Medicare from insolvency. The best that can be hoped for is the cogency, fairness, and transparency of policy decisions. Procedure will matter. In the face of various forms of resistance, however, it is all too imaginable that Medicare will not be given the power to make use of cost-benefit criteria in making its treatment of benefit coverage (which is the present situation). Then patients will be at the mercy of escalating copayments and deductibles, now the chosen method of rationing by Medicare and private insurers. That tactic is in one sense out in the open, but because it has been used incrementally over the years, gradually creeping up, has not provoked loud outcries. It is not impossible as well that we will see what now seems to be the case in the UK as reported by Rudolf Klein: "The best ministers can hope for is that most rationing will continue to take the form of dilution rather than excision and that decisions will be taken in the name of clinical discretion and thus be politically invisible." Some may respond: it cannot happen here. But then no one can say what will happen. Rationing will come, but its method is still up in the air.

References

1. D. Callahan, *Setting Limits: Medical Goals in an Aging Society* (New York: Simon & Schuster, 1987).
2. Federal Hospital Insurance and Supplementary Medical Trust Fund Board of Trustees, 2008 Annual Report, Government Printing Office, Washington, D.C., at 3–4.
3. M. O. Leavitt, "Medicare Drifting Toward Disaster," *Reuters*, April 29, 2008.
4. Congressional Budget Office, Technological Change and the Growth of Health Care Spending, Washington, D.C.: Congressional Budget Office, 2008, at 13.
5. J. K. Shim, A. J. Russ, and S. R. Kaufman, "Risk, Life Extension and the Pursuit of Knowledge," *Sociology of Health and Illness* 38, no. 4 (2006).
6. State Health Facts website, available at <http://www.statehealthfacts.org/comparetable.jsp?ind=290&cat=6&sub=747yr=63&typ=1&sort=a> (last visited November 1, 2011).
7. Centers for Medicaid & Medicaid Services, available at <http://www.cms.hhs.gov/nationalhealthexpenddata/03_nationalhealthaccountsprojected.asp7>.
8. Kaiser Family Foundation, "Comparing Projected Growth of Health Care Expenditures and the Economy," in *Snapshots: Health Care Costs*, Menlo Park, CA, 2006, at 3.
9. G. K. Kollman and D. Noschler, The Financial Outlook for Social Security and Medicare, CRS Report for Congress, Congressional Research Service, Washington, D.C., 2004, at CRS 1–6.
10. D. Cutler, "The Potential for Cost Savings in Medicare's Future," *Health Affairs* 24, Supp. 2 (2005): WR-R78.
11. Congressional Budget Office, The Long-Term Budget Outlook, Washington, D.C., 2003, at 1.
12. A. Garber and D. Goldman, "The Changing Face of Health Care," in H. Aaron and W. Schwartz, eds., *The Impact of Molecular Biology on Medicine and Society* (Washington, D.C.: The Brookings Institution, 2004): at 111.
13. H. Aaron and W. Schwartz, *The Painful Prescription: Rationing Hospital Care* (Washington, D.C.: Brookings Institution Press, 1984).
14. R. Klein, "Rationing in the Fiscal Ice Age," *Health Economics, Policy and Law* 5, no. 4 (2010): 389-396.
15. T. Culyer, "How Nice Is Nice: A Conversation with Tony Culyer," available at <http://healthcarecostmonitor.thehastingscenter.org/admin/how-nice-is-nice-a-conversation-with-anthony-culyer/> (last visited November 1, 2011).
16. J. Fox, "Medicine Should, But Cannot, Consider Costs: Legal Impediments to a Sound Policy," *Buffalo Law Review* 53, no. 2 (2005): at 632.

17. D. Callahan, *Taming the Beloved Beast: How Medical Technology Costs Are Destroying Our Health Care System* (Princeton: Princeton University Press, 2009).

18. P. A. Ubell, "One Size Doesn't Fit All," available at <http://healthcarecost monitor.thehastingscenter.org/peterubel/one-size-doesnt-fit-all/> (last visited November 1, 2011); E. Cassell, "Comparative Effectiveness Research and the Doctor-Patient Relationship," available at <http://healthcarecostmonitor. thehastingscenter.org/ericcassell/comparative-effectiveness-research-and-the-doctor-patient-relationship/> (last visited November 1, 2011).

19. D. Callahan, "America's Blind Spot: Health Care and the Common Good," *Commonwealth*, October 9, 2009, at 13–16.

20. See Callahan, supra note 1; Callahan, supra note 17.

Who Will Care for the Elderly?

The Future of Home Care

By Peggie R. Smith
Buffalo Law Review, July 5, 2013

Introduction

Over the last several years, countless commentaries have posed some version of the question: "Who Will Care for the Elderly?"[1] The question underscores the growing concern with the care needs of an increasingly elderly population as the baby boomers and their parents age over the coming decades. Although the demand for home care services is expected to reach unprecedented highs,[2] the future availability of home care workers does not look promising. Similar to child care, the demand for quality home care outstrips supply—an imbalance caused not only by an aging generation but also by unfavorable working conditions.

This article argues that a comprehensive answer to the question, "Who Will Care for the Elderly?" must represent the interests of elderly individuals who need care and their families, as well as the interests of home care workers, as workers, who should be fairly compensated and provided workplace benefits. Against the backdrop of limited funding for long-term care of the elderly, home care policies in the United States tend to privilege consumers of home care while ignoring the economic interests of women who labor as home care workers.[3] This unfortunate dynamic most recently took center stage in the 2007 Supreme Court decision of *Long Island Care at Home, Ltd. v. Coke.*[4]

The *Coke* decision addressed the rights of home care workers under the Fair Labor Standards Act (FLSA), which guarantees most employees a right to a federal minimum wage and overtime compensation.[5] In a unanimous decision, the Supreme Court ruled that hundreds of thousands of home care workers are not entitled to the most basic of federal labor protections.[6] As this article discusses, the *Coke* decision threatens to further erode the precarious economic status of home care workers and undermine the quality of care that they provide to clients. Proposed federal initiatives could help reverse this trend and improve the employment rights of home care workers.

I. A Snapshot of the Home Care Industry

The substantial growth of America's elderly population is the most significant factor driving the exploding demand for home care.[7] In 1900, the United States population included 3.1 million people aged sixty-five and older, who accounted for 4 percent of the total population.[8] By 2010, the sixty-five–and–older population had swelled to approximately 40 million, a figure that translated into just over 13 percent of the total population.[9] According to projections, approximately 72 million Americans will be sixty-five and older by 2030, representing approximately 20 percent of the total population.[10] The projected climb from 2010 to 2030 tracks the aging of the baby boom generation, which comprises the approximately 76 million people born in the United States from 1946 to 1964.[11] The first wave of boomers turned sixty-five in 2011 and will reach age eighty-four in 2030.[12]

While many elderly individuals lead healthy lives, for others, disability and chronic health problems accompany longevity[13] and create a need for long-term care.[14] Such care involves services that assist the elderly with daily activities, such as dressing, bathing, toileting, eating, shopping, cooking, cleaning, taking medications, and visiting health-care providers.[15] Although family members and other informal, unpaid caregivers represent the most critical source of long-term care to the elderly,[16] the need for formal long-term care remains pressing.[17] The pool of informal caregivers has dwindled as more and more women, who constitute the majority of informal caregivers, have entered the workforce.[18] As women juggle the demands of elder care responsibilities with child care and work, they often require assistance from formal caregivers.

The demand for formal care also stems from elderly individuals with long-term care needs who live alone or who lack family networks to provide assistance.[19] This problem partially reflects the disproportionate number of elderly women who have outlived their spouses and who need long-term care as well as an increasing number of elderly individuals who never had children.[20] Formal care may also become urgent for those elderly persons who reside a substantial distance apart from family members. According to a 2004 study, 15 percent of informal caregivers for the elderly live at least an hour away from the person for whom they provide care.[21]

Home care workers who deliver hands-on assistance to elderly individuals provide the bulk of formal long-term care.[22] According to official statistics, approximately 1.8 million home care workers were employed in 2010.[23] This number, however, likely underestimates the total size of the workforce, as official reports do not capture the many workers who are hired directly by families.[24] A national study of home care workers serving Medicare recipients suggests the degree of undercounting; the study found that 29 percent of the workers were self-employed.[25] While precise numbers are elusive, researchers agree that the expanding need for long-term care has transformed home care into one of the fastest growing occupations in the country, with a projected employment growth rate of close to seventy percent between 2010 and 2020.[26]

Yet even as the demand for home care will continue to climb for the foreseeable future, the industry picture is bleak when viewed from the perspective of home care workers. The typical worker is a low-income woman between the ages of twenty-five and fifty-four.[27] She is unmarried and a mother of children under the age of eighteen.[28] There is a substantial likelihood that she is a woman of color, either African American or Hispanic.[29] There is a 20 percent chance that she speaks a language other than English at home.[30]

In addition, the wages of home care workers are appallingly low, ranking near the bottom of wages earned by employees in the service industry.[31] In 2009, workers received an average hourly wage of less than $10.00, which places many of them below the poverty line.[32] Because home care provides only part-time employment for many workers,[33] this hourly rate yielded median annual earnings of less than $17,000 in 2009.[34] In light of these numbers, close to 40 percent of workers must rely on public assistance such as Medicaid and food stamps for additional support.[35] A lack of benefits, including health insurance, medical leave, and retirement plans,[36] further exacerbates home care workers' poor economic position. In addition, because workers are usually paid only for the time they work in a client's home, they must use their meager earnings to pay for time spent traveling between clients' homes.[37]

Job dissatisfaction among home care workers also hinges on the work's physically demanding and emotionally draining character. Workers experience high rates of workplace injuries[38] and must deal with clients who suffer from cognitive impairments that can result in disruptive, violent behavior.[39] In addition, workers commonly report that, despite their critical role in caring for the elderly, they are often treated with disrespect.[40]

II. The Fight for Compensation and the *Coke* Case

The story of Evelyn Coke vividly illustrates the economic constraints faced by home care workers and some of the legal challenges that must be confronted in order to transform the job into an economically viable occupation. Ms. Coke worked as a home care employee for a home care agency in New York, Long Island Care at Home, for more than twenty years. She often slept in her clients' homes and worked twenty-four-hour shifts.[41] Ms. Coke claimed that Long Island Care at Home failed to pay her minimum wages and overtime wages in violation of the FLSA.[42]

Enacted in 1938, the FLSA establishes minimum employment standards including a minimum wage and overtime compensation for hours worked in excess of forty hours a week.[43] As originally adopted, the FLSA did not reach individuals who worked inside of private homes performing domestic service type work because of doubt about whether they were engaged in interstate commerce.[44] Congress specifically extended coverage to these workers in 1974, when it amended the FLSA to apply to employees "employed in domestic service in a household."[45]

In passing the 1974 domestic service amendments, Congress simultaneously limited their reach by crafting exemptions from the FLSA's minimum wage and overtime provisions for casual babysitters and for persons who "provide companionship services for individuals who (because of age or infirmity) are unable to care for themselves."[46] The legislative history of the 1974 amendments indicates that Congress, in exempting companions, intended to exclude those individuals who, similar to casual babysitters, worked in a casual, non-professional capacity for a private household.[47] The prevailing image of a companion was a neighbor or a friend who would spend time with an elderly person and who, because he or she was not a regular breadwinner, did not require the protection of the FLSA.[48] Thus, as explained by Senator Harrison Williams, the primary sponsor of the amendments, the companionship exemption was intended for "'elder sitters' whose main purpose of employment is to watch over an elderly or infirm person in the same manner that a babysitter watches over children."[49] A companion was also understood as someone who worked directly for the individual household.[50]

This image of a companion stands in stark contrast to most of today's home care workers. Contrary to the one-on-one employment relationship between an employing household and a companion, many home care workers are employed by agencies.[51] Also unlike companions who work on an itinerant basis, home care workers commonly work on a full-time, regular basis.[52] In short, there is little similarity between the casual labor pattern of a neighbor who intermittently works as a companion and the regular, dedicated service performed by home care workers who shoulder significant responsibility for the economic wellbeing of their families.

After the enactment of the 1974 amendments, the Department of Labor (DOL) adopted regulations interpreting the companionship exemption that significantly increased its scope. First, the DOL defined companionship services in broad, sweeping terms to include the performance of a range of household and personal tasks that greatly exceeded the provision of companionship.[53] Second, the DOL provided that the exemption covers not only workers employed by private households but also workers employed by third-party employers, such as home care agencies.[54]

At issue in *Coke* was the validity of the DOL regulation that interpreted the companionship exemption to exclude both home care workers employed by an individual homeowner employer and workers employed by a third-party employer as was the case with Evelyn Coke.[55] The Supreme Court ruled against Ms. Coke and held that because Congress did not clearly express its intentions in 1974 regarding the scope of the exemption, the DOL's interpretation of the exemption was reasonable and entitled to judicial deference.[56]

The *Coke* decision illuminates a troubling fault line in discussions that focus on the importance of work-family policies that can help employed family members address caregiving. In the context of elder caregiving, such discussions all too frequently relegate the labor rights of home care workers to the needs of their elderly clients and the clients' families. Thus, critics claim that extending FLSA protection to home care workers will result in clients and/or their families being unable to afford home care.[57] Not only is this claim greatly exaggerated since public funds, notably Medicare and Medicaid, pay for most of the services provided by home care workers,[58] but more importantly the claim disregards the interests of workers to the most basic of federal labor protections.[59] To be sure, granting home care workers FLSA protection may require state and federal governments to shoulder greater responsibility for the cost of publicly funded home care.[60] However, in a caring society, collective responsibility for long-term care should be vastly preferred to placing the responsibility on the weary shoulders of poor and low-income home care workers by excluding them from minimum labor protections extended to the majority of employees in the United States.[61]

In addition, cost-based concerns fail to consider the costs that will be saved by reducing job turnover among home care workers.[62] Estimates indicate that the average costs to replace a direct care worker range from $4200 to $5200.[63] Fears about skyrocketing costs are also highly exaggerated when one considers that a number of states already include home care workers within the ambit of their own state wage and hour laws.[64] These states recognize the value of providing home care workers with minimum labor protections, and the provision of such protections undermines many of the cost-based objections to extending coverage to third-party employed workers.[65]

The *Coke* decision also underscores the failure of policymakers and others to appreciate the high degree to which the availability of quality home care is inextricably linked to the economic status of the home care workforce. Critics, for example, argue that extending FLSA protection to home care workers will reduce the availability of care for the elderly and, in turn, compromise the quality of care.[66]

Ironically, the current reality suggests that the exact opposite is true. Home care workers are exiting the job—and, as a result, the quality of care is suffering—because of the job's poor working conditions, including low compensation levels.[67] As the American Association of Retired Persons argued in its brief to the Supreme Court on behalf of Ms. Coke, the exemption of home care workers employed by third-party employers from the FLSA operates not to protect the interests of clients but to "compromise" their interests.[68]

Clients are disadvantaged by the severe labor imbalance that characterizes the home care industry.[69] Despite the projected growth of employment in home care jobs and the increased demand for workers, a labor shortage exists in the home care industry. Organizations that provide long-term care invoke the term "crisis" to describe the problems they face in "attracting and retaining" home care workers.[70] Significantly, turnover rates among workers are extremely high. For example, studies indicate that the turnover rate in the home care industry ranges from forty-four to ninety-five percent.[71] Low wages and oppressive job conditions greatly exacerbate the shortage of home care workers. Faced with low-wage and low-status work, it is no surprise that many workers leave the job in search of more sustainable employment opportunities.[72]

Poor compensation not only contributes to a shortage of workers but also endangers the quality of care provided to elderly and disabled persons.[73] A worker's departure can have devastating consequences for a client who must adjust to a new worker and may experience service disruptions that can lead to hospitalization.[74] For other clients, turnover may culminate in their relocation to an institutional setting such as a nursing home.[75] Thus, far from undermining access to quality services, extending home care workers FLSA protection "will strengthen the home care workforce and result in higher quality of care and continuity of care for America's older and disabled persons."[76]

Against this backdrop, it is imperative that steps are taken to protect the rights of home care workers to fair compensation. Providing this protection is essential to help alleviate the vulnerability of workers, redefine home care as valuable labor that merits respect, and link home care quality with improved working conditions.

III. The Need for Federal Reform

Although various state laws extend minimum wage and overtime protections to home care workers,[77] federal action is required to fully address the harmful consequences of the *Coke* decision and improve the rights of home care workers. In 2011, President Barack Obama announced new rules proposed by the DOL to revise the FLSA regulations so as to significantly limit the reach of the companionship exemption.[78] The proposal includes several changes to the existing regulations in order to provide home care workers, especially third-party workers, with greater protection.[79] In advancing the proposed revisions, the DOL emphasized the extent to which existing regulatory interpretations of the FLSA's companionship exemption fail to account for the many changes in the home care industry since 1974.[80] The following discussion focuses on the relevance of three key proposed revisions.

A. Redefining "Domestic Service Employment"

First, the proposal redefines the phrase "domestic service employment" by deleting from the current regulatory definition the requirement that domestic work be performed in or about the home "of the person by whom he or she is employed."[81] The DOL reasoned that this phrase could lead to the erroneous conclusion that the FLSA applied only to those domestic workers employed by individual households and families and not to workers employed by third-party employers.[82] The proposal also updates the illustrative list of domestic workers.[83] Current regulations include as examples of such workers "cooks, waiters, butlers, valets, maids, housekeepers, governesses, nurses, janitors, laundresses, caretakers, handymen, gardeners, footmen, grooms, and chauffeurs."[84] The proposals eliminate various outdated job titles such as "footmen" and "grooms" and adds to the list current occupations such as "nannies" and "home health aides."[85]

B. The Understanding of Companionship Services

The DOL also proposes amending the definition of "companionship services" to more closely align it with congressional intent.[86] A current DOL regulation defines companionship services as services for the "fellowship, care, and protection" of persons who cannot care for themselves.[87] However, the regulation includes services that greatly exceed the essential understanding of a companion as that involving fellowship and protection.[88] For example, the regulation provides that companionship services can include "meal preparation, bed making, washing of clothes, and other similar services."[89] The regulation also allows the exemption to apply when a companion performs general household work, unrelated to the care of the client, as long as such general work "does not exceed 20 percent of the total weekly hours worked."[90] This type of general housework includes household tasks such as vacuuming and dusting.[91]

The proposed regulation seeks to redefine companionship such that it reflects the understanding of a companion evident in the act's legislative history as "someone in the home primarily to watch over and care for the elderly or infirm person."[92] A 1974 House report made clear that congressional intent was not to exclude "employees whose vocation is domestic service" but to apply the exemption only to those for whom such service is a "casual form of employment."[93] "Companionship," as originally understood, explained the DOL, should be confined to situations in which provided services revolve around fellowship activities such as "playing cards, watching television together, visiting with friends and neighbors, taking walks or engaging in hobbies."[94] In limiting the exemption to "casual" companions, the proposal eliminates an unjustifiable distinction that presently exists between domestic workers such as maids, gardeners and handymen, on the one hand, and home care workers, on the other hand. Under current law, the former are entitled to FLSA protection even if they work on a casual basis, while the companionship exemption denies protection to many home care workers, even if they work on a full-time basis.[95]

The proposal also eliminates the current provision that allows the exemption to apply even in instances where a worker spends up to 20 percent of her time performing general household work unrelated to the care of the person.[96] In its place, the DOL proposes a 20 percent allowance for intimate personal care services that are incidental to the provision of fellowship and protection such as making lunch for the elderly person or providing assistance with dressing and occasional grooming.[97] In other words, a companion will continue to be exempt as long as any housework that she does is capped at 20 percent of the total hours worked in a given week and as long as the work is performed on behalf of the care recipient and is of a personal nature.[98] The proposed change reflects the view that general household work, even when done by a companion, should be protected and not subjected to exclusion because it falls within the ambit of the type of work that Congress sought to protect when it amended the FLSA in 1974 to reach domestic workers.[99]

C. Third-Party Employment

The DOL also seeks to revise the regulation at the heart of the *Coke* case which dealt with third-party employment.[100] Under the current regulation on this issue, workers employed by households, as well as those employed by a third-party such as an agency, may be denied FLSA protection based on the companionship exemption.[101]

In opposing application of the exemption to third-party employees, advocates on behalf of the respondent in *Coke* had argued that the 1974 amendments were intended to apply only to domestic workers employed by private households, as opposed to third-party employers.[102] Two factors strongly supported this position. First, domestic workers employed by third parties were already included under the FLSA at the time of the amendments.[103] Thus, applying the exemption to these employees meant that previously covered domestic workers who performed companionship services would be excluded in the aftermath of the amendments. This result seemed illogical given that it completely contradicted Congress's purpose in amending the act to expand coverage.[104] Second, the legislative history of the amendments indicated that Congress understood domestic service employment as "services of a household nature performed by an employee in or about a private home of the person by whom he or she is employed."[105]

Although this argument did not hold sway with the Supreme Court, it persuaded the DOL to propose a revision to the companionship exemption that would limit its application to the "individual, family or household employing the companion or live-in domestic worker, regardless of whether the family member employing the companion or live-in domestic worker resides in the home where the services are performed."[106] As a result, third-party home care workers, like Evelyn Coke, would no longer be subjected to the exemption.

After the DOL issued the proposed rule in December 2011, it received 26,000 comments during the public comment period, two-thirds of which favored the proposed changes.[107] Even as resistance from Republican lawmakers and home care industry groups concerned about profits remains strong,[108] the DOL appears ready to release its final regulations.[109]

Conclusion

The pressing need for formal home care will persist for the foreseeable future, as working families, and employed women in particular, struggle to balance their work obligations and caregiving responsibilities. Yet despite the growing demand for home care, a labor shortage persists.[110]

Turnover rates among home care workers are extremely high and attracting new and qualified workers to the field is an uphill battle. Home care consumers pay a price of the job's instability in the form of inconsistent care, poor quality care, and a lack of available care. This article has maintained that sustainable, long-term improvement on this front requires an approach that connects the availability of quality home care with policies that can help develop and support the home care workforce. As long as workers earn poverty-level wages and lack the resources to afford benefits such as health insurance, the problems of poor quality of care and high turnover rates will persist. While determining how to best resolve this problem is a complicated task, this article has argued that the task should start with the very modest but important step of ensuring home care workers protection under the FLSA, the country's most basic labor law.

Notes

1. See, e.g., Kelly Flynn, But Who Will Care for Me?, N.Y. TIMES (Oct. 10, 2012), http://www.nytimes.com/2012/10/10/booming/10story-booming.html?_r=0; Howard Gleckman, Who Will Care for the Elderly and Disabled?, KAISER HEALTH NEWS (July 20, 2009), http://www.kaiserhealthnews.org/Columns/2009/July/072009Gleckman.aspx; Robyn I. Stone & Joshua M. Weiner, Who

Will Care for Us? Addressing the Long-Term Care Workforce Crisis, URBAN INST., 19 (Oct. 2001), http://www.urban.org/UploadedPDF/Who_will_Care_for_Us.pdf; Nora Super, Who Will Be There to Care? The Growing Gap between Caregiver Supply and Demand, NAT'L HEALTH POL'Y FORUM, 1-17 (Jan. 23, 2002), http://www.nhpf.org/library/background-papers/bp_caregivers_1-02.pdf.

2. See BURT S. BARNOW ET AL., OCCUPATIONAL LABOR SHORTAGES: CONCEPTS, CAUSES, CONSEQUENCES, AND CURES 148 (2013) (discussing the projected growth in the home care industry); Home Health and Personal Care Aides, BUREAU OF LABOR STATISTICS, US DEP'T OF LABOR, OCCUPATIONAL OUTLOOK HANDBOOK (2012–13 ed.) [hereinafter OCCUPATIONAL OUTLOOK HANDBOOK 2012–13], http://www.bls.gov/ooh/healthcare/home-health-and-personal-care-aides.htm (noting that "[e]mployment of home health aides is expected to grow by 69 percent from 2010 to 2020, much faster than the average for all occupations," and that "[e]mployment of personal care aides is expected to grow by 70 percent from 2010 to 2020, much faster than the average for all occupations").

3. See Judith Feder, Paying for Home Care: The Limits of Current Programs, in FINANCING HOME CARE: IMPROVING PROTECTION FOR DISABLED ELDERLY PEOPLE 27, 44 (Diane Rowland & Barbara Lyons eds., 1991) (reviewing state and federal expenditures on home care and noting their limitations); Richard Kaplan, Cracking the Conundrum: Toward a Rational Financing of Long-Term Care, 2004 U. ILL. L. REV. 47, 62-64 (highlighting the limitations of Medicare to address the long-term care needs of older Americans); id. at 69-72 (noting structural features in Medicaid that limit its ability to fund long-term care); see also Long-Term Care Financing: Growing Demand and Cost of Services are Straining Federal and State Budgets: Testimony Before the H. Subcomm. on Health, Comm. on Energy and Commerce, 109th Cong. 11 (2005) (statement of Kathryn G. Allen, Director, Health Care-Medicaid and Private Health Insurance Issues) [hereinafter Long-Term Care Financing], http://www.gao.gov/new.items/d05564t.pdf (highlighting the consequences of inadequate funding for long-term care on elderly individuals).

4. 551 US 158 (2007).

5. Fair Labor Standards Act of 1938, 29 USC. §§ 206-207 (2006).

6. Coke, 551 US at 170, 173-74.

7. See OFFICE OF THE ASSISTANT SEC'Y FOR PLANNING & EVALUATION, US DEP'T OF HEALTH & HUMAN SERVS., THE FUTURE SUPPLY OF LONG-TERM CARE WORKERS IN RELATION TO THE AGING BABY BOOM GENERATION: REPORT TO CONGRESS, 4-5 (2003) [hereinafter FUTURE SUPPLY], http://aspe.hhs.gov/daltcp/reports/ltcwork.pdf.

8. WAN HE ET AL., US DEP'T OF HEALTH & HUMAN SERVS. & US DEP'T OF COMMERCE, 65+ IN THE UNITED STATES: 2005, at 9 (2005), http://www.census.gov/prod/2006pubs/p23-209.pdf.

9. ADMIN. ON AGING, US DEP'T OF HEALTH & HUMAN SERVS., A PROFILE OF OLDER AMERICANS: 2011, at 2 (2011), http://www.aoa. gov/aoaroot/aging_statistics/Profile/2011/docs/2011profile.pdf.

10. Id. at 3.

11. JAMES T. PATTERSON, GRAND EXPECTATIONS: THE UNITED STATES, 1945–1974, at 77 (1997) (describing the increase in birth rates that started in 1946 and leveled off in 1964); see also FUTURE SUPPLY, supra note 7, at 7-8 (discussing the effect that aging baby boomers will have on the demand for caregiving).

12. HE ET AL., supra note 8, at 6. The population growth of elderly Americans has been the most pronounced among individuals eighty-five and older. See id. This segment of the elderly population, which is the fastest growing, included 4.7 million people in 2003. Id. It is expected to double to 9.6 million in 2030, and to double yet again to 20.9 million in 2050, the point at which all of the remaining boomers will be eighty-five and older. Id.

13. See Long-Term Care: Aging Baby Boom Generation Will Increase Demand and Burden on Federal and State Budgets: Testimony before the S. Special Comm. on Aging, 107th Cong. 3 (2002) (statement of David M. Walker, Comptroller General of the United States), available at http://www.gao.gov/ new.items/d02544t.pdf (highlighting medical conditions among the elderly that have led to an increase in demand for long-term care services).

14. FUTURE SUPPLY, supra note 7, at 3-5; H. Stephen Kaye et al., The Personal Assistance Workforce: Trends in Supply and Demand, 25 HEALTH AFF. 1113, 1115 (2006); Peggie R. Smith, Elder Care, Gender, and Work: The Work-Family Issue of the 21st Century, 25 BERKELEY J. EMP. & LAB. L. 351, 356-57 (2004) [hereinafter Smith, Elder Care].

15. HE ET AL., supra note 8, at 58 (distinguishing between activities of daily living which include personal care tasks such as bathing, eating, toileting, and dressing, and instrumental activities which include "household management tasks like preparing one's own meals, doing light housework, managing one's own money, using the telephone, and shopping for personal items").

16. See ROBYN I. STONE, LONG-TERM CARE FOR THE ELDERLY WITH DISABILITIES: CURRENT POLICY, EMERGING TRENDS, AND IMPLICATIONS FOR THE TWENTY-FIRST CENTURY, 8 (2000), http:// www.milbank.org/reports/0008stone/ LongTermCare_Mech5.pdf; Kaye et al., supra note 14, at 1113.

17. Lynn F. Feinberg, Issue Brief: State Support for Family Caregivers and Paid Home Care Workers, NGA CTR. FOR BEST PRACTICES, 5 (2004), http:// www.subnet.nga.org/ci/assets/4-caregivers.pdf ("Twenty-eight percent of community-based elders receive assistance from both family and paid in-home workers, and eight percent of elders receive care solely from paid in-home workers.").

18. See US GEN. ACCOUNTING OFFICE, GAO/PEMD-96-5, LONG-TERM CARE: SOME STATES APPLY CRIMINAL BACKGROUND CHECKS

TO HOME CARE WORKERS, 4 (1996) [hereinafter LONG-TERM CARE] (connecting the increased reliance on home care with projections "indicat[ing] that labor force participation will continue to increase among women, who have traditionally provided much of the informal care for the elderly").

19. Steven J. Katz et al., Gender Disparities in the Receipt of Home Care for Elderly People With Disability in the United States, 284 J. AM. MED. ASS'N 3022, 3022 (2000) ("[C]hanges in the pattern of living arrangements will increase the number of elderly people living alone and thus reduce the availability of informal care."); Diane Rowland, Measuring the Elderly's Need for Home Care, 8 HEALTH AFF. 39, 48 (1989) ("[M]ore than one in four elderly people with multiple impairments live alone. For this group, the absence of a resident caregiver is likely to result in a greater need for formal home care services.").

20. See LONG-TERM CARE, supra note 18, at 4 ("Among those in need of home care, reliance on paid home care workers is also expected to rise, partly because adults in the baby boom generation have had smaller numbers of children and will therefore have fewer available to provide or supervise their care in old age."); see also Smith, Elder Care, supra note 14, at 360-61 (discussing the gendered dimension of elder care as it relates to elderly women who have outlived their husbands).

21. Smith, Elder Care, supra note 14, at 367-68 (referencing a study conducted by the National Council on Aging).

22. MATURE MKT. INST., MILES AWAY: THE METLIFE STUDY OF LONG-DISTANCE CAREGIVING, 3 (2004), https://www.metlife.com/assets/cao/ mmi/ publications/studies/mmi-miles-away-long-distance-caregiving.pdf.

23. The 1.8 million figure reflects the combined total for home-health and personal-care aides. OCCUPATIONAL OUTLOOK HANDBOOK 2012–13, supra note 2.

24. See STEVEN L. DAWSON & RICK SURPIN, DIRECT-CARE HEALTH WORKERS: THE UNNECESSARY CRISIS IN LONG-TERM CARE, 12 (2001), http://phinational.org/sites/phinational.org/files/clearinghouse/Aspen. pdf ("[B]eneath the formal sector lies a gray-market workforce of paid caregivers who are hired directly by consumers, but whose income is not reported. The size of this unreported workforce is significant but unquantifiable."); ROBYN I. STONE, LONG-TERM CARE WORKFORCE SHORTAGES: IMPACT ON FAMILIES, 2 (2001) [hereinafter STONE, WORKFORCE SHORTAGES], http://caregiver.org/caregiver/jsp/content/pdfs/op_2001_10_ policybrief_3.pdf ("[M]any home care workers are hired privately and official federal statistics may not include them."); see also US DEP'T OF HEALTH & HUMAN SERVS., NURSING AIDES, HOME HEALTH AIDES, AND RELATED HEALTH CARE OCCUPATIONS—NATIONAL AND LOCAL WORKFORCE SHORTAGES AND ASSOCIATED DATA NEEDS, 9 (2004) [hereinafter HOME HEALTH AIDES], http://phinational.org/sites/ phinational.org/files/clearinghouse/RNandHomeAides.pdf (observing that

there is "a sizable gray market of direct care workforce who consumers hire directly").

25. See STONE, WORKFORCE SHORTAGES, supra note 24, at 2.

26. OCCUPATIONAL OUTLOOK HANDBOOK 2012–13, supra note 2.

27. James Cooper & Diane Cooper, Crisis in Workforce Supply—Read All About It!, 13 ANNALS OF LONG-TERM CARE 23, 24 (2005) (adding that relative to workers in other jobs, the typical paid direct-care worker is "more likely to be nonwhite. Only 10-20 percent of direct care workers are male. Home care aides tend to be older than aides in other settings, and less likely to be native-born US citizens."); Rhonda J. V. Montgomery et al., A Profile of Home Care Workers from the 2000 Census: How It Changes What We Know, 45 GER-ONTOLOGIST 593, 595 (2005) (explaining that typical direct-care workers are women who are "much less likely to be under the age of 25 and more likely to be 65 years or older").

28. US GEN. ACCOUNTING OFFICE, GAO-01-750T, NURSING WORK-FORCE: RECRUITMENT AND RETENTION OF NURSES AND NURSE AIDES IS A GROWING CONCERN: TESTIMONY BEFORE THE S. COMM. ON HEALTH, EDUCATION, LABOR & PENSIONS, 107th Cong. 22 (statement of William J. Scanlon, Director, Health Care Issues) (2001), available at http://www.gao.gov/new.items/d01750t.pdf ("Nursing home and home health care aides are also two to three times more likely as other work-ers to be unmarried and have children at home."); STONE, WORKFORCE SHORTAGES, supra note 24, at 2 ("Compared to the workforce in general, nursing home and home health care aides are more likely to be non-white, unmarried and with children under age 18 at home.").

29. DAWSON & SURPIN, supra note 24, at 12 (observing that "86 percent of [direct-care workers] are women, [and that] 30 percent are women of color"); Montgomery et al., supra note 27, at 595 ("[T]he home care industry tends to have somewhat fewer African American workers and proportionally more Hispanic or Latino workers.").

30. Montgomery et al., supra note 27, at 595.

31. See Application of the Fair Labor Standards Act to Domestic Service, 76 Fed. Reg. 81190, 81192 (proposed Dec. 27, 2011) (to be codified at 29 C.F.R. pt. 552) [hereinafter FLSA Application].

32. PARAPROFESSIONAL HEALTHCARE INST., WHO ARE DIRECT-CARE WORKERS?, 2-3 (2011) [hereinafter "WHO ARE DIRECT CARE WORKERS?"], http://phinational.org/sites/phinational.org/files/clearinghouse/PHI percent20Facts percent203.pdf (reporting a median hourly wage of $9.46 for personal care aides and $9.85 for home health aides).

33. Id. at 2.; see also BERNADETTE WRIGHT, AARP PUB. POLICY INST., DIRECT CARE WORKERS IN LONG-TERM CARE, 1 (2005), http://www.hcbs.org/files/75/3748/directcare.pdf (reporting that "30.5 percent of home care aides . . . work part time").

34. WHO ARE DIRECT-CARE WORKERS?, supra note 32, at 2.

35. Steven Greenhouse, Wage Protection for Home Care Workers, N.Y. TIMES, Dec. 16, 2011, at B2; see also Susan Harmuth, The Direct Care Workforce Crisis in Long-Term Care, 63 N.C. MED. J. 87, 89 (2002) (highlighting a government report indicating that "nurse aides working in home care and nursing homes are twice as likely as workers in other occupations to receive public benefits, particularly food stamps and/or Medicaid-covered health benefits").

36. DAWSON & SURPIN, supra note 24, at 6 ("The quality of direct-care jobs tends to be extremely poor. Wages are low and benefits few; ironically, most direct-care staff do not receive employer-paid health insurance."); Rebecca Donovan, "We Care for the Most Important People in Your Life": Home Care Workers in New York City, WOMEN'S STUD. Q., Spring/Summer 1989, at 56, 62 (reporting on the lack of medical benefits available to home care workers).

37. See PAUL SOHN ET AL., NATIONAL EMPLOYMENT LAW PROJECT, FAIR PAY FOR HOME CARE WORKERS: REFORMING THE US DEPARTMENT OF LABOR'S COMPANIONSHIP REGULATIONS UNDER THE FAIR LABOR STANDARDS ACT, 8 (2011), available at http://nelp.3cdn.net/ba11b257b1bb32f70e_4rm62qgkj.pdf.

38. See Brian J. Taylor & Michael Donnelly, Risks to Home Care Workers: Professional Perspectives, 8 HEALTH, RISK & SOC'Y 239, 245 (2006) ("[H]ome care workers face[d] many and varied hazards ranging across access issues, hygiene and infection, manual handling, aggression and harassment, domestic and farm animals, fleas and safety of home equipment.").

39. BUREAU OF LABOR STATISTICS, US DEP'T OF LABOR, OCCUPATIONAL OUTLOOK HANDBOOK 450 (2010–11 ed.) (commenting that some home care clients "are pleasant and cooperative; others are angry, abusive, depressed, or otherwise difficult"); see generally Peggie R. Smith, The Pitfalls of Home: Protecting the Health and Safety of Paid Domestic Workers, 23 CANADIAN J. OF WOMEN & L. 309 (2011) [hereinafter Smith, The Pitfalls of Home] (discussing the health and safety issues confronting home care workers).

40. Donovan, supra note 36, at 62-63 (observing that workers resent their "second-class position" and feel undervalued).

41. The Fair Home Health Care Act: Hearing on H.R. 3582 Before the Subcomm. on Workforce Protections and the H. Comm. on Education & Labor, 110th Cong. 3 (2007) (statement of Hon. Lynn C. Woolsey, Chairwoman, Subcomm. on Workforce Protections).

42. Long Island Care at Home, Ltd. v. Coke, 551 US 158, 164 (2007).

43. Fair Labor Standards Act of 1938, 29 USC. §§ 206(a)(1), 207(a)(1) (2006).

44. Patricia Mulkeen, Comment, Private Household Workers and the Fair Labor Standards Act, 5 CONN. L. REV. 623, 626 (1973).

45. 29 USC. § 206(f)(1) (2006) (including domestic service workers in the minimum wage provision); 29 USC. § 207(l) (2006) (including domestic service workers in the overtime provision).

46. 29 USC. § 213(a)(15) (2006).
47. See Brief for Law Professors and Historians as Amici Curiae Supporting Respondents at 12-13, Long Island Care at Home, Ltd. v. Coke, 551 US 158 (2007) (No. 06-593) [hereinafter Brief for Law Professors and Historians].
48. Id.
49. Application of the Fair Labor Standards Act to Domestic Service, 66 Fed. Reg. 5481, 5482 (proposed Jan. 19, 2001) (quoting Sen. Williams during the 1974 FLSA Amendments).
50. See Brief for Law Professors and Historians, supra note 47, at 4-11.
51. Brief for the Urban Justice Center et al. as Amici Curiae Supporting Respondent at 7, Long Island Care at Home, Ltd. v. Coke, 551 US 158 (2007) (No. 06-593) (citing Rhonda J.V. Montgomery et al., A Profile of Home Care Workers from the 2000 Census: How It Changes What We Know, 45 GERONTOLOGIST 593, 597 (2005)).
52. See WRIGHT, supra note 33, at 1.
53. 29 C.F.R. § 552.6 (2012).
54. 29 C.F.R. § 552.109(a).
55. Long Island Care at Home, Ltd. v. Coke, 551 US 158, 164 (2007).
56. Id. at 174-75.
57. See Greenhouse, supra note 35.
58. See FLSA Application, supra note 31, at 81,232 ("Medicare and Medicaid together paid over one-half of the funds to freestanding agencies (37 and 19 percent, respectively). State and local governments account for 20 percent, while private health insurance accounts for 12 percent. Out-of-pocket funds account for 10 percent of agency revenues.").
59. See id.
60. See id. at 81,223 (noting that "because approximately 75 percent of expenditures on home health services are reimbursed by Medicare and Medicaid, the effect of the rule depends vitally on how Medicare and Medicaid respond to the increase in the cost of providing home health services"); see also Greenhouse, supra note 35 (stating the opinion of then Labor Secretary Hilda Solis that any increased costs associated with the proposal would be "modest").
61. See, e.g., FLSA Application, supra note 31, at 81, 232 (discussing the necessity of protecting such workers for both clients and the field).
62. Brief for AARP and Older Women's League as Amici Curiae Supporting Respondent at 13, Long Island Care at Home, Ltd. v. Coke, 551 US 158 (2007) (No. 06-693) [hereinafter AARP and Older Women's League] (citing DORIE SEAVEY, THE COST OF FRONTLINE TURNOVER IN LONG-TERM CARE, BETTER
63. Id.
64. See FLSA Application, supra note 31, at 81,203-04 (overviewing the extent to which state minimum wage and overtime provisions apply to home care workers).
65. See id. at 81,197 ("The fact that these state statutes exist negates many of the

objections raised in the past regarding the feasibility and expense of prohibiting third parties from claiming the companionship and live-in worker exemptions.").

66. See Brief for the United States as Amicus Curiae at 16, Long Island Care at Home, Ltd. v. Coke, 551 US 158 (2007) (No. 04-1315) (highlighting various groups that submitted amicus briefs in *Coke* which indicated that the decision would increase the cost of home care and disrupt services for the elderly and disabled); Jonathan D. Colburn, Home Health Firms Watch Developments in Overtime Case, SAN FERN. V. BUS. J., Jan. 30, 2006, at 9.

67. See FLSA Application, supra note 31, at 81,229 ("Job satisfaction, and the desire to remain in a given position, is highly correlated with wages, workload, and working conditions.").

68. AARP and Older Women's League, supra note 62, at 4.

69. See SEAVEY, supra note 62, at 15.

70. STONE, WORKFORCE SHORTAGES, supra note 24, at 1.

71. FLSA Application, supra note 31, at 81,231. While researchers agree that turnover in home care is a major problem, estimates of the problem vary. See, e.g., DAWSON & SURPIN, supra note 24, at 1 (reporting turnover rates among direct-care workers range between 40 and 100 percent annually); CAROL RAPHAEL, LONG-TERM CARE: CONFRONTING TODAY'S CHALLENGES, 1 (2003), http://www.academyhealth.org/files/publications/ltcchallenges.pdf (reporting a 28 percent turnover rate for home health aides).

72. Harmuth, supra note 35, at 89.

73. See SEAVEY, supra note 62, at 15.

74. See, e.g., HOME HEALTH AIDES, supra note 24, at v ("In areas where levels of service have been reduced, elderly or chronically ill persons deprived of access to care must either remain in more restrictive, more costly environments . . . or seek care from family or friends. Both quality of care and quality of life suffer as people are denied services, or services are provided by persons less qualified or experienced."); SEAVEY, supra note 62, at 15 ("Strong arguments can be made that turnover adversely affects continuity of care and care recipient relationships, causing disruptions that prevent or interfere with the development of relationships critical to both client and caregiver.").

75. See Ron Osterhout & Rick Zawadski, On Homecare Workforce, POL'Y & PRACTICE, Mar. 2006, at 30.

76. AARP and Older Women's League, supra note 62, at 15.

77. See supra note 64 and accompanying text.

78. See Greenhouse, supra note 35. The current proposed revisions mark the fourth time that the DOL has proposed amending the FLSA regulations on domestic service in a manner that would limit applicability of the companionship exemption to third-party domestic workers. See FLSA Application, supra note 31, at 81,196 (indicating that the Department earlier proposed revisions in 1993, 1995, and 2001). The 2001 proposed revisions, issued under President William Clinton's administration, were withdrawn by the Bush administration

before they became final. See Application of the Fair Labor Standards Act to Domestic Service, 67 Fed. Reg. 16,668, 16,668 (proposed Apr. 8, 2002) (to be codified at 29 C.F.R. pt. 552).

79. See FLSA Application, supra note 31, at 81,190.
80. See id.
81. Id. at 81,192.
82. See id.
83. 29 C.F.R. § 552.3 (2012); see also FLSA Application, supra note 31, at 81,192 (referencing Senate Report No. 93–690, at 20).
84. 29 C.F.R. § 552.3; see also FLSA Application, supra note 31, at 81,192 (referencing Senate Report No. 93–690, at 20).
85. FLSA Application, supra note 31, at 81,192.
86. See id. at 81,190, 81,192.
87. 29 C.F.R. § 552.6.
88. See id.
89. Id.
90. Id.
91. See id.
92. FLSA Application, supra note 31, at 81,193.
93. Id. (referencing H.R. REP. NO. 93-913, at 36 (1974)).
94. Id.
95. The exemption only applies to domestic workers like home care workers who "provide companionship services for individuals who (because of age or infirmity) are unable to care for themselves." 29 USC. § 213(a)(15) (2006).
96. FLSA Application, supra note 31, at 81,193.
97. Id. at 81,193-94.
98. Id. (stating that "incidental services must be performed attendant to and in conjunction with the provision of fellowship and protection and in close physical proximity to the aged or infirm individual" and adding that "[s]hould the provision of these incidental services exceed 20 percent of the total hours worked in any workweek, then the exemption may not be claimed for that week and workers must be paid minimum wage and overtime").
99. See id. at 81,193.
100. Long Island Home Care, Ltd. v. Coke, 551 US 158 (2007).
101. See id.
102. Respondent's Brief in Opposition at 21, Long Island Care at Home, Ltd. v. Coke, 551 US 158 (2007) (No. 06-593); Brief for Law Professors and Historians, supra note 47, at 4.
103. See Application of the Fair Labor Standards Act to Domestic Service, 39 Fed. Reg. 35,383, 35,385 (Oct. 1, 1974) ("Employees who are engaged in providing . . . companionship services and who are employed by an employer other than the families or households using such services . . . [were] subject to the [FLSA] prior to the 1974 Amendments."); FLSA Application, supra note 31, at 81,196 ("Congress did not intend for the 1974 Amendments, which sought

to extend the reach of the FLSA, to exclude workers already covered by the Act. The focus of the floor debate concerned the extension of coverage to categories of domestic workers who were not already covered by the FLSA, specifically, those not employed by an enterprise-covered agency.").

104. See Brief for Law Professors and Historians, supra note 47, at 5 ("[I]t seems unlikely that Congress, while aiming to protect more domestic service employees, would have simultaneously excluded previously included domestic service employees without any reference to doing so in the Amendments' legislative history.").

105. See H.R. REP. NO. 93-913, at 35 (1974) (emphasis added); S. REP. NO. 93-690, at 20 (1974) (emphasis added); S. REP. NO. 93-300, at 22 (1973) (emphasis added).

106. FLSA Application, supra note 31, at 81,196.

107. See Sandra Butler, Providing Labor Protections for Home Care Workers, SCHOLARS STRATEGY NETWORK, 2 (June 2012), http://www.scholarsstrategynetwork.org/sites/default/files/ssn_basic_facts_butler_on_labor_protection_0.pdf.

108. In June 2012, Republicans proposed a new law, the "Companionship Exemption Protection Act," which would preserve the Coke ruling and continue to deny home care workers FLSA protection. S. 3280, 112th Cong. (2012); see also Home Care Aides Await Decision on New Labor Rules, NPR (Feb. 3, 2013), http://www.npr.org/2013/02/03/171000803/health-care-aides-await-labor-decision-on-minimum-wage (describing opposition to the proposal from companies that employ home care workers).

109. See VNAA Policy Team, DOL Sends Home Health Companionship Final Rule to OMB, VISITING NURSE ASS'N OF AM. (Jan. 22, 2013), http://vnaa.org/article_content.asp?edition=3&section=1&article=134 (noting that the Office of Management and Budget has ninety days to issue the final rule).

110. See Harmuth, supra note 35, at 93 ("The crisis is already here and, in the absence of appropriate and effective action, shortages will only get worse.").

Reframing the Language of Long-Term Care Can Shape Policy, Improve Public Perception

By Victoria R. Ballesteros and Athan G. Bezaitis
Generations, Spring 2011

Americans remain uninformed and unsure of what to do about long-term care. Stating the case in plain language will help steer them in the right direction.

Last October, President Barack Obama signed The Plain Writing Act of 2010, (H.R. 946), requiring the federal government to write all new publications, forms, and publicly distributed documents in a clear, concise, well-organized manner that follows the best practices of "plain language writing" (Congressional Research Service, 2010). The point was to better engage citizens in the work of their government, and to avoid turning people off with the jargon and complicated, bureaucratic wonk-speak of policy insiders.

Those dedicated to improving policy and reshaping our nation's long-term-care system should take note. Noble efforts [have been made] to address the needs of older adults and individuals in conversations about affordable long-term care options that currently exist, as well as those that will soon become available to support elders. This means telling stories and crafting messages more accessible to those not versed in the details of policies and programs on aging, and their associated payment systems.

The public has largely been excluded from these discussions, leaving everyday Americans confused about the range or lack of potential medical care and supportive service options. Older people and their family members are often misinformed about who will pay for needed care and services; and, in general, they are afraid to discuss aging and options for receiving support if the need arises. The Community Living Assistance Services and Supports (CLASS) provision of the Affordable Care Act (ACA) creates a public, voluntary long-term-care insurance program. Yet those who stand to gain the most from this program are tuned out. Planning for long-term care isn't even on their radar.

The American Public Speaks

In June 2009, The SCAN Foundation commissioned a national survey to understand public opinion toward long-term care and its association with healthcare reform.

The poll overwhelmingly demonstrated people's concern about being able to afford long-term-care services in the future, and showed broad-based support for improving coverage for home- and community-based services. Nine out of ten Americans (92 percent) said it was important to improve insurance coverage for services that help people remain in their homes instead of going into skilled nursing facilities. The findings crossed party lines; majorities of Republicans (90 percent), Independents (89 percent), and Democrats (97 percent) reported that improving coverage to help people remain in their homes was important (Lake Research Partners, 2009).

Furthermore, eight in ten Americans (80 percent) supported improving insurance coverage for home- and community-based long-term-care-services as part of healthcare reform, again with support crossing party lines. Lastly, and perhaps most important, a large majority (78 percent) of Americans felt health-care reform legislation would benefit them or a family member if it included improved coverage for home- and community-based long-term-care services.

Even younger Americans, ages 18 to 34, saw a personal benefit (85 percent) if healthcare reform improved coverage for long-term-care services. These findings again crossed the political spectrum, with Americans who identify as Republican (68 percent), Independent (67 percent), and Democrat (90 percent) saying they would benefit personally (Lake Research Partners, 2009).

Following the ACA's passage in March 2010, The SCAN Foundation and the UCLA Center for Health Policy Research commissioned a poll to find the level of understanding, attitudes, and beliefs of California voters ages 40 and older on long-term care. Conducted by Lake Research Partners and American Viewpoint, survey responders once again expressed consternation about how to afford services to care for themselves and their loved ones. The majority of voters ages 40 and older were worried about being able to afford long-term care, concerned about losing their savings to pay for it, and looking to their elected officials to improve its affordability. Concerns about these issues crossed not only party lines, but also income levels, race, and gender (Lake Research Partners and American Viewpoint, 2010). These findings were indicative of a strong desire to have legislators take action to improve the system of care.

Armed with these poll results, The SCAN Foundation next conducted a series of twelve focus groups across the country, followed by polling data, to find out how adults ages 40 and older understand and talk about these issues with one another in a non-threatening, "kitchen-table" discussion. Tapping individuals from urban and rural settings and seeking diverse backgrounds and experiences, the primary goal was to gauge individual attitudes about aging, long-term care, and planning for long-term-care services.

Focus group findings indicated most people are unsure of what the phrase "long-term care" even means, and are afraid of looking ahead to a time when they might need such assistance. They cannot or will not envision themselves ever being functionally impaired or planning for these needs. When informed that 70 percent of Americans ages 65 and over will need some form of assistance at some point in their lives (The SCAN Foundation, 2010), people expressed concern because they did not know how to prepare for such an event.

What Resonates, What Works?

In December 2010, The SCAN Foundation commissioned another national survey of voters ages 40 and older to further gauge language, messaging, and attitudes about aging. The findings were consistent with prior polling and focus group work, but several key points emerged that can serve as building blocks for encouraging a national dialog around long-term care.

Several phrases resonate well with the public. When pressed to think about the future, people want to age with "dignity, independence, choice," and at home. Most people prefer to think that if the time comes when they will need everyday assistance, they could get by "with a little help," and believe it should be available to them through "a network of supportive services." People also expressed a desire to be happy when they age. And, those taking the survey responded best to a positive framework that focuses on a vision of what could be, rather than to negative portrayals of a fragmented or broken system.

In other words, when talking about long-term-care issues, it's important to talk about what people want and what can be achieved rather than scaring them or focusing on the system's problems, which often leaves them feeling helpless and powerless. If we can move people to think about securing their ability to age with dignity in a place of their choosing in the same way most of us acknowledge the importance of planning for retirement, we will be successful in reframing the perception of long-term care.

This work signals a broad opportunity for all stakeholders interested in transforming care for vulnerable elders to engage the public with information and education, and provide them with concrete actions to take. The lesson for us is clear as we work together to support the implementation of CLASS and other key provisions of the ACA that can improve the connectivity between medical care and supportive services. It is imperative that we avoid overcomplicating the already complex issues of long-term care or long-term services and supports with language that is hard to understand.

Without a new lexicon that "takes the fear out of aging" as reported in our focus groups, we won't gain the public's attention, and opportunities for a public outcry to improve care for vulnerable elders will be lost.

But don't take our word for it—or that of the Obama Administration. The public has spoken: It's what they want.

References

Congressional Research Service. 2010. "Bill Summary & Status, 111th Congress (2009–2010), H.R. 946." http://thomas.loc.gov/cgi-bin/bdquery/z?d111: HR00946:@@@D&summ2=4&. Retrieved February 17, 2011.

Lake Research Partners. 2009. "New Poll Shows Americans More Likely to Favor Health Care Reform if it Improves Coverage for Long-Term Care Services." Final report to The SCAN Foundation. www.thescan foundation.org/sites/default/files/Media%20 Report%20final%20070609.pdf. Retrieved February 17, 2011.

Lake Research Partners and American Viewpoint. 2010. "New Poll Shows California Voters 40 and Older Largely Unprepared for Costs of Long-Term Care Services." Final report to The SCAN Foundation. www.thescanfoundation.org/sites/default/files/ TSF-UCLA%20Poll%20Results_1.pdf. Retrieved February 17, 2011.

The SCAN Foundation. 2010. "Who Needs and Who Uses Long Term Care? Fact Sheet No. 4." www. thescanfoundation.org/sites/default/files/Fact_Sheet_No._4_Final_0.pdf. Retrieved February 17, 2011.

The Aging of the Baby Boom and the Growing Care Gap: A Look at Future Declines in the Availability of Family Caregivers

By Donald Redfoot, Lynn Feinberg, and Ari Houser
AARP, August 13, 2013

The majority of long-term services and supports are provided by family members. But the supply of family caregivers is unlikely to keep pace with future demand. The following report defines a "caregiver support ratio" as the number of potential caregivers aged 45–64 for each person aged 80 and older. The report uses this support ratio to estimate the availability of family caregivers during the next few decades. In 2010, the caregiver support ratio was more than 7 potential caregivers for every person in the high-risk years of 80-plus. By 2030, the ratio is projected to decline sharply to 4 to 1; and it is expected to further fall to less than 3 to 1 in 2050, when all boomers will be in the high-risk years of late life.

Understanding the effects of the relative size of the baby boom (those born between 1946 and 1964), compared to preceding and succeeding age cohorts, is essential to anticipating the demand for long-term services and supports (LTSS) for this cohort and the potential availability of family caregivers. Tracking the availability of potential caregivers provides a roadmap of the magnitude and timing of the challenges that we will face in the next few decades, as the caregiver gap widens.

People aged 80 years and older are the most likely to need LTSS. As the population in this age group increases during the next 20 years, the number of people in the primary caregiving years (ages 45–64) is projected to remain flat, due in part to changing family size and composition. As a result, the availability of potential family caregivers (mostly adult children) to arrange, coordinate, and provide LTSS is expected to decline dramatically and overall care burdens will likely intensify—especially as baby boomers move into late old age.

Family Caregivers: The Backbone of Long-Term Services and Supports

Family caregivers—including family members, partners, or close friends[1]—are a key factor in the ability to remain in one's home and in the community when disability strikes. More than two-thirds (68 percent) of Americans believe that they will be able to rely on their families to meet their LTSS needs when they require help,[2] but this belief may collide with the reality of dramatically shrinking availability of family caregivers.

If fewer family members are available to provide everyday assistance to the growing numbers of frail older people, more people are likely to need institutional care—at great personal cost—as well as costs to health care and LTSS programs. Greater reliance on fewer family caregivers to provide home- and community-based services could also add to costs borne by family members and close friends—in the form of increasing emotional and physical strain, competing demands of work and caregiving, and financial hardships.

In recent years, the role of family caregivers has greatly expanded from coordinating and providing personal care and household chores to include medical or nursing tasks (such as wound care and administering injections). These difficult nursing tasks were provided in hospitals and nursing homes and by home care providers, but increasingly, family members are called on to perform these tasks with little training or professional support.[3] As health care and LTSS shift from institutional to home-based care, the burdens on family caregivers will likely increase without adequate supportive services for caregiving families.

Measuring the Future Availability of Family Caregivers

One basic measure of the potential availability of caregivers is the ratio of the number of people in the most common caregiving age range divided by the number of older people most at risk of needing LTSS. To calculate this ratio, we used the ages of 45–64 as the most common age range for caregivers. The "average" family caregiver is a 49-year-old woman who works outside the home and spends about 20 hours per week providing unpaid care to her mother for nearly 5 years. Nearly two-thirds of family caregivers are female (65 percent).

More than 8 in 10 are caring for a relative or friend aged 50 or older.[4]

Cohort size also affects the availability of paid direct care workers, such as nurse aides, home health aides, and personal and home care aides. Paid caregivers often provide essential, hands-on help to family caregivers struggling to provide good care to loved ones. More than half (57 percent) of home health aides are aged 45 and older.[5] Direct care workers who are self-employed or working directly for private households are, on average, 48 years old.[6]

We used ages 80 and older as our measure of the risk of needing LTSS. Seven in 10 (70.5 percent) people aged 80 and older had some kind of disability in 2010, compared to one in five (19.7 percent) people aged 45–54.[7] More than half (55.8 percent) of people aged 80 and older have a severe disability, and nearly one in three (30.2 percent) need assistance from others with one or more activities of daily living (ADLs), such as bathing, dressing, or using the toilet, or instrumental activities of daily living (IADLs), such as using the telephone, preparing meals, or paying bills.[8]

This Insight on the Issues uses data from Regional Economic Models, Inc. (REMI) to calculate a national caregiver support ratio as well as caregiver support ratios for each state by dividing the population aged 45–64 by the population aged 80 and older. The REMI model uses historical data for 1990 through 2010, and the model's most current population projections are used to calculate the ratios from 2011 to 2050. A brief summary of the assumptions of the projections can be found in Appendix A. See Appendix B for national and state historical and projected care-giver support ratios.

Caregiver Support Ratios Are Projected to Decline Dramatically as Boomers Transition from Caregivers to Care Recipients

The following discussion of findings is organized by 20-year periods, each of which is characterized by distinctive trends. Each section looks at the implications of changes in the caregiver ratio and other drivers of change in LTSS demand, to anticipate the challenges we will face as a nation to meet that demand.

- The period from 1990 to 2010 was marked by boomers aging into the prime caregiving years, with the result that the caregiver ratio was high and increasing.

- The period from 2010 to 2030 will be a period of transition as boomers age into old age and the caregiver ratio declines—especially when the oldest boomers begin to reach age 80 in the 2020s.

- The period from 2030 to 2050 will include all remaining boomers aging into the high-risk years of 80-plus, and the caregiver ratio is expected to continue to drift downward.

1990–2010

Despite large increases in the oldest population, the caregiver support ratio increased slightly as boomers boosted family caregiving.

Despite the attention given to the graying of the baby boomers and their potential future effect on health care and LTSS, little attention has been paid to the role that boomers have already played and are still playing as caregivers for their aging parents. From 1990 to 2010, the 80-plus population increased by 62 percent, but the number of potential caregivers aged 45–64 increased more rapidly—by 77 percent—as boomers aged into the peak caregiving years.

As a result, the number of potential caregivers for every person aged 80-plus increased from 6.6 in 1990 to 7.2 in 2010, the year in which the caregiver ages of 45–64 corresponded to the ages of the baby boomers.

Research has demonstrated the critical importance of family support in maintaining independence and reducing nursing home use among older people with disabilities.[9] The increasing caregiver support ratio, declining rate of widowhood (due, in large part, to the narrowing longevity gap between men and women), along with socioeconomic improvements and declines in disability,[10] have been major factors in favorable trends in the use of LTSS during the 1990s and 2000s. Between 1984 and 2004, institutional use declined by 37 percent among the older population, as the number of older people living in the community with two or more needs for assistance with ADLs rose by two-thirds.[11]

These trends have had major implications for public programs that provide LTSS assistance. Medicaid costs for institutional care would have been an estimated $24 billion higher in 2004 had utilization rates remained unchanged after 1984.[12] By 2010, the number of older people who received Medicaid assistance for nursing home services had declined by 26 percent from its peak in 1995, which translates into savings of tens of billions of dollars per year.[13]

While it is impossible to document the exact portion of these savings that is due to family caregiving, the high rates of family support among the growing number of older people with high levels of disabilities who live in the community suggest that such support has been a critical factor in the dramatic decline of institutionalization and Medicaid use during the past couple of decades.[14]

Trends varied somewhat from state to state, but generally exhibited favorably high caregiver support ratios. The ratio increased or stayed the same in 39 states and the District of Columbia, and increased by 1.0 or more potential caregivers per person aged 80-plus in 21 states. The caregiver ratio decreased in the other 11 states, but only 3 states with high ratios to start with (Alaska, Hawaii, and Nevada) saw declines of more than 0.5 caregivers for each person aged 80-plus (see Appendix B).

The increase in the caregiver support ratio reflects fertility patterns among the cohorts who aged into the 80-plus range between 1990 and 2010. The cohort who turned 80 years old in 1990 came into adulthood as the Great Depression of the 1930s struck. Because it was not a favorable time for family formation or child-bearing, nearly one in four (24.2 percent) women aged 80–84 in 1990 never had any children. By 2010, the percentage of women aged 80–84 who were childless had dropped by more than half to 11.6 percent, as women who had come into adulthood in the post–World War II years gave birth to the baby boom. The average number of children borne by women aged 80–84 increased from 2.3 in 1990 to 3.1 in 2010.[15]

The most important predictor of having someone to count on when an individual needs help in LTSS is being married, because spouses and adult children most often arrange, coordinate, and provide care and social support. Spousal support has increased as the rates of widowhood declined dramatically during the 1990s and 2000s. In 1990, 8 out of 10 women (81 percent) aged 85-plus were widowed—a rate that declined to 73 percent among women aged 85-plus in 2010. Among women aged 75–84, the decline was even sharper—from 65 percent to 46 percent.

Among men aged 85-plus, the widowhood rate declined from 40.5 percent to 36 percent; the rate declined from 21 percent to 14 percent among those aged 75–84.[16]

2010–2030

The caregiver support ratio is expected to plummet as boomers transition from caregivers into old age.

The decades of the 2010s and 2020s will be a period of transition, as boomers age out of the peak caregiving years and the oldest boomers age into the 80-plus high-risk years.

The departure of the boomers from the peak caregiving years will mean that the population aged 45–64 is projected to increase by only 1 percent between 2010 and 2030. During the same period, the 80-plus population is projected to increase by a whopping 79 percent.

The number of potential caregivers per person aged 80-plus is expected to decline fairly slowly during the 2010s—from 7.2 to 6.1 by 2020—as the declining numbers of boomers in the prime caregiver ages will be offset somewhat by the relatively small cohorts turning 80-plus who were born during the birth dearth of the Great Depression. But the pace of the decline is expected to accelerate during the 2020s—from 6.1 to 4.1 in 2030—especially when the oldest boomers start turning 80 years old in 2026.

In all states, the projected ratio of potential caregivers to people aged 80 and older will decline between 2010 and 2030 (see Appendix B). Sixteen states are projected to experience declines of 50 percent or more in the caregiver ratio by 2030.

The declining caregiver ratio once again reflects changes in the fertility rates of successive cohorts. Only 11.6 percent of the women who were 80–84 years old in 2010 were childless, but that will increase to 16.0 percent for those who are 80–84 years old in 2030.[17] The average number of children has declined from 3.1 among women aged 80–84 in 2010 to 2.0 among women who will be in that age group in 2030.

Further declines in widowhood are likely to be offset by increases in divorce for future cohorts of older women and men. As a result, the percentage of women who are projected to spend 10 years or more unmarried after age 65 will decrease only slightly, from 64 percent (among the cohort of women who will be 80–89 years old in 2010) to 60 percent (among women who are that age in 2030). This percentage will remain fairly constant among succeeding cohorts. Among men in these age cohorts, the percentage who are projected to spend 10 years or more unmarried will increase substantially, from 29 to 36 percent.[18]

The impact of these demographic changes will be further complicated by recent data that indicate the declines in disability rates may have stalled and even reversed among the young old and pre-retirees, largely because of increases in obesity.[19] The implications of these trends can be observed in projections of future demand for LTSS. The number of "frail older people" (those aged 65-plus with any disability) is projected to increase from 11 million in 2010 to 18 million in 2030.[20] The percentage of frail older people who are childless is projected to rise from 14 to 18 percent during this period, and the percentage of frail older people who have only one or two adult children is projected to increase from 38 to 49 percent.[21]

These numbers suggest that the increasing frail older population will have fewer potential family caregivers on whom they can rely.

2030–2050

The caregiver ratio is expected to decline further as boomers complete the transition to the high-risk years of 80 and older.

Meeting the LTSS needs of the baby boom has been called "the 2030 problem,"[22] because of the large number of boomers who are entering late old age at that time. The steep decline in the caregiver support ratio that accelerated in the 2020s will continue through the 2030s, as boomers cascade over the 80-year-old threshold. The 80-plus population is projected to increase by 44 percent between 2030 and 2040, while the number of caregivers aged 45–64 is projected to increase only 10 percent. In the 2040s, the ratio is expected to begin to bottom out, as the population aged 80-plus is projected to increase 17 percent and the aged 45–64 population increases 8 percent.

The caregiver ratio is projected to decrease from 4.1 to 2.9 between 2030 and 2050, when all boomers will enter the high-risk years of late old age. Once again, all 50 states and the District of Columbia are expected to experience further declines in the caregiver support ratio (see Appendix B).

The percentage of women who remain childless is projected to increase from 16.0 percent, among those aged 80–84 in 2030, to 18.8 percent of those of the same age in 2050, and the average number of children will decrease slightly, from 2.0 to 1.9.[23] Projecting marital status that far into the future is difficult, but the increased rates of divorce after age 50 suggest less marital stability in old age among boomers. The divorce rates of people aged 50 and older doubled between 1990 and 2010, especially among boomer cohorts.[24]

One in three baby boomers are currently unmarried, an increase of 50 percent since 1980.[25] Boomers are a substantial part of the 1.2 million people aged 65 or older who will live alone and will have no living children or siblings in 2020, up from 682,000 in 1990.[26] Childlessness among the older population with disabilities is projected to increase to 21 percent in 2040, and another 49 percent will have only one or two children.[27]

Conclusion

Demography is not destiny[28]—the policy decisions we make during the next decade will make a big difference in our ability to meet the challenges associated with the aging of the baby boom. But demographic trends certainly define the challenges we will face and establish the magnitude of the solutions that will be needed. The year 2010 was a watershed, as the caregiver support ratio climaxed and began a long, steep decline that will define the demand for LTSS for older people for decades to come.

The supply of family caregivers is unlikely to keep pace with demand to assist the growing number of frail older people in the future. In just 13 years, as the baby boomers age into their 80s, the decline in the caregiver support ratio will shift from a slow decline to a free fall.

From 7 potential caregivers per frail older person today, the caregiver ratio is projected to shrink to just 4 in 2030. The care gap is expected to widen even more as the ratio continues declining to 2.9 by 2050, when we have three times as many people aged 80 and older as there are today. These national trends will be reflected in major declines in the caregiver support ratio in all 50 states and the District of Columbia.

Rising demand and shrinking families to provide support suggest that the United States needs a comprehensive person- and family-centered LTSS policy that would better serve the needs of older persons with disabilities, support family and friends in their caregiving roles, and promote greater efficiencies in public spending. The challenges that face us are real, but they are not insurmountable—if we begin now to lay the foundation for a better system of LTSS and family support for the future.

Appendix A. Methodology

We used data from Regional Economic Models, Inc. (REMI) PI+ v1.4 model to calculate a national caregiver support ratio as well as caregiver support ratios for each state (see Appendix B), by dividing the population aged 45–64 by the population aged 80 and older. The REMI model uses historical data for 1990 through 2010, and projects demographic and economic conditions from 2011 to 2060.

The demographic projection component of the REMI model incorporates birth and survival rates by sex, race, age, and state. It also includes international and interstate migration by sex, race, age, and state.

Birth and survival rates are calculated by taking the changes in birth and survival rates from the Census Population Projection Assumptions file (national data only). These changes are applied to the last historical year birth and survival rates by sex, race, age, and state to form the forecasted state-level rates.

The international migration projections by race for the country (also from the census assumptions file) are divided among the states in the same proportion as the last historical year. Interstate migration is a calculation of the model and is responsive to macroeconomic conditions and historical interstate migration data. Additional detail on the methodology is available at http://www.remi.com.

The table in Appendix B below gives historical (1990 and 2010) and projected (2030 and 2050) caregiver support ratios for each state and the nation as a whole. One may observe that the state-to-state variation is much higher in the historical years than in the projected years. This is to be expected, as the projections represent a "middle case" based on assumptions that are uniform across states. The moderating influence of many years of such projections reduces interstate variance in the projected ratio. In actuality, states are likely to deviate from the baseline projection in unpredictable ways; because of this, it is not recommended to draw comparative inferences for the small differences in caregiver support ratios among states in 2030 or 2050.

Appendix B. Caregiver Support Ratios by State, 1990–2050

State	Support Ratio, by Year			
	1990	2010	2030	2050
United States	6.6	7.2	4.1	2.9
Alabama	6.8	7.8	3.9	3.2
Alaska	26.2	18.3	5.3	3.1
Arizona	6.8	7.0	2.6	1.8
Arkansas	5.6	7.0	3.9	3.2
California	7.6	7.7	4.4	2.7
Colorado	8.0	9.3	4.5	2.7
Connecticut	6.4	6.3	3.9	2.8
Delaware	7.9	7.4	3.5	2.8
District of Columbia	6.6	7.0	6.4	4.0
Florida	4.9	5.5	2.9	2.3
Georgia	8.5	10.1	4.8	3.1
Hawaii	8.7	6.1	2.9	2.1
Idaho	6.5	7.6	4.0	3.0
Illinois	6.5	7.1	4.9	3.3
Indiana	6.6	7.2	4.3	3.2
Iowa	4.6	5.6	3.3	2.3
Kansas	4.9	6.3	3.8	2.7
Kentucky	6.7	8.0	4.1	3.1
Louisiana	7.4	8.3	4.4	3.4
Maine	5.9	6.9	3.4	3.0
Maryland	8.6	8.1	4.2	2.8
Massachusetts	5.6	6.4	4.4	3.2
Michigan	7.3	7.0	4.1	3.3
Minnesota	5.4	6.9	4.3	2.7
Mississippi	6.2	8.0	4.1	3.3
Missouri	5.4	6.9	3.8	2.9
Montana	6.2	7.1	3.5	2.9
Nebraska	4.6	6.1	4.1	2.8
Nevada	12.4	10.0	3.4	2.0
New Hampshire	6.8	8.1	3.8	2.9
New Jersey	7.1	6.8	4.3	2.9
New Mexico	8.0	8.0	3.2	2.5
New York	6.5	6.6	4.8	3.5
North Carolina	7.7	8.0	3.9	2.7
North Dakota	4.5	5.5	4.2	3.0
Ohio	6.8	6.7	4.0	3.3
Oklahoma	5.8	7.4	3.8	3.1
Oregon	6.0	6.9	3.9	2.8
Pennsylvania	6.0	5.8	3.9	3.3
Rhode Island	5.3	5.7	3.9	3.0
South Carolina	8.6	8.3	3.6	2.9
South Dakota	4.4	5.8	3.9	2.9
Tennessee	6.9	8.1	4.1	3.2
Texas	7.6	9.2	4.8	3.0
Utah	7.6	8.3	5.8	3.4
Vermont	6.3	7.5	3.4	2.9
Virginia	8.4	8.5	4.2	2.8
Washington	6.9	7.9	4.4	2.8
West Virginia	6.2	6.8	3.4	3.1
Wisconsin	5.5	6.7	4.0	2.9
Wyoming	7.8	8.7	3.9	2.6

Source: AARP Public Policy Institute calculations based on REMI (Regional Economic Models, Inc.) 2013 baseline demographic projections.

Note: Data for 1990 and 2010 are historical; data for 2030 and 2050 are projected. Because of the uncertainty inherent in any model-based long-term population projections, we do not recommend comparing states for 2030 or 2050.

Notes

1. The term *family caregiver* is broadly defined and refers to any relative, partner, friend, or neighbor who has a significant relationship with, and who provides a broad range of assistance for, an older person or an adult with chronic or disabling conditions.

2. T. Thompson et al., *Long-Term Care: Perceptions, Experiences, and Attitudes among Americans Age 40 or Older* (Chicago, IL: The Associated Press-NORC Center for Public Affairs Research, 2013). Accessed at http://www.apnorc.org/PDFs/Long%20Term%20Care/AP_NORC_Long%20Term%20Care%20Perception_FINAL%20REPORT.pdf.

3. S. C. Reinhard, C. Levine, and S. Samis, *Home Alone: Family Caregivers Providing Complex Chronic Care* (Washington, DC: AARP; New York, NY: United Hospital Fund, October 2012). Funded by The John A. Hartford Foundation.

4. National Alliance for Caregiving (NAC) and AARP, *Caregiving in the U.S. 2009* (Bethesda, MD: NAC [National Alliance for Caregiving]; Washington, DC: AARP, November 2009). Funded by the MetLife Foundation.

5. G. Khatutsky et al., *Understanding Direct Care Workers: A Snapshot of Two of America's Most Important Jobs* (Washington, DC: Assistant Secretary for Planning and Evaluation, U.S. Department of Health and Human Services, March 2011).

6. PHI (Paraprofessional Healthcare Institute), Who Are Direct-care Workers? Facts 3 (New York, NY: PHI, February 2011 Update).

7. M. W. Bault, Americans with Disabilities: 2010 (Washington, DC: U.S. Census Bureau, U.S. Department of Commerce, July 2012).

8. Ibid.

9. C. Noel-Miller, "Spousal Loss, Children, and the Risk of Nursing Home Admission," *Journal of Gerontology* 65B(3) (2010) pp. 270–280. See also D. Lakdawalla and T. Philipson, "Aging and the Growth of Long-Term Care," Working Paper No. 6980 (Washington, DC: National Bureau for Economic Research, 1999).

10. D. Redfoot and A. Houser, More Older People with Disabilities Living in the Community: Trends from the National Long-Term Care Survey, 1984–2004, AARP Public Policy Institute Report No. 2010-08 (Washington, DC: AARP, September 2010). For the most recent update on disability trends among the very old, see also V. Freeman, B. Spillman, P. Andreski, J. Cornman, E. Crimmins, E. Kramarow, J. Lubitz, L. Martin, S. Merkin, R. Shoeni, T. Seeman, and T. Waidman, "Trends in Late Life Activity Limitations in the United States, An Update from Five National Surveys," *Demography*, Vol. 50, Issue 2 (April 2013), pp. 661–671.

11. Ibid.

12. Ibid.

13. D. L. Redfoot, The Good News about Medicaid Costs and an Aging Population (June 28, 2013). AARP Public Policy Institute blog: http://blog.aarp.org/2013/06/28/the-good-news-about-medicaid-costs-and-an-aging-population/.

14. A. Houser, M. J. Gibson, and D. L. Redfoot, Trends in Family Caregiving and Paid Home Care for Older Persons with Disabilities in the Community: Data from the National Long-Term Care Survey, AARP Public Policy Institute Report No. 2010-09 (Washington, DC: AARP, September 2010).

15. D. L. Redfoot and S. M. Pandya, Before the Boom: Trends in Long-Term Supportive Services for Older Americans with Disabilities, AARP Public Policy Institute Report No. 2002-15 (Washington, DC: AARP, 2002). On cohort fertility rate comparisons, see also S. E. Kirmeyer and B. E. Hamilton, "Childbearing Differences among Three Generations of U.S. Women," NHCS Brief No. 68 (Washington, DC: National Center for Health Statistics, August 2011).

16. Ibid. Updated with data from the U.S. Census Population data for 2010.

17. Redfoot and Pandya, op cit.

18. R. Johnson, "Private Resources and the Financing of Long-Term Care," presentation to the Institute of Medicine Forum on Aging, Disability, and Independence, June 12, 2013.

19. See Freeman et al., op cit. See also D. Lakdawalla, D. Goldman, J. Bhattacharya, M. Hurd, G. Joyce, and C. Panis, "Forecasting the Nursing Home Population," Medical Care 41(1) (2003), pp. 8–20.

20. These projections are from the Urban Institute's DYNASIM3 model. See M. M. Faureault and K. E. Smith, A Primer on the Dynamic Stimulation of Income Model, DYNASIM3 (Washington, DC: Urban Institute, 2004). Accessed at http://www.urban.org/UploadedPDF/410961_Dynasim3Primer.pdf.

21. R. W. Johnson, D. Toohey, and J. M. Weiner, Meeting the Long-Term Care Needs of the Baby Boomers: How Changing Families Will Affect Paid Helpers and Institutions (Washington, DC: The Urban Institute, May 2007).

22. J. R. Knickman and E. K. Snell, "The 2030 Problem: Care for Aging Baby Boomers," Health Services Research 37(4) (2002), pp. 849–884.

23. Redfoot and Pandya, op cit., updated with data from the U.S. Census fertility tables at http://www.census.gov/hhes/fertility/data/cps/2010.html.

24. S. L. Brown and I-Fen Lin, "The Gray Divorce Revolution: Rising Divorce among Middle-aged and Older Adults, 1990–2010," Journals of Gerontology Series B: Psychological Sciences and Social Sciences 67(6) (2012), pp. 731–741.

25. I. Fen-Lin and S. L. Brown, "Unmarried Boomers Confront Old Age: A National Portrait," The Gerontologist 52(2) (2012), pp. 153–165.

26. R. Stone, Long-Term Care: Coming of Age in the 21st Century, Wisconsin Family Impact Seminars (1999). Accessed at http://www.familyimpactseminars.org/s_wifis12c01.pdf.

27. Johnson et al., op cit.

28. R. Friedland and L. Summer, Demography Is Not Destiny (Washington, DC: National Academy on an Aging Society, January 1999).

Boomers' Aging Parents May Yield a Tax Deduction

Associated Press, January 25, 2013

Members of the sandwich generation—caught between supporting elderly parents whose assets are nearly exhausted and adult children without jobs—might find some relief come tax time.

The bottom line is, who's a dependent? Your kindergarten-age son, your adult daughter, her grandparents, or maybe an elderly uncle or aunt?

"There's a changing family dynamic because of the economy," said Bob Meighan, vice president of TurboTax, an online tax preparation service.

More people are living longer. According to the U.S. Census Bureau, the number of older Americans increased by 9.7 percent from 2000 to 2010, when there were about 40 million people age 65 or older. A longer lifespan puts added strain on retirement accounts, which have already taken a hit in the roller-coaster economy.

As a result, many baby boomers find themselves supporting their elderly parents, in some cases footing the bill for assisted living or nursing home care.

Meanwhile, the unemployment rate for adults age 20 to 24 was 13.7 percent in December, considerably higher than the overall rate of 7.8 percent.

Unable to find work, many young adults are returning home—or never leaving, relying on Mom and Dad for food, lodging and more.

What does this mean for taxes?

"A lot of filers are going to have to pay particular attention," Meighan said. More people may rely on tax software to help get them through the dependency issue.

Depending on individual circumstances, taxpayers may be able to claim both their parents and their children as dependents.

"The rules are very pro-taxpayer," said Mark Steber, chief tax officer at Jackson-Hewitt Tax Services. If you are taking care of someone and the IRS defines that clearly—age, income, residency tests and support—you should be able to claim the exemption, he says.

It comes down to the definition of dependent.

The Internal Revenue Service makes a distinction between a qualifying child and a qualifying relative.

To be a qualifying child, the person would have to be a child, stepchild, foster child or sibling, and under the age of 19, or 24 if in college, who has lived with you for at least half the year. The taxpayer would have to provide at least half the support.

A qualifying relative can be a child who doesn't meet the qualifying child requirement, a parent or stepparent, grandparent, niece or nephew, aunt or uncle or in-laws, according to the IRS. They do not necessarily have to live with you, but you do have to provide at least half the support for that person. And that person's income cannot exceed the personal exemption—$3,800 in 2012.

"Unlike a qualifying child, a qualifying relative can be any age," the IRS says in its Publication 17.

Taxpayers can take an exemption of $3,800 for each qualified child or relative who is a dependent.

Here are some examples from the IRS:

> "Your mother received $2,400 in Social Security benefits and $300 in interest. She paid $2,000 for lodging and $400 for recreation." If you spend more than $2,400 to support her, supplementing what she spends, and her annual income is less than $3,800, you can claim her as a dependent and take the full value of the exemption.

> "Your brother's daughter takes out a student loan of $2,500 and uses it to pay her college tuition. She is personally responsible for the loan. You provide $2,000 toward her total support. You cannot claim an exemption for her because you provide less than half of her support."

Usually the items that go into determining support are the cost of housing, food, clothing and medical costs, including doctor bills and medicine.

But it's not just the personal exemption that could help taxpayers. Individual taxpayers might qualify and get the "extra benefit" of filing as head of households if they legally can claim children, parents or relatives as a dependent, said Jackie Perlman, principal tax research analyst for H&R Block .

For example, the 15 percent tax bracket applies to taxable income up to $47,350 for heads of households and $35,350 for individual returns. At the 25 percent tax bracket, it's $133,300 for heads of households and $85,650 for single filers.

Steber said taxpayers have to understand that it's not just nuclear family members who might qualify. Think beyond children and parents. If you're providing half the support for an aunt or uncle, niece or nephew whose income for the year was under $3,800, you may be able to claim them as dependents.

2

The Economics of Senior Health Care

© Jim Gehrz/MC/Landov

Kathy DeYoung has chosen to work past the normal retirement age and is in sales at the Coach store in Edina, Minnesota.

What Aging Costs

As the percentage of the US population over the age of sixty-five increases, health care costs have a growing economic impact. In 2010, about 13 percent of the population (40 million people) was age sixty-five and over. But by 2030, nearly 20 percent of the population (72 million people) will be in this age group. This rapid shift means a corresponding increase in costs to care for the aging population.

Overall, the economic position of Americans age sixty-five and older is slightly better than past generations. In 2010, about 9 percent of older Americans lived below the poverty line, down from 15 percent in 1974. During that same period, the median household income increased from $21,100 to $31,410 (both amounts expressed in 2010 dollars), while the percentage of high-income households increased from 18 percent to 31 percent.

Many Americans age sixty-five and older live on fixed incomes such as Social Security and retirement pensions, and they must cover many expenses within these constraints. Approximately 40 percent of older households, for example, struggle with housing cost burden and spend more than 30 percent of their income on housing and utilities. However, one very large—and growing—cost for Americans age sixty-five and over is health care.

The average annual health care costs for individuals on Medicare rose from $9,850 in 1992 to $15,709 in 2008. These costs varied by race and ethnicity, as well as by income. Individuals with less than $10,000 in income incurred average annual health care costs of $21,924, while those with incomes above $30,000 incurred an average of $13,149. Costs also varied significantly based on whether individuals had any chronic health conditions or resided in a long-term care facility.

Medicare, Supplemental Insurance, and Out-of-Pocket Expenses

Most Americans age sixty-five and older obtain their health insurance through the federal government's Medicare program. Medicare offers a variety of plans, most of which operate similarly to private insurance policies. The beneficiary pays a premium to secure the policy, and the policy pays a portion of the health care cost as specified by the chosen plan. As with private insurance, the Medicare policy may be subject to deductibles, co-pays, and benefit caps.

Regardless of the plan selected, Medicare only covers part of health care costs, and it provides no coverage for dental services or long-term care. As a result, many Medicare recipients need supplemental insurance to be able to pay for services not covered. Some people have policies provided by a former employer, and others need to purchase supplemental insurance themselves on the private market. Low-income individuals may receive supplemental coverage from the government in the form of Medicaid, and the percentage of older Americans with Medicaid coverage increased from 10 percent in 2000 to 12 percent in 2009. Around 9 percent of Medicare enrollees do not have any form of supplemental insurance.

In 2008, Medicare paid for about 60 percent of health care costs for its enrollees, including all hospice care, plus most hospital, physician, and home health care costs. Enrollees paid about 18 percent of their costs out of pocket, excluding any supplemental insurance premiums, which can be quite expensive. Medicaid covered about 7 percent, and private insurance policies covered about 15 percent for others.

The percentage of older Americans incurring out-of-pocket health care expenses increased from 83 percent in 1977 to 94 percent in 2009. In 2009, 41 percent of those expenses were for prescription drugs alone. Additionally, older individuals are spending a growing percentage of their household income on health care services. This is especially true for those with an income below 125 percent of the poverty level, whose spending increased from 12 percent of their total income in 1977 to 22 percent in 2009. For individuals with incomes above this threshold, the percentage remained relatively steady at an average of 5 percent of their annual income.

Access to timely and affordable health care is extremely important, as preventative care can detect chronic conditions, such as cancer and heart disease, in their early stages, which allows for more effective treatment. This may in turn help keep overall health care costs down as the population ages. Between 1992 and 1997, the percentage of older Americans reporting that they delayed getting health care because of the cost decreased from about 10 percent to 5 percent, and has remained relatively constant since. The percentage of those who reported they had difficulty obtaining care was consistently around 2–3 percent. However, if out-of-pocket costs continue to rise, older Americans may once again delay seeking health care because of the expense, potentially leading to an increase in chronic conditions and reduced quality of life.

Prescription Drugs

As new medications have become available to treat a multitude of health conditions, prescription drug costs for older Americans have skyrocketed. In 1992, the cost was around $700 annually, but increased to $2,834 in 2008. These costs varied significantly by individual—approximately 6 percent incurred no prescription drug costs in 2008, while 15 percent incurred $5,000 or more in the same year.

Most Medicare plans did not cover prescription drugs until the Medicare Part D prescription drug plan took effect in January 2006. Since then, the average out-of-pocket cost for prescription medication decreased from 60 percent in 1992 to 23 percent in 2008. The costs covered by private insurance policies, however, decreased during this same time period, suggesting that public programs are picking up more of the cost. By June 2006, 18.2 million individuals (51 percent of general Medicare beneficiaries) had enrolled in the Medicare Part D prescription drug plan, which took effect on January 1, 2006. By October 2011, this number increased to 23.8 million (58 percent of beneficiaries), 6.4 million of whom were also receiving other low-income subsidies.

Chronic Health Conditions and Functional Limitations

Between 1960 and 2009, average life expectancy increased by a little more than five years. While this brings many benefits, it can also bring more chronic health conditions and functional limitations. As individuals live longer with these conditions, they incur more costs for expensive medical treatment and assistance to maintain a livable quality of life.

Common chronic health conditions associated with aging include cardiovascular disease, lower respiratory disease, hypertension, cancer, osteoarthritis, and diabetes. Many of these conditions are on the rise. For example, diabetes—a notoriously expensive long-term health condition—increased from 13 percent in 1997 to almost 21 percent in 2009. This is particularly important because the presence or absence of chronic conditions causes significant variations in average annual health care costs. In 2008, older Americans with no chronic health conditions reported an annual average of $5,520, while those with five or more conditions reported an annual average of $24,658. In 2008, older Americans with no chronic conditions incurred average prescription drug costs of $1,230, while those with five or more conditions cost about $5,300.

Many older Americans also report experiencing functional limitations in their daily life activities. These can include relatively minor limitations such as using the telephone, light or heavy housework, meal preparation, shopping, or managing money; or more significant limitations such as bathing, dressing, eating, getting into or out of a chair, walking, or using the toilet. In 2009, about 41 percent of older Americans enrolled in Medicare reported experiencing at least one functional limitation, and about 4 percent were living in long-term care facilities due to these limitations.

Maintaining a certain quality of life in spite of such limitations has a significant economic impact. Individuals living independently within their communities may require home health care to complete basic tasks. In 2010, the average cost of a home health aide was twenty-one dollars per hour; non-medical assistance cost on average nineteen dollars per hour. This cost increases significantly if placement in a long-term care facility is required. As average life expectancy increases, individuals can expect to live longer with these limitations, thus incurring larger expenses to obtain the necessary assistance. This may be of particular concern because the AARP Public Policy Institute predicts a sharp decline in the number of available family caregivers per individual in the coming years. In 2010, there were more than seven available caregivers for each individual aged eighty and older. But by 2050, that number will drop to less than three. This will likely mean greater demand for professional—and therefore paid—caregivers, as well as a potential shortage of supply.

Long-Term Care

The necessity of long-term care presents its own set of economic challenges. Most Americans age sixty-five and older rely on Medicare to provide their health coverage, but Medicare plans do not cover the greater cost of long-term care facilities. Individuals must either carry their own private long-term care insurance policies, or be prepared to pay the entire expense out of pocket.

Unfortunately, this comes at a steep price. In 2010, the average cost for long-term care was $6,235 per month for a semiprivate room in a nursing home, and $3,293 per month for a unit with one bedroom in an assisted living facility. This cost could potentially be enormous. In 2013, the Centers for Disease Control and Prevention (CDC) reported that the average length of time since nursing home admission was 835 days. Overall, individuals residing in long-term care facilities incur much higher average annual health care costs than individuals living in the community ($61,318 versus $13,150).

In 2009, about 52 percent of long-term care service costs were paid for by Medicaid, while 41 percent were paid for out of pocket. The potentially enormous expense of long-term care raises legal and policy issues as well as personal ones. For example, some families help bankrupt older relatives by transferring their money into trusts or gifting it away, so the older individual can qualify for Medicaid assistance to pay for long-term care. To counteract this, Congress established a look-back period, which examines the older individual's finances in the five years prior to entering the long-term care facility. This makes it harder to hide assets, since actions would need to happen more than five years prior to entering a long-term care facility; however, many families are simply including this approach as part of their long-term estate plans.

Government Impact

The overwhelming reliance of Americans age sixty-five and older on government-sponsored health care programs will present more problems as the size of this population increases rapidly in the coming years. The availability of funds for Medicare coverage is highly dependent on the financial health of the federal government, and is vulnerable to spending cuts and benefit reductions. In addition, the growing trend of individuals hiding assets in order to qualify for Medicaid coverage of long-term care places further strains on programs that already experience funding shortfalls.

The uneven distribution of the aging population across the United States presents a more localized challenge. States such as Florida, Maine, Pennsylvania, and West Virginia have the highest percentage of people age sixty-five and over (more than 15 percent each as of 2012). And even within these states, the older populations are not evenly distributed—some counties and towns have a much higher proportion of older residents than others. As a result, state, county, and local governments must account for the potential economic effects of a large population of older residents, including smaller income taxes bases and higher expenditures on health and recreational programs for seniors.

Conclusion

The United States faces a significant economic challenge in the coming decades due to the combination of rising health care costs and the rapid growth of the population over the age of sixty-five. Overall, people are living longer, healthier lives than previous generations. Unfortunately for many, those later years may require expensive medical care and living assistance that can strain their financial resources, as well as those of the federal Medicare program. The United States must address the growing need for trained health care providers, as well as any budget issues that could impede timely access to the services that will be required by the rapidly aging population.

Aging Baby Boomers Face Shortage of Caregivers

By Jeanna Smialek
Bloomberg News, September 27, 2013

Carolyn Gay, a certified nursing assistant of 20 years, says she wants to inspire teens to become caregivers to the elderly.

"I'm getting older, and in another 10 years I'm going to need one of these girls to look after me," said Gay, 72, a Polk County, Fla., resident who speaks at area high-school career days. But it's not always an easy choice to advocate, she said. "It's embarrassing to explain why the wages for this job are so low."

Well-prepared helpers for seniors and disabled Americans soon could be harder to find. The current work force is aging, and low pay may make the career unattractive to entrants, said Catherine Ruckelshaus, legal co-director of the National Employment Law Project, which focuses on low-wage workers. Immigration changes that could alleviate future shortages are stalled in Congress. And while state rules exist, there are no federal training standards for personal-care aides.

Need is escalating: By 2020 the US will require 1.6 million more direct-care workers than in 2010, based on an analysis of Bureau of Labor Statistics data by the New York- based Paraprofessional Healthcare Institute. That's a 48 percent increase for nursing, home-health and personal-care aides over the decade.

"If people want their parents and grandparents to be able to be cared for at home, and they want that opportunity themselves, we need to make this job a competitive job in the marketplace," said Steven Edelstein, national policy director at PHI, a nonprofit that provides consulting services and workforce development for home health-care workers and groups. "If we care about the quality of the services, we need to care about the training of the work force."

The challenge is to make caregiving attractive as a profession while still providing affordable care, as responses to a Labor Department rule issued last week showed. Minimum-wage and overtime protections will be extended to most in-home care workers, Secretary of Labor Thomas Perez said.

The change will apply parts of the Fair Labor Standards Act to many who aid the elderly and disabled in their homes. That work force is 90 percent female and 56 percent minority, according to an analysis by the Washington-based Institute for Women's Policy Research.

On average, home-health aides make $10.49 an hour, nursing assistants earn $12.32 and personal-care aides are paid about $10, based on Bureau of Labor Statistics estimates.

While workers usually earn more than the federal minimum wage of $7.25 an hour, when they serve multiple clients their travel time often isn't compensated and those extra hours could take them below that level, Edelstein said, adding this stands to change with the new rule.

Regulations often take effect 60 days after being issued. This rule is delayed until January 1, 2015, to give families that use home-care workers and state Medicaid programs time to prepare, according to Laura Fortman, principal deputy administrator for the Labor Department's wage and hour division.

The US Chamber of Commerce and Republican Representatives John Kline of Minnesota and Tim Walberg of Michigan are among those who say the change could make home help too expensive.

"While the delivery of care has changed in recent years, the crucial need for affordable in-home companion care has not," the lawmakers said in a September 17 press release. "Faced with higher costs, some individuals will have no choice but to leave their homes and enter institutional living."

About 75 percent of home-care services are paid for with public dollars, PHI estimated based on US Census Bureau data from 2010.

A semi-private room in a nursing home costs about $6,235 per month, based on 2010 data compiled by the US Department of Health and Human Services, or about $75,000 annually.

In-home health aides cost $21 an hour on average, based on the data. That means a 40-hour week of care would cost $840, and a year about $44,000. Round-the-clock care, however, would be more expensive.

The new overtime-pay requirement could hurt home-care businesses, since many clients require more than 40 hours worth of care, said Jay Perron, vice president of government affairs and public policy at the Washington-based International Franchise Association.

If companies rotate caregivers to avoid paying time-and-a-half overtime, it could interrupt continuity of care, said Perron, whose group's members include Interim HealthCare, a care, hospice and medical-staffing company, among other home-care franchises.

Such businesses usually make about a 5 percent to 7 percent profit margin after insurance, background checks and other costs, Perron said, and so have limited room to pay higher wages.

"Home-care companies will have little choice but to employ workers part time rather than full time as Medicaid payment rates and consumers with limited incomes cannot afford higher costs," said Andrea Devoti, chairman of the National Association for Home Care & Hospice, a Washington-based nonprofit.

At the same time, the overtime rule could protect caretakers from being overworked, and having national requirements may improve industry oversight, Ruckelshaus said. Fifteen states provide both wage and hour protections to direct-care workers and an additional six and Washington, D.C., require minimum wage, yet she said many lack resources for enforcement.

Poverty Among Seniors Getting Harder to Ignore

By Jonathan Walters
Governing.com, January 13, 2013

The gap between what seniors *need* to live on versus what they *have* might land squarely on state and local governments.

If you are a senior citizen in Seminole County, Florida, you might consider yourself lucky. The county is home to the Seniors Intervention Group, a coalition of not-for-profit organizations and businesses dedicated to ensuring that the county's older population doesn't get lost behind closed doors in poverty and neglect. The group provides help ranging from cash assistance and transportation, to home repair, retrofitting and cleanup.

The genesis of the Seniors Intervention Group can be traced to a single person: Zach Hudson, who joined the city of Lake Mary's police department in 2007. Shortly after arriving on his beat, Hudson began noticing something troubling. He'd go to a call involving an elderly resident victimized by fraud or some other crime and would discover what could arguably be described as a more serious issue than the one he was being asked to investigate: far too many seniors in Lake Mary who were just barely scraping by.

"I went to the home of a mother who was in her 90s living with her daughter who was in her 70s, and they had no electricity and very little food," says Hudson. "They were cutting pills in half to save money." When he tried to get them help, he discovered that, in essence, there wasn't any.

No state, county or city agency was there to step in and pay the electric bill, fill the refrigerator with food or secure adequate medication. In matters of acute physical or mental health problems, says Hudson, there were some potential support services available. But when it came to simple, basic poverty—elders who had fallen through the cracks due to a lack of resources—help was hard to find.

"We have 10,000 people turning 65 every day," says Hudson. "And the fastest growing segment of homeless are among the elderly. Can you imagine being 85 and homeless?"

"The data on boomer finances is troubling," agrees Margaret Neal, head of the Institute on Aging at Portland State University in Oregon. "The fact that we just aren't saving enough for retirement is concerning."

That fact has set up an interesting tension when it comes to the study of aging in the US. On the one hand, there has been a considerable amount of work on how to make communities more livable and friendly for the elderly—how streetscapes, co-housing, public transportation, food supply, recreation centers, volunteer opportunities, continuing education and so forth, can all be blended to make for a rich and positive aging experience. Less attention has been paid to the darker side of aging. Many elders are ill-prepared to shoulder the cost of retirement, and the gap between what seniors *need* to live on versus what they *have* might land squarely on state and local governments.

Take, for example, a recent report from Clark County, Washington, on the impact of the aging population there. Finalized last February, the report is an exhaustive but relatively upbeat assessment on what the county should be doing to prepare. It includes a wide variety of recommendations. Some would cost significant amounts of money ("Provide bus rapid transit or light-rail transit service to areas where the density and ridership will support it"); other recommendations would require new levels of intergovernmental coordination ("Develop a village to village program to encourage aging-in-place"); and others are flat-out hopeful exhortations ("Encourage the development of a geriatric mobile outreach program"). Still, the county has been able to make progress on a handful of the report's recommendations, says Marc Boldt, the county commissioner who pushed for the study, none of which have cost much money. They include a voluntary age-friendly building code, some park improvements and a new approach to subdivision planning that discourages cul-de-sacs. The county has also helped launch a Web-based service that connects elders who need help with things like shopping and lawn care with volunteers willing to step up.

But then the report gets much more real—and the recommendations a whole lot thornier—with the introduction of an "Elder Economic Security Index" for Washington counties. The index looks at the costs of independent living for elders, including their household size, health status, geographical location and whether they rent or own their home. Then it uses that data to calculate the level of income necessary to support an independent, age-in-place lifestyle. According to the report, "The Elder Index, with its modeled scenarios for older adults living in different circumstance, shows the difficulties low- and moderate-income elders confront in meeting their living expenses. In every county in the state, elders who live at the federal poverty level, or who are totally dependent on the average Social Security payment in 2009, need housing and health-care supports to make ends meet. Long-term care adds significant costs."

As the Elder Index lays out, older people who own their homes outright, who are in relatively good health and who reside in areas where the cost of living isn't too high can get by on a relatively modest amount of money. But throw in a mortgage and poor health, and the amount of income needed to live independently quickly skyrockets.

Looking at the looming fiscal crisis among the elderly and the limited government resources available, Boldt says, "I think we're going to have to acknowledge that other cultures do this much better than we do" regarding intergenerational caretaking. "We're where we are because our parents helped us, so maybe it's time to help them out with things like housing, having a cottage in the backyard."

When it comes to the story of aging in America, there are two bottom lines. The first is that everyone is getting older. That of course brings attendant health and mobility issues, as well as added costs. (According to one of the bleaker assessments on the American Medical Association website, by age 65, two-thirds of Americans will have at least one chronic disease and will be seeing seven different doctors; a fifth of elders will have five or more chronic diseases and will be tangled up with 14 doctors.) The second bottom line is that a huge proportion of our rapidly aging population simply isn't going to have the financial resources to live out their lives in independent comfort and security.

The data on poverty—and potential poverty—among the elderly are sobering. AARP has documented an alarming increase in home foreclosures among those over age 50, with 2011 witnessing 1.5 million of them, a 23 percent increase from 2007. And the problem is getting worse. "Americans 65 and older sustained the *largest* increases in poverty of any group in 2009," according to a 2011 AARP report on the relative readiness of local governments to handle their rapidly aging populations. Affordable housing opportunities—obviously a key alternative for middle- and low-income elders—declined from 2005 to 2011, the report said. Meanwhile, local governments facing their own fiscal difficulties have scaled back on things like property tax breaks for the elderly.

There's a simple, fundamental reason for the looming economic insecurity among elders: They haven't saved enough money. "It's a very bleak picture," says Alicia Munnell, director of the Center for Retirement Research at Boston College. According to the latest data, says Munnell, people ages 55 to 64 have approximately $120,000 total on which to retire. "You can imagine how long that's going to last."

It's not the cost of living that's really the problem here, says Munnell. It's the cost of trying to stay alive. Things like the cost of food, housing, heat and other day-to-day necessities will certainly contribute to fiscal hardship, says Munnell, but they'll be nothing compared to the cost of health care. Total US health-care expenditures will surpass $3 trillion in 2014 and reach $4.8 trillion in 2021, according to the Centers for Medicare & Medicaid Services. "If we could somehow bend the health-care cost curve, that would make a lot of difference," says Munnell. "Other than that I can't see that this is anything but bad news."

Meanwhile, Munnell's center recently updated what's known as the National Retirement Risk Index, which measures the share of working households that are "at risk" of an inability to maintain pre-retirement living standards upon leaving the work world. They found that the working household risk index jumped from 44 percent in 2007 to 53 percent in 2010. That's nearly a 25 percent increase. "Even if households work to age 65 and annuitize all their financial assets, including the receipts from reverse mortgages on their homes," says the report, "more than half are at risk of being unable to maintain their standard of living in retirement."

That finding squares almost exactly with what states now using the Elder Economic Security Initiative (EESI) have calculated by way of income insecurity among the elderly. Besides Washington, 16 other states have deployed the EESI, which was developed by the organization Wider Opportunities for Women. The EESI is an adaptation of another index the organization had developed around the time of welfare reform, says Acting President and CEO Shawn McMahon, when the organization decided to take on what it viewed as the fuzzy math of the US Census Bureau's poverty rate. "We asked, 'What does a family *really* need to be independent?'" says McMahon. "In the mid-2000s we realized we needed to ask the same question for elders." The answer? A lot more. Fifty-two percent of seniors are economically insecure.

There are, of course, significant variables in all of this. Single women and minorities are disproportionately represented as income insecure. Meanwhile, one of the Retirement Center report's key assumptions around the Retirement Risk Index is based on a figure that's rapidly gliding north: that 65 is the magic and essential age at which Americans all throw in the towel. Another possible bright spot, according to data from the Institute on Aging, is that more than half of all new small business startups are being launched by those 55 and older.

But even given the likelihood that Americans will be working longer and retiring at an older age, poverty experts like McMahon despair over the relative readiness of states and localities to deal with the looming needs—and costs—associated with an aging population.

The pressure on states and localities will be especially acute in light of the federal government's unwillingness to "reform any known system in favor of elders," McMahon says. If anything, the feds are trying to figure out how to cap or at least better control entitlement costs, whether it's Medicaid, Medicare or Social Security.

McMahon does, however, appreciate the fact that the issue of poverty among the elderly is at least starting to come up more often on the country's radar. He cites, for example, a new law passed by the California Legislature requiring so-called "triple A's"—area agencies on aging—to use the EESI as part of their long-range policy planning. Other states, he says, have used the EESI to make the case for things like increases in supplemental security income and home heating assistance.

Others are a little more sanguine. Matt Thornhill, who runs an elder-focused market research firm in Richmond, Virginia, called the Boomer Project, is working with AARP on amassing a database of state and local action related to dealing with the wave of aging boomers. It's a sign, says Thornhill, that state and local governments are at least waking up to the demographic wave starting to roll over them.

But the question remains: Will the response to the needs of an aging population be a multisector and intergovernmental mosaic, or a haphazard mishmash that will inevitably leave the most unfortunate impoverished elderly to fall through the cracks?

"I wish I could say otherwise, but I think the current system is going to persist," says McMahon, "with this mix of often inadequate private-sector donations, church charity and local nonprofit efforts to fill gaps that good incomes and governments used to fill."

McMahon adds, though, that he sees "some hope" in the fact that more people are at least becoming more attuned to the historic demographic shift that's occurring, and the financial challenges that will come with it. So even the most pessimistic agree that the message of a looming and huge group of impoverished seniors is starting to get through. That's the good news. The very real bad news is that what many would like to characterize as the silver cloud of opportunity represented by rapidly aging boomers at the moment appears to be defined by a decidedly dark lining.

The Older Americans Act and US Seniors

By Greg Kaufman
The Nation, June 21, 2013

Honoring our grandparents, our elders—in these divisive times, at least we hold this value in common, right?

As children, we dutifully sat through long visits or lectures from older relatives, teachers, neighbors or family friends; and then wised up to learn that some of these relationships would prove to be our most enduring.

It's enough to make you think that maybe—just maybe—this shared experience would lead to a steadfast commitment from policymakers to ensure that those who cared for us, fought for us, and raised us are able to meet their basic needs.

But if you attended Senator Bernie Sanders's hearing on reducing senior poverty and hunger through the Older Americans Act (OAA) on Wednesday, you were in for a rude awakening.

Signed into law by President Lyndon Johnson in 1965 at the same time as Medicare and Medicaid, the OAA provides federal funding for essential senior services like job training, caregiver support, transportation, preventative healthcare, meals and protection from abuse and financial exploitation. Funding for the legislation has failed to keep pace with inflation and population growth for decades. Under sequestration, an additional $40 million will be cut from senior meal programs alone, which means that as many as 19 million fewer meals will be available to seniors who need them.

Sanders, chairman of the Senate Subcommittee on Primary Health and Aging, noted in his opening remarks that OAA "programs not only work to ease isolation, hunger and suffering, they also save taxpayers substantial sums of money."

"It doesn't take a genius to figure it out," said Sanders, with characteristic bluntness. "If you're malnourished, you're going to get sick more often. You may end up in the emergency room at great expense to Medicaid...If you're weak and you fall and break your hip, you end up in the hospital, at an expense of tens and tens of thousands of dollars...We can feed a senior for an entire year for the cost of one day in a hospital."

It emerged as the central theme of the hearing—that shortchanging OAA programs isn't simply a failure on moral grounds, it's bad economic policy.

Ellie Hollander is president and CEO of the Meals on Wheels Association of America, a nonprofit organization representing local senior nutrition programs in all fifty states. She noted a recent study by the Center for Effective Government, which found that for every $1 in federal spending on Meals on Wheels, there is as much as a $50 return in Medicaid savings alone.

"There is an unrecognized but substantial return on investment," said Hollander. "[OAA] programs enable seniors to continue living at home, averting far more costly healthcare alternatives such as hospitals and nursing homes. This reduces Medicare and Medicaid expenses, potentially saving billions of dollars."

But these meals—delivered directly to an individual's home or to groups at places such as senior centers—currently reach only 2.5 million of the 8.3 million elderly who struggle with hunger.

"The resources fall substantially short," said Hollander, noting that demand is increasing and that the senior population will double to more than 70 million people by 2030. She said that real funding levels (adjusted for inflation) for OAA nutrition programs have decreased 18 percent since 1992, while the population of those age 60 and older has increased 34 percent over that same period.

Howard Bedlin, vice president of public policy at the National Council of Aging—a nonprofit service and advocacy organization focusing on economically disadvantaged seniors—testified that there are now more than 23 million economically insecure Americans over 60. They struggle with rising energy and healthcare bills, diminished savings and job loss. The recession caused median wealth for people between ages 55 and 74 to decline by approximately 15 percent, and for those over 65—many of whom now need to continue working or go back to work just to stay afloat—unemployment is at its highest rate since the Great Depression.

The OAA's Senior Community Service Employment Program is "the nation's only workforce program designed exclusively [for] vulnerable seniors," said Bedlin. Nearly 90 percent of participants live in poverty (on less than $11,000 annually), and one-third of them are homeless or at risk of homelessness. While these seniors receive job training that in some cases prevents homelessness, they also perform millions of hours of community service for local organizations struggling with their own budget cuts—"with a value to states and communities estimated at over $1 billion." Due to a lack of resources, the number of seniors served by the program has declined by 34 percent since FY 2010, and the program now has waiting lists in many cities.

Bedlin also addressed the fact that nursing home costs are now $84,000 annually so "it doesn't take long to essentially go bankrupt" due to long-term care. But the OAA's Home and Community-Based Supportive Services help people avoid this situation and remain in their homes, by providing for needs such as transportation, case management, adult daycare and chore assistance.

Bedlin also singled out OAA's cost-saving role in funding evidence-based "fall prevention programs." One in three seniors falls every year, and falls are the leading cause of fatal and nonfatal injuries for people ages 65 and older. The resulting injuries are projected to cost the nation $60 billion in 2020. Research has shown that several local, OAA-supported programs have reduced falls by 30 to 55 percent— which saves money and lives.

Senator Elizabeth Warren pointed to the Pension Counseling and Information Program—which helps seniors recover lost pensions—as one that could be reaching many more seniors with a modest investment. As companies merge, move or change names, people are sometimes unable to obtain the benefits that they worked for, and can't afford legal assistance to help them recover what they've earned. This OAA program funds six regional counseling projects that help individuals in 29 states.

Nancy Altman, co-director of Social Security Works, testified that the counseling program has recovered more than $175 million in pension benefits for 50,000 clients since 1993—a return of $8 dollars for every federal dollar spent on the program. The current federal cost is $1.6 million, and those monies are used to leverage private and foundation resources, as they are with all OAA programs.

Altman said that some of the states not covered by the six regional projects have a high senior population, such as Florida. If all fifty states were served, Altman believes pension benefits recovered for seniors would likely double.

For Warren, the need to support OAA programs is clear.

"What is our measurement of who we are as a people other than how we treat those who are more vulnerable?" she said. "This is a place where good economics merges with the decisions that are right for us as a country."

Sanders and seventeen cosponsors have introduced a bill to reauthorize the OAA with a funding increase of 12 percent over FY 2010 levels, the amount required to begin to catch up with population growth and inflation over the past decade. (The funding that year was approximately $2.3 billion, accounting for just 0.06 percent of the federal budget; with the proposed increase it would be about 0.07 percent.) He said that "level funding just continues the downward spiral."

"I happen to believe that if 100 million people were watching this panel today, there would be overwhelming support for this program and significantly increasing funding," said Sanders. "So I urge and ask people all over this country to stand up for seniors right now, stand up for cost-effective government."

Cutting Retiree Health Care

Robert Barkin
American City and County Exclusive Insight, June 11, 2013

This article appeared in the June 2011 issue of American City and County *with the title, "Cutting Retiree Health Care."*

Faced with a $75 million unfunded liability for the cost of providing health care coverage for retired city workers, Columbia, Mo., officials decided that the retiree health plan had to change. With the agreement of the retirees, the city lowered the liability to $4.5 million and began funding it through annual contributions to a trust.

Now, retirees at age 65 or older, who are eligible for Medicare, are no longer covered under the city's health plan. Those retirees under 65, who remain in the plan, receive a partial subsidy but pay a higher contribution rate than the amount paid by active employees. "We had to get our liability down to something manageable," says Margrace Buckler, the city's human resources director. "Our policy is to offer retirement health but at a reasonable cost."

Around the nation, from the smallest towns to the largest states, government leaders are taking a hard look at the government employee benefits they offer to their retired employees, as a means of tackling current financial strains as well as reducing a gaping liability on their balance sheets. "Public sector organizations are hurting right now," says Neil Reichenberg, executive director of the Alexandria, Va.-based International Public Management Association for Human Resources (IPMA-HR). "They are facing serious budgetary challenges. They are looking to cut, and retirement health benefits are on the list."

Specific Reductions Planned

While governments scramble to fill their budget holes, some observers, like Reichenberg, also are worried that cutting valued government employee benefits will have a long-term effect on recruiting and retention of skilled workers, who historically have been attracted by rich benefits, even if their salaries lagged the private sector. "There's a feeling that if the private sector doesn't get a benefit, they shouldn't give it to the public sector," he says. "But there are different challenges in the public sector, bigger issues. I think with all pensions and retirement health benefits, there's a race to the bottom. No one asks what will be the impact on long-term recruiting and retention."

A quick scan of government action on retiree health plans reveals wide-ranging reductions in a variety of forms:

- In Los Angeles, city workers will contribute to their retirement health benefits for the first time starting July 1. Under the agreement, approved by 80 percent of the 19,000 eligible employees, employees will contribute 4 percent from their salaries toward retirement health benefits, and, in return, the city promised to avoid furloughs. The accord will save the city $396 million over the next four years. The health-care contributions, along with additional government pension payments, mean employees will be putting aside 11 percent of their salaries for retirement benefits, up from 6 percent.

- In Illinois, thousands of retired state employees could see their health insurance premiums rise dramatically under a series of payment options being considered in 2011 by state lawmakers. Under the proposals, retired employees would begin paying about 50 percent of the state's $686 million in retiree health insurance expenses, up from the 9 percent they currently pay. The premium payments also would cut into the state's retiree health insurance liability, now estimated at more than $30 billion.

- Maryland Gov. Martin O'Malley has proposed scaling back some health benefits, increasing prescription drug costs and requiring retirees to work longer and pay more in contributions to help alleviate the state's dismal funding situation. Maryland has underfunded state retirees' health benefits by roughly $16 billion and is now proposing that employees work longer for fewer benefits. The state pays 83 percent of retirees' health plan costs, compared to 77 percent for active employees.

- In the Village of Tinley Park, Ill., a community of about 60,000 residents outside Chicago, trustees are considering an ordinance that would require new village employees to pay the entire cost of their retirement health coverage. Currently, the village pays half of a retired employee's health premiums. "We made a study of 12 comparable villages, and only two had retiree health benefits," says Patricia Leoni, a trustee and chair of the Budget and Administration Committee, who estimated that the savings would amount to about $500,000 a year. "We were looking at taking some cost-cutting measures and still be competitive. This is huge."

The cost-cutting activity reflects a transition in the government approach to pay for retiree health care benefits. After accounting standards in 2004 began to require that governments state the full value of the retiree health care benefit on their balance sheets, governments considered setting aside funds to prefund the benefit. In the last few years, though, governments have shifted to reduce the cost of the benefit through changes in eligibility, the benefit and employee cost sharing.

According to an August 2010 study by the Washington-based Center for State and Local Government Excellence (SLGE), a public sector policy research organization, 39 percent of local governments surveyed had eliminated or planned to eliminate retiree benefits for new hires, 11 percent had increased the retirement age, and 36 had increased or planned to increase the years of service required to vest into the retirement health benefit. In a follow-up survey last month, SLGE found that of the 52 percent of local governments that had changed their health plans, about 25 percent had shifted more costs from the employer to the retiree— not as prevalent of a change as cost-shifting to active employees (72 percent)—but still significant. Another 8 percent had shifted to a defined contribution model (e.g., health savings account) and another 3 percent had eliminated retiree health care altogether.

At a May conference in Washington on legislative changes that will affect health care, a leading authority on health care reform said that the exchanges that will be established in 2014 under the Patient Protection and Affordable Care Act may eventually eliminate the whole category of retirement health insurance benefits. "Governments may just say, 'Here's a reimbursement, go buy coverage,'" said Mark Nielsen of the Groom Law Group.

Few States Save Enough

It is not surprising that governments are taking and considering such steps to rein in the costs of their retiree health plans, given that an earlier, similar change in the accounting rules for companies led to the virtual elimination of retiree health care plans in the private sector. Even with the financial meltdown since 2008, health care coverage for retirees was offered by 69 percent of public sector employers, according to a 2011 survey by the Brookfield, Wis.-based International Foundation of Employee Benefit Plans. The same survey showed that only 36 percent of corporations offer retiree health care coverage.

Yet public sector employers clearly are struggling to fund the cost of the benefit. The data from state governments, which offer plans to their own employees and often to local government employees as well, is daunting. An April 2011 study by the Washington-based Pew Center on the States calculated that states had a total liability of $635 billion in fiscal year 2009, but had saved only about $31 billion—slightly less than 5 percent of the total cost. The situation has worsened since fiscal year 2008, when states had $587 billion in liabilities and $32 billion in assets.

Based on the most recent data, states made only 36 percent of the $47 billion in contributions required by their own actuaries for the long-term bill. Five states— Alaska, Arizona, North Dakota, Utah and Washington—made full contributions. Even worse, just two states—Alaska and Ohio—accounted for nearly 62 percent of all the money set aside to fund retiree health care as of fiscal year 2009.

Nineteen states had set aside nothing to pay for their promises and continue to fund the benefits on a pay-as-you-go basis, covering medical costs or premiums as current retirees incur them. For states offering modest benefits, that may cause little problem. But for those that have made significant promises, the future fiscal burden could be enormous if more savings are not set aside or costs are not better managed. "Everything is on the table as far as costs are concerned," says Leslie

Scott, director of the Lexington, Ky.-based National Association of State Personnel Executives (NASPE). "In this current fiscal crisis, states are looking at everything. Obviously, health care is a huge, huge cost."

Locals Eliminate the Benefit

The drive to bring down costs in retiree health care also is prevalent at the local level, in communities large and small. Faced with a bill for retiree health care that ran about $140,000 over the budgeted amount of $595,000, officials in St. Charles, Mo., have redesigned their plan.

Future employees of the city will no longer be eligible for health care during retirement, but current employees will continue to receive coverage. "Promises made, promises kept," says Councilman David Beckering.

Still, the city is talking to a retirees' group about other changes in the program. "The message is very clear," Beckering says. "We have to figure out how to cut costs."

He notes that at the local Boeing Company plant, where he worked for many years, the retiree benefits are not as generous as those for city employees. "Even when we reduce the program, it will be better than Boeing," he says, which makes him unconcerned about remaining competitive for talent. "For every opening, we get so many more police and fire applications than we'll ever need," he says.

Charlotte, N.C., has eliminated the retiree health care plan for all employees hired since July 1, 2009. In addition, the city requires an employee contribution toward the retiree health care benefit, with a subsidy keyed to the employee's tenure. "Retirement health care cost sharing helps preserve retiree insurance," says Anna Ellis, the city's employee benefits manager. "We offer quality coverage at an affordable premium. With everything going on, we expect there to be a little bit more cost shifting."

In surrounding Mecklenberg County, N.C., new employees lost eligibility for the retirement health care benefit in July 2010, but the benefit was retained for current employees because of the legal risk of removing a benefit that had already been promised, says Chris Peek, human resources director. "Over time, we hope to gradually phase out the benefit," he says. "The [annual actuarial required contribution] is a big challenge."

Peek questions whether the elimination of the retiree health care benefit will hurt the county's ability to attract and retain top-quality employees. "We don't find it high on the list of benefits that new employees are looking for," he says. "Young employees today want portability. The feedback we're getting is that this benefit is not why they come to the county."

Trying to Compete

Scott, from NASPE, says that states are seeking to balance their need for financial stability with the promises that have been made to their employees. "They don't want to be insensitive to the workers," she says, "but they are facing a revenue shortfall."

She notes that studies have shown that public sector workers are paid less for equivalent jobs than those in the private sector and that benefits have been a very attractive means of finding good employees. For example, IT workers are essential for their operations, but hard to find and keep. "It's very difficult to be competitive to what the private sector can offer," she says.

Reichenberg, of IPMA-HR, worries that local and state governments, having eliminated the premium benefits, will have a hard time finding employees once the economy picks up and there is less available labor in the market. "There is a bigger issue," he says. "How do you remain the employer of choice, once you cut all the benefits that make you the employer of choice? It's a difficult issue for an organization, but not one that people want to consider while we're in a recession."

Myth: The Aging Population Is to Blame for Uncontrollable Health Care Costs

Journal of Health Services Research & Policy, October 2011

FACT: The proportion of Canadians 65 years of age and older is increasing as the baby-boom generation reaches retirement age.

FACT: Older adults need more medical services than younger people.

Taken together, these snippets of reality can conjure a frightening image, in which the health care costs of the aging population balloon until the system becomes unsustainable, necessitating cuts to services and/or tax increases. But health care costs don't inflate uncontrollably just because there are more seniors. 'Boomerangst', as it has been cleverly dubbed, isn't based in reality, so say the experts.

The Cost of Aging

Health care costs generally increase with age. When the Canadian Health Services Research Foundation first busted this myth in 2002, Canada was spending $8,208 per year per senior versus $1,428 (in 2008 dollars) per person under the age of 65. By 2008, these figures had grown to $10,742 and $2,097, respectively. Among older seniors, the data are even more telling. Seniors 80 years of age and older cost the system $18,160 per capita, more than three times the cost of seniors aged 65 to 69.[1]

Estimates of how the aging population will affect health care costs vary considerably, with some predicting doom and gloom and others a minor blip on the radar.[2] Only time will tell the true story, but developing credible predictions is a core component of responsible health systems planning.

Some of the best research shows that, although health care costs will begin to rise as baby boomers age, the impact will be modest in comparison to that of other cost drivers, such as inflation and technological innovation.[3,4] Economic models suggest that growth in health care costs due to population aging will be about 1 percent per year between 2010 and 2036[5] (although it has been argued that the assumptions used in these models make for rosy predictions). These low figures can be reassuring, but with the public share of health care spending topping $120 billion as it did in 2008,[1] even growth of 1 percent translates into a lot of money.

Aging and Sustainability

There are two issues at play when it comes to age and health care delivery. First, the older we are the more health care we use. While the overall population is using more care than ever, seniors are using proportionally more care than younger age groups, which is why seniors cost the system more. They are more likely than younger people to have chronic conditions (and more of them) such as heart disease, dementia and diabetes, which require longer hospital stays and more physician visits.[6] Having multiple chronic conditions may also involve the use of many different drugs to treat each condition separately. Research has shown that such treatment regimens are often not managed properly, leading to adverse drug reactions and further hospitalisation.[7]

With respect to sustainability, it's the more rapid growth in age-specific health care utilization for seniors that may be cause for concern. Studies have shown that per capita use of medical, surgical and diagnostic specialists is increasing more for seniors than for younger people, and services provided to seniors are altogether more costly.[8] An 80-year-old today is twice as likely to have cataract surgery, a knee replacement, and/or a coronary bypass as in 1990.[9]

Some of these increases in utilization relate to medical and technological advances (for example, equipment for new surgical techniques or increased use of medical imaging technology).[10] Others relate to age-specific health care needs, which will increase in tandem with the aging population (for example, the number of seniors with dementia is expected to double by 2038).[11] Without changes in policy, care delivery, prevention or treatment for those with dementia, the economic implications of this greater utilization could be considerable.

Second, dying is expensive. Research shows that we cost the health care system the most in our final years of life—and, obviously, our likelihood of dying increases as we age.[12] In fact, the high (and rising) service use by older people is in many ways a reflection of their greater probability of dying.

Restructuring Care for Seniors

Ensuring that age-specific increases in utilization do not spiral out of control will require tough decisions, which may include disinvesting from some services and investing more in others. It will also mean designing systems that make sense for the care of seniors. Arguably, there are too many seniors in acute care settings because community supports (whether residential care, assisted living or home care) are not available. Our reliance on alternate level of care (ALC) beds (i.e., nonacute patients residing in acute care beds waiting for admission elsewhere)[13] demonstrates the need for stronger continuing care supports.

A move toward integrated continuing care delivery can produce sizeable cost savings, create efficiencies, and improve the quality of care and caregiver satisfaction.[6, 14, 15] Supporting the education, recruitment and retention of caregivers to help with home support is an essential element of a broader labor strategy to meet seniors' care needs while controlling costs.

Conclusion

While the impact of the aging population alone won't bankrupt the health care system, there is still a need to get age-specific cost increases under control, especially those related to death and dying. The good news is that problems expected to arise from population aging can be managed with smart changes to care delivery for the elderly. It's the other issues—such as the growing cost of health care services and the increased costs arising from technological innovation—that are causing expenditures to escalate. These are the cost drivers that require our foremost attention.

Notes

1. Canadian Institute for Health Information. National Health Expenditure Trends, 1975–2010. Ottawa, Canada: CIHI, 2010.
2. Infrastructure Canada. Population Aging and Public Infrastructure: A Literature Review of Impacts in Developed Countries. Ottawa, Canada: Government of Canada, 2010.
3. Evans RG. Sustainability of Health Care: Myths and Facts, 2010. Retrieved 15 September 2010 from: http://medicare.ca.
4. Constant A, Petersen S, Mallory CD, Major J. Research Synthesis on Cost Drivers in the Health Sector and Proposed Policy Options. CHSRF series of reports on cost drivers and health system efficiency: Paper 1. Ottawa, Canada: CHSRF, 2011.
5. Mackenzie H, Rachlis MM. The Sustainability of Medicare. Canadian Federation of Nurses Unions, 2010. Retrieved 27 August 2010 from: http://www.nursesunions.ca.
6. Denton FT, Spencer BG. "Chronic health conditions: changing prevalence in an aging population and some implications for the delivery of health care services." *Canadian Journal on Aging* 2010; 29: 11–21.
7. Canadian Institute for Health Information. Seniors and the Health Care System: What Is the Impact of Multiple Chronic Conditions? Ottawa, Canada: CIHI, 2011.
8. Barer ML, Evans RG, McGrail KM, Green B, Hertzman C, Sheps SB. "Beneath the calm surface: the changing face of physician-service use in British Columbia, 1985/86 versus 1996/97." *Canadian Medical Association Journal* 2004; 170: 803–07.
9. Lee M. How Sustainable Is Medicare? A Closer Look at Aging, Technology and Other Cost Drivers in Canada's Health Care System. Vancouver, Canada: Canadian Centre for Policy Alternatives, 2007.
10. Canadian Institute for Health Information. Medical Imaging in Canada, 2007. Ottawa, Canada: CIHI, 2008.
11. Alzheimer Society of Canada. Rising Tide: The Impact of Dementia on Canadian Society, 2010 Retrieved 20 December 2010 from: http://www.alzheimer.ca.
12. Payne G, Laporte A, Foot DK, Coyte PC. "Temporal trends in the relative cost of dying: evidence from Canada." *Health Policy* 2009; 90: 270–76.

13. Velhi K. Presentation at CIHR Café Scientific: How Canada's aging population will impact the health care system, 24 November 2010.

14. Hollander MJ, Chappell N. Final Report of the National Evaluation of the Cost-Effectiveness of Home Care. Victoria, BC: National Evaluation of the Cost-Effectiveness of Home Care, 2002.

15. Hollander MJ, Chappell NL, Prince MJ, Shapiro E. "Providing care and support for an aging population: briefing notes on key policy issues." *Health Care Quarterly* 2007; 10 (3): 34–45.

Outsourcing the Elderly:
Low-Cost Care Made in India

By Laurie Goering
Chicago Tribune, August 3, 2007

After three years of caring for his increasingly frail mother and father in their Florida retirement home, Steve Herzfeld was exhausted and faced with spending his family's last resources to put the couple in an affordable nursing home.

So he made what he saw as the only sensible decision: He "outsourced" his parents to India.

His 89-year-old mother, Frances, who suffers from advanced Parkinson's disease, now receives daily massages, physical therapy and 24-hour help getting to the bathroom, all for about $15 a day. His father, Ernest, 93, an Alzheimer's patient, has a full-time personal assistant and a cook who has won him over to a vegetarian diet healthful enough that he no longer needs cholesterol medication.

Best of all, the plentiful drugs the couple require cost less than 20 percent of what they do at home, and salaries for their six-person staff are so low that the pair now bank $1,000 a month of their $3,000 Social Security payment. They aim to use the savings as an emergency fund, or to pay for airline tickets if family members want to visit.

"I wouldn't say it's a solution for everybody, but I consider it the best solution to our problem," said Herzfeld, 56, a management expert who made the move to India with his parents, and now, as "care manager rather than the actual worker" has time for things such as bike rides to the grocery and strolls in the botanical gardens with his father.

The outsourcing of medical care to India already includes limited use of Indian radiology technicians to read X-rays digitally transmitted from U.S. hospitals, as well as a number of surgical procedures performed more cheaply in India and other Asian nations.

With the cost of nursing homes, home nurses and medications painfully high in the United States, the elderly and their caregivers long have looked abroad for better solutions. Many families now drive regularly to Mexico or Canada to buy more affordable drugs, or hire recent immigrants—some of them illegal—to help them look after frail parents.

A growing number of aging couples have bought retirement homes in Mexico, where help is cheap and Medicare-funded health care a quick drive across the border.

Herzfeld never thought he'd head abroad, too. When his mother broke a hip in 2004, he drove to their home in Pompano Beach from his home in North Carolina, figuring he'd stay awhile and help his parents get back on their feet. But like so many other caregivers, he found himself still on the couch in his parents' spare bedroom three years later, wondering where his life had gone and how he was going to find the energy to go on.

"I started to see him breaking down after three years working 24 hours a day," said longtime friend Eric Shaffer, who runs an international software design firm with offices around the world, including one in Pondicherry, a former French colony on India's southern coast. "He was in a chess game with no move. Nothing was good."

At wit's end, Herzfeld began investigating nursing homes, but found that the $6,600-a-month cost at the cheapest one he could find near family members would bankrupt his parents quickly. Herzfeld's father also refused to take what he called "welfare" from his family or from the government.

Herzfeld had other concerns: "I've seen nursing homes, and it's a hell of a way to end your life," he said. "I wouldn't want someone to do that to me."

So when Shaffer suggested by phone that Herzfeld consider a move to India, "I said right away, 'There's an idea!'" he said.

Herzfeld, single and a longtime follower of Transcendental Meditation, previously had spent five years in India, first studying and later teaching courses on management at an MBA program in Hyderabad. He admired India's longtime, though recently slipping, respect for the elderly, and he quickly realized that Pondicherry— a haven for aging hippies from around the world—might just work.

The graceful old town, with its orange-blooming flamboyant trees and coconut palms, was foreigner-friendly and on the ocean, a big attraction for his father. The weather was much like Florida's, and many people spoke French, a language his Swiss-born father speaks fluently. Best of all, nursing care and rent were cheap, and Shaffer already was there, promising to help rent a house and hire staff. Herzfeld decided to make the move.

Hours after arriving in India, Herzfeld's jet-lagged father tried to chase his new Indian personal aide out of the bathroom—the youth had been instructed to help him with the toilet—and fell, cracking his head on the bathtub. The family spent the first night in the hospital as Ernest was stitched up.

The three also had a few bouts with India's infamous intestinal bugs as they adjusted to a new diet, and Ernest broke his nose when he tripped over his aide— diligently sleeping just outside the bedroom door—on a midnight refrigerator raid.

Eight months later, however, the family is settled in.

Herzfeld's mother has a daily hour-long session with a physical therapist, who flexes her stiff legs and gets her up on her feet briefly with a walker. A nurse, on duty all day, braids flowers into the old woman's gray hair, massages her legs and arms, holds her hand while she watches television and feeds her meals. A massage therapist gives both of the aged Americans a daily full-body massage, and a cook fixes them simple Indian meals.

Ernest spends much of the day watching cable television in an overstuffed chair, reading a couple of local English-language papers. He sometimes catches a rickshaw to the beach or botanical gardens with his aide or his son.

Asked how he likes India, he says he has seen enough and is "ready for a change." But he admits to liking the food and speaking French, not to mention the pretty, young sari-clad attendants hovering around him.

But India, where life expectancy still hovers around 60 years, lacks many physicians experienced in gerontology. The family keeps in touch with relatives and friends via e-mail and Internet videophone but hasn't persuaded anybody to visit.

"They still think of India as being on another planet," Herzfeld said, speaking of family and friends. "It's a step above asking them to come to Baghdad, but not much."

Every time he looks at the bills—less than $2,000 a month for food, rent, utilities, medications, phones and 24-hour staffing—Herzfeld thinks he's done the right thing for his parents and himself.

"It can be done," he said. "This is working."

3

Caring for Elder Parents

© Patrick Farrell/MCT/Landov

John Shoendorf, left, takes a walk with his father, Harold, in Coral Gables, Florida.

Obligations to Young and Old

The United States is a nation that values youth—its vitality, its energy, its enthusiasm, and its possibilities. The United States is also a relatively young nation with a young identity and culture. Perhaps this is why the United States has had an under-developed ethos of how to include its elderly in the rest of the population. Where do the old go in a culture oriented toward the young? Where is their place? How does America accord them respect, a voice, and honor their perceptions, preferences, decisions, and judgments? Epidemiologists have predicted the swelling of the aging segment of the population for decades, but it is only now being practically dealt with.

American culture is learning how to care for its elderly population. Americans have, of course, always cared about the elderly, but a major challenge is caring for an increasing number of elderly people who are living longer than previous generations. Another obstacle is that adults now have to care for both their older parents and their own children at the same time, what sociologists refer to as a "sandwich generation." For many other cultures, this sandwiching is not uncommon, and family members of different generations often live together. Tri-generational households were, in fact, common in the United States until World War II, when they slowly gave way to the emerging cultural value that young people need their own place and their parents should not stand in the way of their children's progress. By the early twenty-first century the effects of this social change are still playing out, both culturally and economically.

The baby boomer generation often encapsulates a broader population of older persons, even those old enough to predate this sociological phenomenon. This large demographic encompasses a wide range of elderly persons and is reshaping how aging is viewed. One of the most important aspects of aging in America relates to managing the long-term effect of the baby boom—the eighteen-year bulge in the population, which started with a rise in annual births in 1946 and ended with a plateau of annual births in 1964. Gerontologists have indicated that the national response to this aging group will have widespread effects on the nation for future generations.

According to the *Congressional Quarterly Researcher*, between seventy-six and seventy-eight million Americans are in this group. Fluctuations in these numbers that have resulted from deaths are balanced by immigrants entering the country, maintaining this sizeable segment of the US population. The oldest in this group are approaching seventy years old, and most of them do not think of themselves as elderly. Collectively, they are staying in the workforce longer and are more active and less sedentary than the generations that lived before them. Despite public health concerns about rises in obesity, diabetes, arthritis, and heart disease as America ages, this segment enters the elder years with better health, greater vitality, less morbidity, and more work productivity than all preceding generations. With their net worth estimated at more than $5 trillion, they are also investing wealth into the overall economy to a degree no previous generation has. Consequently, every major retailer's marketing strategy has a segment that specifically targets them.

Within this apparently affluent segment, there exists lopsided distribution of wealth to a degree never before seen in any previous generation. Economists believe that the wealthiest third will be able to retire in varying degrees of comfort; the top 10 percent hold two-thirds of all the assets this segment holds. Comfort is a relative term, but the middle third should also be able to maintain more than a modicum. The great concern is for the bottom third who own no assets, and, therefore, they may never be able to retire.

Another monetary concern is that this sizeable group works may actually strain the government's ability to hold fiduciary economies together. Today, the elderly consume 8.5 percent of the nation's total economic output. By the time the youngest of this segment, now in their mid-fifties, reach seventy, the elderly will be consuming approximately 15 percent.

Many economists believe there is no way to spare Medicare, Medicaid, or Social Security from bankruptcy. Many other economists, however, believe the long-term economic national forecast is good. The disagreement among economists reflects the complexity of that social science, and the fact that its predictive validity is never certain. What is certain is that this cohort of the country—the baby boomer generation—has reshaped the nation at every point and fueled one of the greatest economic expansions in world history. The real fear of nuclear mutual annihilation during the Cold War along with the mass loss of life during the Korean War and Vietnam War prevented boomers from being raised during a time of peace and stability.

The elderly of the twenty-first century do not conceptualize retirement as a form of retreat. They retire later than their predecessors, and the reasons why fall into a few broad categories. A primary reason is that of necessity—they cannot afford to retire. Social Security is based on a formula that sixty-five will be the standard retirement age, but most boomers' personal economic formulas require that their actual retirement age will be closer to seventy and, in some cases, a little beyond. Adjusting for inflation, many in the boomer generation have experienced declining rates of family income. A large percentage of aging boomers, therefore, do not have the means to retire. The situation is more demanding on boomers who simultaneously support their children who are unable to find work after college and cannot become financially independent, and the boomers' aging parents who are becoming increasingly dependent on them.

Moreover, many boomers want to continue working, and many employers value the experiential wisdom in these most senior of laborers. They are valued for their critical reasoning ability and for bringing a historical perspective to the workplace that is often beneficial to sorting out the challenges of rapid market and business changes. Some fields, such as government and nursing, are disproportionately represented by boomers, and employers try to incentivize delaying retirement to keep their work forces intact.

The elderly are also beginning new careers as some retire from their last job in order to embark on new occupations they have always wanted to try. For example, an elderly person may choose to enter a dream retail business, or volunteer their time as a means to give back for the successes a life of sustained hard work has provided.

A challenge common among boomers is dealing with their own aging parents. While it is good to encourage elders to live life to the fullest and to try new things, the reality is that the effects of getting old will inevitably limit these new horizons. Normal aging, disease, and injury can affect physical and intellectual prowess. When considering their parents, members of the baby boom generation see the risks of falls, improper medications, mismanaged funds, and inadequate nutrition and hygiene. They therefore emphasize the need to be prudent, cautious, and play it safe. Seniors, on the other hand, are focused on the anxiety and vulnerabilities attached to dependency, and the loss of personal freedoms they have enjoyed their entire lives.

Critical risk points exist, including managing chronic health conditions, quickly responding to acute conditions that arise without notice, and medical follow-up and medication compliance. Other issues include boomers not trusting that aging parents will understand what their physicians are telling them, or that they will ask their doctors the right questions, and worrying about whether or not bills are being paid and monthly incomes accounted for. An important and divisive example of this is that of car ownership and driving. Senior citizens over the age of seventy-five account for a relatively high number of traffic and pedestrian fatalities in the United States, and they are more likely to be found at fault than younger drivers.

For baby boomers, owning a car and being licensed to drive it are essential ingredients of what it means to be an adult in American society. And yet except for a few, the most potentially dangerous routine activity most people engage in is driving. What is often thought of as a mindless habit is actually a mentally complex activity, requiring sustained attention—driving requires strong perception to make judgments and take coordinated action. These skills diminish insidiously with normal aging. If drivers live long enough, they will reach the point where they are no longer capable of safely operating a motor vehicle. This critical risk point is a sad realization for the elderly, and it is also a worrisome problem for their boomer children. The decision of adult children to limit or stop their aging parents from driving is difficult, but often necessary regardless of the parent's driving record.

Each risk point requires negotiation, sensitivity, clarity, and respect. Making these decisions—whether they are about recommended surgery, getting help into the home, moving into the boomers' home, taking medication, avoiding certain chores, even basics like bathing and toileting—requires the understanding that each of these are a process that takes time. Boomers, in their sincere desire to establish safety and to help, can mistakenly rush the process and damage their relationships with their elderly relatives by trying to force them into compliance. Seniors are often reluctant to give in. They have worked hard to earn their own place and take pride in being independent. Fueled with often unacknowledged anxiety, guilt, and shame, they may deny and avoid the process. The process of making these changes works best when boomers genuinely empathize with what the elderly are being asked to give up. Often it includes physical freedom to come and go, having another make the scores of choices required in a typical week, and the dignity of having a purpose and place. It is usually a lot more than boomers would consider giving up themselves.

Baby boomers expect to handle the challenges of their own aging in style and triumph. They are an economic, political, and sociological force that prefers to lead than be led. Members of the baby boom generation also often support two other generations—one younger with the promise and prospects of emancipated adulthood not yet fully realized, and the other older facing the final phase of their lives.

The Sandwich Generation: Rising Financial Burdens for Middle-Aged Americans

By Kim Parker and Eileen Patten
PewSocialTrends.org, January 30, 2013

Overview

With an aging population and a generation of young adults struggling to achieve financial independence, the burdens and responsibilities of middle-aged Americans are increasing. Nearly half (47 percent) of adults in their 40s and 50s have a parent age 65 or older and are either raising a young child or financially supporting a grown child (age 18 or older). And about one-in-seven middle-aged adults (15 percent) is providing financial support to both an aging parent and a child.

While the share of middle-aged adults living in the so-called sandwich generation has increased only marginally in recent years, the financial burdens associated with caring for multiple generations of family members are mounting. The increased pressure is coming primarily from grown children rather than aging parents.

According to a new nationwide Pew Research Center survey, roughly half (48 percent) of adults ages 40 to 59 have provided some financial support to at least one grown child in the past year, with 27 percent providing the primary support. These shares are up significantly from 2005. By contrast, about one-in-five middle-aged adults (21 percent) have provided financial support to a parent age 65 or older in the past year, basically unchanged from 2005. The new survey was conducted Nov. 28-Dec. 5, 2012 among 2,511 adults nationwide.

Looking just at adults in their 40s and 50s who have at least one child age 18 or older, fully 73 percent have provided at least some financial help in the past year to at least one such child. Many are supporting children who are still in school, but a significant share say they are doing so for other reasons. By contrast, among adults that age who have a parent age 65 or older, just 32 percent provided financial help to a parent in the past year.

While middle-aged adults are devoting more resources to their grown children these days, the survey finds that the public places more value on support for aging parents than on support for grown children. Among all adults, 75 percent say adults have a responsibility to provide financial assistance to an elderly parent who is in need; only 52 percent say parents have a similar responsibility to support a grown child.

One likely explanation for the increase in the prevalence of parents providing financial assistance to grown children is that the Great Recession and sluggish recovery have taken a disproportionate toll on young adults. In 2010, the share of young adults who were employed was the lowest it had been since the government started collecting these data in 1948. Moreover, from 2007 to 2011 those young adults who were employed full time experienced a greater drop in average weekly earnings than any other age group.[1]

A Profile of the Sandwich Generation

Adults who are part of the sandwich generation—that is, those who have a living parent age 65 or older and are either raising a child under age 18 or supporting a grown child—are pulled in many directions.[2] Not only do many provide care and financial support to their parents and their children, but nearly four-in-ten (38 percent) say both their grown children and their parents rely on them for emotional support.

Who is the sandwich generation? Its members are mostly middle-aged: 71 percent of this group is ages 40 to 59. An additional 19 percent are younger than 40 and 10 percent are age 60 or older. Men and women are equally likely to be members of the sandwich generation. Hispanics are more likely than whites or blacks to be in this situation. Three-in-ten Hispanic adults (31 percent) have a parent age 65 or older and a dependent child. This compares with 24 percent of whites and 21 percent of blacks.

More affluent adults, those with annual household incomes of $100,000 or more, are more likely than less affluent adults to be in the sandwich generation. Among those with incomes of $100,000 or more, 43 percent have a living parent age 65 or older and a dependent child. This compares with 25 percent of those making between $30,000 and $100,000 a year and only 17 percent of those making less than $30,000.

Married adults are more likely than unmarried adults to be sandwiched between their parents and their children: 36 percent of those who are married fall into the sandwich generation, compared with 13 percent of those who are unmarried. Age is a factor here as well, since young adults are both less likely to be married and less likely to have a parent age 65 or older.

Presumably life in the sandwich generation could be a bit stressful. Having an aging parent while still raising or supporting one's own children presents certain challenges not faced by other adults—caregiving and financial and emotional support to name just a few. However, the survey suggests that adults in the sandwich generation are just as happy with their lives overall as are other adults. Some 31 percent say they are very happy with their lives, and an additional 52 percent say they are pretty happy. Happiness rates are nearly the same among adults who are not part of the sandwich generation: 28 percent are very happy, and 51 percent are pretty happy.

Sandwich-generation adults are somewhat more likely than other adults to say they are often pressed for time. Among those with a parent age 65 or older and a dependent child, 31 percent say they always feel rushed even to do the things they have to do. Among other adults, the share saying they are always rushed is smaller (23 percent).

For members of the sandwich generation who not only have an aging parent but have also provided financial assistance to a parent, the strain of supporting multiple family members can have an impact on financial well-being.[3] Survey respondents were asked to describe their household's financial situation. Among those who are providing financial support to an aging parent and supporting a child of any age, 28 percent say they live comfortably, 30 percent say they have enough to meet their basic expenses with a little left over for extras, 30 percent say they are just able to meet their basic expenses and 11 percent say they don't have enough to meet even basic expenses. By contrast, 41 percent of adults who are sandwiched between children and aging parents, but not providing financial support to an aging parent, say they live comfortably.

Family Responsibilities

When survey respondents were asked if adult children have a responsibility to provide financial assistance to an elderly parent in need, fully 75 percent say yes, they do. Only 23 percent say this is not an adult child's responsibility. By contrast, only about half of all respondents (52 percent) say parents have a responsibility to provide financial assistance to a grown child if he or she needs it. Some 44 percent say parents do not have a responsibility to do this.

When it comes to providing financial support to an aging parent in need, there is strong support across most major demographic groups. However, there are significant differences across age groups. Adults under age 40 are the most likely to say an adult child has a responsibility to support an elderly parent in need. Eight-in-ten in this age group (81 percent) say this is a responsibility, compared with 75 percent of middle-aged adults and 68 percent of those ages 60 or older. Adults who are already providing financial support to an aging parent are no more likely than those who are not currently doing this to say this is a responsibility.

On the question of whether parents have a responsibility to support their grown children, personal experience does seem to matter. Parents whose children are younger than 18 are less likely than those who have a child age 18 or older to say that it is a parent's responsibility to provide financial support to a grown child who needs it (46 percent vs. 56 percent). And those parents who are providing primary financial support to a grown child are among the most likely to say this is a parent's responsibility (64 percent).

Financial Support for Aging Parents and Grown Children

While most adults believe there is a responsibility to provide for an elderly parent in financial need, about one-in-four adults (23 percent) have actually done this in the past year. Among those who have at least one living parent age 65 or older, roughly one-third (32 percent) say they have given their parent or parents financial support in the past year. And for most, this is more than just a short-term commitment.

About seven-in-ten (72 percent) of those who have given financial assistance to an aging parent say the money was for ongoing expenses.

Similar shares of middle-aged, younger and older adults say they have provided some financial support to their aging parents in the past year. It is worth noting that many parents age 65 or older may not be in need of financial assistance, so there is not necessarily a disconnect between the share saying adult children have a responsibility to provide for an aging parent who is in need and the share who have provided this type of support.

Overall, Americans are more likely to be providing financial support to a grown child than they are to an aging parent. Among all adults, 30 percent say they have given some type of financial support to a grown child in the past year. Among those who have a grown child, more than six-in-ten (63 percent) have done this.

Here the burden falls much more heavily on adults who are middle-aged than on their younger or older counterparts. Among adults ages 40 to 59 with at least one grown child, 73 percent say they have provided financial support in the past year. Among those ages 60 and older with a grown child, only about half (49 percent) say they have given that child financial support. Very few of those under age 40 have a grown child.

Of those middle-aged parents who are providing financial assistance to a grown child, more than half say they are providing the primary support, while about four-in-ten (43 percent) say they are not providing primary support but have given some financial support in the past 12 months. Some 62 percent of the parents providing primary support say they are doing so because their child is enrolled in school. However, more than one-third (36 percent) say they are doing this for some other reason.

The focus in this report is on the financial flows from middle-aged adults to their aging parents and their grown children. Of course, money also flows from parents who are 65 or older to their middle-aged children. While the new Pew Research survey did not explore these financial transfers, previous surveys have found that a significant share of older adults provide financial help to their grown children. A Pew Research survey conducted in Sept. 2011 found that among adults 65 and older with at least one grown child age 25 or older, 44 percent said they had given financial support to a grown child in the past year.[4]

Beyond Finances: Providing Care and Emotional Support

While some aging parents need financial support, others may also need help with day-to-day living. Among all adults with at least one parent age 65 or older, 30 percent say their parent or parents need help to handle their affairs or care for themselves; 69 percent say their parents can handle this on their own.

Middle-aged adults are the most likely to have a parent age 65 or older (68 percent say they do). And of that group, 28 percent say their parent needs some help. Among those younger than 40, only 18 percent have a parent age 65 or older; 20 percent of those ages 60 and older have a parent in that age group. But for those in their 60s and beyond who do still have a living parent, the likelihood that the parent will need caregiving is relatively high. Fully half of adults age 60 or older with a living parent say the parent needs help with day-to-day living.

When aging adults need assistance handling their affairs or caring for themselves, family members often help out. Among those with a parent age 65 or older who needs this type of assistance, 31 percent say they provide most of this help, and an additional 48 percent say they provide at least some of the help.

In addition to helping their aging parents with day-to-day living, many adults report that their parents rely on them for emotional support. Among all adults with a living parent age 65 or older, 35 percent say that their parent or parents frequently rely on them for emotional support, and 33 percent say their parents sometimes rely on them for emotional support. One-in-five say their parents hardly ever rely on them in this way, and 10 percent say they never do.

Even among those who say their parents do not need help handling their affairs or caring for themselves, 61 percent say their parents rely on them for emotional support at least sometimes. For those whose parents do need help with daily living, fully 84 percent report that their parents rely on them for emotional support at least some of the time.

Not surprisingly, the older the parent, the more likely he or she is to require emotional support. Among adults with a parent age 80 or older, 75 percent say their parents turn to them for emotional support frequently or sometimes. This compares with 64 percent among those who have a parent ages 65 to 79.

Emotional support also flows from parents to grown children, even children who are financially independent. Overall, 33 percent of parents with at least one child age 18 or older say their grown child or children depend on them frequently for emotional support. An additional 42 percent say their grown children sometimes rely on them for emotional support.

When it comes to grown children, there is a link between financial and emotional support. Among parents who say they are providing primary financial support to their grown child or children, 43 percent say their children frequently rely on them for emotional support and 45 percent say they sometimes do. By comparison, only 24 percent of those who say they do not provide any financial support to their grown children say their children frequently rely on them for emotional support, and 39 percent say their children sometimes rely on them for this type of support.

Boomers Moving out of the Sandwich Generation

Today members of the Baby Boomer generation and Generation X are represented in the "sandwich generation." But the balance has shifted significantly. When the Pew Research Center explored this topic in 2005, Baby Boomers made up the majority of the sandwich generation. They were more than twice as likely as members of the next generation—Generation X—to have a parent age 65 or older and be supporting a child (45 percent vs. 20 percent). Since 2005, many Baby Boomers have aged out of the sandwich generation, and today adults who are part of Generation X are more likely than Baby Boomers to find themselves in this situation: 42 percent of Gen Xers have parent age 65 or older and a dependent child, compared with 33 percent of Boomers.[5]

This report will focus largely on adults ages 40 to 59, loosely defined as "middle aged." While this group may not share a generational label, many of its members do have a shared set of experiences, challenges and responsibilities given the unique position they inhabit, sandwiched between their children and their aging parents.

Middle-aged adults who make up the core of the sandwich generation are living out these challenges and, in the process, perhaps ushering in a new set of family dynamics. Most middle-aged parents with grown children say their relationship with their children is different from the relationship they had with their own parents at a comparable age. Half say the relationship is closer, while 12 percent say it's less close and 37 percent say the relationship is about the same. Older adults (those ages 60 and older) are less likely than middle-aged parents to say they have a closer relationship with their grown children than they had with their own parents (44 percent), and they are more likely to say the relationship is about the same (45 percent).

The remainder of this report will look at the basic building blocks of intergenerational relationships in more detail. The first section will look at attitudes about financial responsibilities and the reality of financial transfers. The second section will look at caregiving for older adults. How many older adults need assistance with day-to-day living, and who is providing that care? The third section will look at emotional ties across generations and explore the extent to which aging parents rely on their children and grown children rely on their parents for emotional support.

About the Data

Findings in this report are based primarily on a telephone survey conducted by the Pew Research Center. The survey was conducted Nov. 28 to Dec. 5, 2012, with a nationally representative sample of 2,511 adults age 18 and older. A total of 1,506 interviews were completed with respondents contacted by landline telephone and 1,005 with those contacted on their cellular phone. Data are weighted to produce a final sample that is representative of the general population of adults in the United States. Survey interviews were conducted in English and Spanish under the direction of Princeton Survey Research Associates International. Margin of sampling error is plus or minus 2.2 percentage points for results based on the total sample at the 95 percent confidence level.

The report also draws on findings from a previous Pew Research Center survey. That survey was conducted Oct. 5 to Nov. 6, 2005, with a nationally representative sample of 3,014 adults age 18 and older. All interviews were conducted by landline telephone. Data were weighted to produce a final sample that was representative of the general population of adults in the continental United States. Survey interviews were conducted under the direction of Princeton Survey Research Associates International, in English and Spanish. Margin of sampling error was plus or minus 2 percentage points for results based on the total sample at the 95 percent confidence level.

Notes

1. For a more detailed discussion of young adults and the impact of the Great Recession, see Pew Research Social & Demographic Trends, "Young, Underemployed and Optimistic," Feb. 9, 2012.

2. Throughout this report, the "sandwich generation" is defined as those adults with at least one living parent age 65 or older and who are either raising a child younger than 18 or providing financial support (either primary support or some support in the past year) to a grown child age 18 or older. Stepmothers/stepfathers who "played an important role" in the respondent's life are included in cases where the mother/father is deceased. Stepchildren are included for respondents who volunteer that they have a stepchild and say they consider themselves to be his or her parent or guardian. The sample size for this group is n = 553.

3. Throughout the report, respondents who have at least one living parent age 65 or older and say that they have provided financial support to a parent in the past 12 months are considered to be supporting a parent age 65 or older. In some cases, a respondent may have two living parents—one age 65 or older and one younger than 65—and may have provided financial support only to the younger parent. It is not possible to determine the exact age of the parent receiving the financial assistance.

4. See Pew Research Center for the People & the Press, "The Generation Gap and the 2012 Election," Nov. 3, 2011.

5. As in previous Pew Research Center reports, Baby Boomers are those adults born between 1946 and 1964, and Generation X applies to those born between 1965 and 1980. For a more detailed discussion of the generations and their demographic and political characteristics, see Pew Research Center for the People & the Press, "The Generation Gap and the 2012 Election," Nov. 3, 2011.

Caring for Aging Parents: Should There Be a Law?

By Francine Russo
Time, June 22, 2013

China's government thinks so, and as the population of elderly in nearly every society starts to swell, such eldercare laws are becoming more common. But are they effective?

What kind of care and devotion is expected of adult children toward their aging parents? Not surprisingly, siblings can hold fiercely different positions about what they "should" do. Some make huge sacrifices of time and money to comfort and care for mom; others rarely show their faces even when parents pine for them. But if families can't resolve these difficult issues, can governments do any better?

In China, a new law that went into effect this month requires children to provide for the emotional and physical needs of their parents, which includes visiting them often or facing fines and potential jail time. One woman who was found negligent in visiting her 77-year-old mother has already been charged under the Law on Protection of the Rights and Interests of the Elderly and was ordered to visit her mother at least once every two months, and on at least two national holidays a year.

Enforcing the law will certainly be challenging, and critics have raised the very real possibility that in an effort to alleviate some of the impending burden that 200 million people over the age of 60 represent for the Chinese government, the law may end up causing more familial strife and resentment toward elderly parents. While no government can legislate loyalty or love, more legislatures are finding it necessary to mandate responsibilities, especially those of the financial kind.

In Ukraine (and other former Soviet-bloc nations), says Katherine Pearson, a law professor at Penn State, children are "obliged to display concern and render assistance." In practical terms, that translates to needy elderly being able to sue their children for financial support. And a sister can sue her brother for not paying his share of mom's costs.

Much closer to home, laws in 20 US states require family members, for the most part adult children, to support their financially needy relatives, which can include elderly parents who no longer have an income or disabled adult children who are unable to support themselves. Most of these statutes, which are among the original laws of the states, have not been in active use since the Great Depression. In fact, most states repealed them from the 1950s through '70s when older people began reaping the benefits of Social Security and Medicare.

Since 1994, however, Pearson says lawsuits in Pennsylvania and South Dakota against adult children by a needy parent or a care provider like a hospital have required adult children to come up with the money for their parents' care bills. Some nursing homes have used the laws to win judgments as high as $90,000 against adult children, says Pennsylvania elder-law attorney Jeffrey Marshall. "It's a 'gotcha' law," says Pearson, "because most people don't know about it until after it goes wrong."

Such statutes are a relic of the Elizabethan Poor Laws, which colonists from England introduced to America. They were enacted in the first half of the 20th century, at a time when it was more common for multigenerational families to live near each other, or even in the same house, and to be economically interdependent. Life expectancies were lower back then, however, so there were far fewer frail old people, and those few were usually cared for at home by a daughter.

The social revolutions of the 20th century changed this social landscape in the US and in much of the world. Parents live much longer, often with chronic conditions for which they need medical care. Women as well as men are in the workplace, and adult children may live hundreds or even thousands of miles away from their parents. That's what prompted the law in China; with so many of the younger generation seeking better employment and financial opportunities away from home, elderly parents are increasingly left behind to fend for themselves.

This collision of new realities with responsibilities to parents has struck even in Japan, a traditional Confucian society, where filial piety is a cherished value and the traditional role of a wife has been to care for her husband's parents. But Japan has the world's fastest aging population—nearly a quarter of the population is over 65, and in a sign that the silver wave is already washing over the nation's shores, adult diapers are projected to outsell baby diapers by 2020, according to the *Nikkei* newspaper.

Huge numbers of caregivers are needed, but with traditional daughters-in-law now disappearing into the workforce, in 2000 the Japanese government created a universal long-term care program to help families pay for hired caregivers. And, despite the traditional reverence for elders, says AARP analyst Don Redfoot, women—many of them presumably daughters-in-law—lobbied against a provision that would have allowed the elderly to pay family members to care for them.

More affluent European countries rely primarily on some sort of government support for eldercare, with varying degrees of potential family involvement. Norway provides universal long-term care to everyone. In France, the elderly receive a payment similar to Social Security, which increases according to the recipient's income and care needs. In Germany, a social-insurance approach like Medicare helps pay for long-term care. Unlike in Japan, this money can be used to pay family members for care services.

But these insurance programs only provide financial support, and do little, if anything, to address what the Chinese call the "spiritual needs" of the old. China's law, therefore, was intended to exert moral pressure on sons and daughters to attend to their parents—seeing retired parents, that legislation makes clear, is your job.

And what if that job becomes too burdensome, or even impossible to maintain?

Even without laws, most children do feel some responsibility or even a positive wish to take care of their parents. The real problem, particularly in the US and increasingly elsewhere, is that adult kids are caught between time, career, family and geographical demands that they can't always resolve in favor of spending more time with grandma and grandpa.

That means that from China to South Korea to South Carolina, governments may create programs to mandate care for the elderly, but, says Lori Brown, a sociologist at Meredith College in North Carolina, they are often still isolated and alone. "And the most isolated elderly," she says, "have the most depression, lower quality of life, and die earlier."

If legislating such loneliness away isn't the answer, what is? Some social programs reduce elders' loneliness by visit from volunteers. Many children arrange for their parents to attend day programs for the elderly, where they will have the chance to interact with others and engage in activities to stimulate their social and cognitive skills. And they are increasingly hiring aides who not only can help older people perform daily tasks but serve as companions for them as well. In Japan, for example, companies that provide "companions" for the elderly are flourishing. Home Instead Senior Care's Japanese franchises have grown at an average rate of over 10% since 2006. It's no substitute for a child's companionship, but the reality of current financial and social demands makes it an acceptable stand-in for many people. "We might not want to pass laws like the one in China, but we could certainly do with some awareness campaigns about caring for not only our family members who are older but everyone who is elderly," says Brown. Especially if we remember that one day each of us will find ourselves in need of such societal support and attention.

The Dilemma of Taking Care of Elderly Parents

By Lillian Rubin
Salon.com, November 26, 2011

Aging boomers are agonizing over how to help Mom and Dad. I should know—my daughter is one of them.

It has become the baby boom generation's latest and, in some ways, most agonizing life crisis: what to do when the parents who once took care of you can no longer take care of themselves. Raise your hand if you're one of the 60-year-olds reading this who has one or more living 80-year-old parents.

Listen in on a group of middle-aged children of the elderly, and you'll hear that even the most casual mention of aging parents is likely to open up a Pandora's box of anxieties. These are stories told with tears, with exasperation, and sometimes, when they can take a step back, with laughter. Not funny ha-ha mirth, but more like the hysterical laughter we all experience at those moments when we're forced to come to grips with the absurdity of life and our own helplessness.

Even if their parents are still doing fine, middle-aged children need only look around at friends and neighbors to be reminded that these anxieties will become theirs one day. Indeed, most of the children I spoke with in the research for my book, *60 On Up: The Truth About Aging in America*, actively worry about their aging parents, often well before their parents need any help.

I see it with my own 63-year-old daughter, who wants me—her 87-year-old mother—to be in touch when I leave town, even if only for a few days or a week, who calls when she's traveling though she never did before, whose anxiety announces itself over the phone lines when we haven't talked for a while: "Are you OK?" I tell her I'm fine, ask her to stop worrying. "It's my turn to worry," she replies.

She and her husband have regularly spent some weeks each year in adventurous travel abroad. Now, she's reluctant to go away for so long and resists going anyplace where she'll be out of reach for more than a day or two. When I tell her that her anxieties are overblown, that her fears are unfounded, that I want her to go and enjoy herself, she looks at me and says, "It has nothing to do with what you want. It's what I need."

It's a response that moves me to tears, while a little corner of my brain thinks, "Yes, I know, but that's your problem. It has nothing to do with what I need right now."

When she read these words in an earlier draft of this article, she called. "I think you left something out here, Mom." I'm quiet, puzzled, waiting for the rest, until she goes on to remind me that when she phoned to say they were back after their last overseas trip, my immediate response was one of great relief—"as if," she says, "you were holding your breath the whole time we were gone. You actually told me that you were relieved and that you didn't really like it anymore when I'm so far away for so long."

I resist at first, wanting to tell her she's making more of it than I meant. Then I remember the rush of unshed tears when I heard her cheery, "We're home!" at the other end of the phone line, remember, too, how comforted I felt to know she was nearby again, relieved of an anxiety I hadn't even fully known was there.

"But I also meant it when I said I don't want my feelings about this to determine how you live your life," I say.

"I know," she says, "but that's only because you think you always have to be the mom. I love you for it, but it can be a pain when I feel like I'm getting mixed signals and when you try to protect me when I don't need your protection."

Another reader—the adult child of another mother—to whom I sent an earlier version of this article, sends an email pointing to this passage and says, "It would be nice if you'd expand on what you do need. Parents tend not to say what they need, and we children are left to try to figure it out, which leads to problems when we make mistakes."

These issues between parents and children, the mixed messages on both sides—children who say they want to help but who already have too many demands on their time and energy, parents who say they don't need anything but clearly do—are an old story. It's not news either that adult children have always worried about their parents, that they've always cared for them in their old age, and that the role reversal is inevitably a wrenching emotional experience for all concerned.

But the demographic and cultural context in which this takes place is vastly different now than it was a century ago. Then, few women worked outside the home, so someone was available to care for an ailing parent. Today, a changed culture combined with economic need has put most women in the labor force alongside their men, which means that there's no one at home to take care of Mom or Dad when they need it. Then, life expectancy at birth was just over 48 years; today, it's close to 80. Then, so few lived to 65 that there is no record of life expectancy at that age. Today, if we make it to 65, we can expect to live another 20 years. And one-third of those over 65 need some help in managing their daily lives; by the time they reach 85 (the fastest-growing segment of our population today), that number jumps to well over one-half.

The result: Middle-aged adults may well spend more years caring for a parent than they did for their children.

Those in their 60s and 70s, who looked forward to these years with their promise of freedom from the responsibilities that bound them before, are now asking: "When do I get to live my life for myself?" The younger ones, who at middle age are already stretched thin by their own financial problems—worried about how they'll provide for their children's education, whether they'll ever have enough for their own retirement, how they'll live the rest of their lives—are asking: "How can I do it all?"

No one wants to ignore parental needs, but unless there are financial resources well beyond what most families can dream about, how to meet those needs is a problem with no easy solution. For the children, it can mean bringing their parents into their homes and, among other things, dealing with a spouse's grumblings about the intrusion in their lives, teenagers' complaints about giving up the privacy of their rooms and coming home to Grandma or Grandpa after school—a tempest that sometimes strains marriages to the breaking point.

If there's one word to describe the dominant feeling on both sides of the bridge that connects the generations at this stage of life, it's "ambivalence." "I love my parents, but…" That's a line I hear spoken repeatedly as women and men struggle with the duality of their feelings—their love for their parents; their sense of obligation; their guilt that, no matter how much they do, it never seems to be enough; their difficulty in coping with their own needs, with their jobs, their families, their fears about their future and, not least, the inability to see an end in sight. The parents' stories are the mirror image of their children's. "I love my children, I know they want to help, but…" The words say they appreciate their children's concern while they feel it as an infringement on their autonomy.

Children grumble about how hard it is to reason with their parents, about how they resist any change even when it seems clearly necessary. Parents complain about unwelcome intrusions, about being talked to as if they were incompetent children. "It's what happens when you're old. You lose all credibility, and people treat you as if you're half brain-dead," observes an 86-year-old father heatedly. "It's damn insulting, and I don't like it any better when my children do it. Worst part of it is, they don't get it. They just write you off as being difficult."

His 79-year-old wife agrees but speaks with more understanding of the difficult situation in which they all find themselves, welcoming her daughter's caring while also resenting her interference. "I know she doesn't agree with our decision to stay in our house, but that's only because she wants us someplace she thinks is safe, so she doesn't have to worry." She hesitates a moment as if considering whether to go on or not, then adds, "I don't know exactly how to say this, but sometimes I think the kids are selfish, too. I mean, I know they love us and want the best for us, but is it an accident that what they think is best is what will relieve them, whether it's really good for us or not?"

An accusation that's not without some merit, but one also that doesn't take account of the complex and conflicting feelings both generations juggle. Looked at from the parents' side, there may, in fact, be something self-serving in the way children push parents to give up their home, their cars, their lives, so that they can stop worrying about them. Some even acknowledge it. But step into the children's shoes, and you wonder: Who's selfish? Is it selfish of parents to insist on maintaining their lives and the home of a past they can no longer live easily without considering the price children pay?

True, parents didn't count the cost, whether financial or emotional, when they gave themselves over to caring for their children. But parents *chose* that life. It wasn't forced on them by circumstances outside their control, and the legitimacy of their authority to do so was unquestioned. But taking care of Mom and Dad profoundly interrupts the lives of adult children who have no authority to control or manage the situation unless their parents willingly hand it over. "I feel like I'm being torn to pieces," cries a 48-year-old woman as she struggles to balance her care and concern for her 70-something parents who need help and don't have the financial resources to pay for it.

Her parents' response: "We just want her to stop nagging us and let us live our lives the way we want to." I remind them that their daughter says they can't afford to continue to live their lives as they have.

"That's our problem," her mother replies, hotly. "We've managed until now. We'll manage again."

It's a no-win situation. Parents commonly resist their children's attempts to intervene, but they are often in denial about the depth of their decline and can't or won't see what's plain to others: They need help. If children back off from the conflict, their parents can fall through the cracks. If they don't, parents are often resentful and difficult. "They think because their father died, I need them to tell me how to run my life—where to live, how to spend my money. It's ridiculous. I love them and I don't want to get upset and argue with them, so I finally just stopped listening when they talk. Sometimes when I know it's one of them calling, I don't answer the phone."

It's an upside-down version of the familiar passive-aggressive drama between parent and adolescent child: "Where are you going?" "Out." "Who are you going with?" "Nobody." "What are you going to do?" "Nothing." Just as parents must decide when to intervene and demand answers, so adult children sometimes have no choice but to take control.

"My mother is furious with me because I insisted on moving her into an assisted-living place," says a 70-year-old man mournfully. Then, his sadness turning to anger, "For God's sake, she's 89 years old and has arthritis so bad she can hardly move. I don't think she'll ever forgive me, but when I found her on the floor because she fell and couldn't get up, there was nothing else to do."

There is no right and wrong here, no black and white; there are only shades of gray in situations so murky that it's nearly impossible for either parents or children to know just when it's the right time to take a step, make a move. Children, who think they see the line more clearly, push their parents to a decision, mostly out of loving concern but also because they need some relief from the worry and the burden. Parents fight more tenaciously to hold on to what's left, as each step of their decline poses another threat to their sense of self. They tell themselves they'll know when the time has come; then one day they slip, fall and can't get up. Or at some unseen, unfelt moment, they slide past the time when they were mentally capable of making a reasoned choice. For a disease of the mind doesn't arrive with the drama of a broken hip; it travels stealthily, taking little bits and pieces as it moves through the brain, each one seeming inconsequential in itself until one day the person has slipped over the edge.

What to do? I have no easy answers. What I do know is that one of the great challenges facing both the nation and its families is how to take care of our parents and grandparents—a problem that is increasing exponentially as 78 million baby boomers have begun to move into the ranks of the elderly. In an article last month in the *New York Times* about the failures of Medicare—what it does that it shouldn't do, what it doesn't do that it should—Jane Gross tallies some of the social cost: "Right now, there are 47 million Medicare beneficiaries, costing a half trillion dollars a year, or one-fifth of the nation's health spending. In 2050, the population on Medicare will number 89 million. How scary is that?"

Scary enough to push us to lift our voices for some radical change in the way healthcare is delivered in our nation. I know, I know. We're living in a moment when the rise of the political right, and the consequent gridlock in Washington, has even made it socially and politically acceptable to propose the abolition of Medicare and Social Security as we've known them. But that doesn't mean we must suffer in silence. Rather, we—both parents and children—have to make ourselves heard on behalf of the kinds of changes that will lift some of the strain from the backs of both generations. At minimum, a change in Medicare policy that would allow for long-term care, whether outside or inside the home, without requiring that the recipient be impoverished—a policy shift that would ease the financial anxieties of both generations and surely assuage some of their psychological anxieties as well. At best, a national universal healthcare system that, like those in every other Western democracy, would ensure healthcare for all Americans and wouldn't break the bank, as our present for-profit system threatens to do.

Meanwhile, take a deep breath and come to terms with the reality that our new longevity is both a blessing and a curse—a blessing because we live longer, healthier lives than we ever dreamed possible, a curse because old age sucks. It always has, and it always will, because it is, by definition, a period of decline that takes a toll on those who are old and those who love them. The only difference now is that, because we live so long, our children suffer it right alongside us.

"This was supposed to be my time," says a 75-year-old retired widower whose 94-year-old mother has been living with him for 13 years. "It's hard not to think, *What about me?* I've had some heart problems, and I think about that and know that, well, you know, I could die anytime and I'll never have had the chance to live these years like I wanted to."

The Guilt of Caring for Elderly Parents

By Suzanne Koven
Boston Globe, February 25, 2013

Four years ago, at 8 p.m. on Valentine's Day, my mother died. A few hours earlier I had taken a brief break from my vigil in the hospice to wander through an excessively air-conditioned Florida mall. The kiosks were overflowing with heart-shaped Mylar balloons, stuffed bears, and chocolate roses. As I surveyed the depressingly cheerful Valentine's paraphernalia, I thought: I really should bring her something.

It was a ridiculous thought, since my mother was in a coma and had no use for balloons or bears. Why did I feel obligated to do something more for Mom just then—as if the years my brothers and I had spent flying back and forth to be with her, the thousands of phone calls, the long hours spent at countless hospital bedsides had not adequately expressed our loyalty and affection?

I've been revisiting this question lately, because a number of my middle-age patients have told me that taking care of their parents is a major source of stress. Baby boomers have parents who are living longer than ever. Plus, many of those boomers had children later in life than their parents did, so they may be juggling eldercare and childcare at the same time—all in an economy where their kids' employment prospects and their own retirement plans feel uncertain.

The funny thing is, though, that when my patients describe the nature of the stress they feel in caring for their parents, they often don't mention financial issues or even the daily pressure of fitting their parents' doctors' appointments, errands, and other needs into already jammed schedules. What they almost always mention is the emotion I felt that day in the mall: guilt.

Many of my patients experience a new or renewed closeness with their parents while helping to care for them. This was certainly the case with me and my mother. In the last years of her life, we spent more time together, and at a slower pace. Sometimes a visit consisted of hours spent in our bathrobes, talking over cups of coffee.

But underlying this closeness was a feeling that my visits, however long or frequent, weren't long or frequent enough. I said to a patient recently, when she told me how guilty she felt about not calling her mother more often, that she could keep her mother on speaker phone all day long, and still feel guilty. She agreed.

Some of this is survivor's guilt. In the years when my mother became increasingly infirm, she would revel in my descriptions of office politics and kids' sleepovers and exotic vacations. "What a full life you lead!" she would exclaim. She'd say she wished she could get in a time machine and go back to the 1960s, when she, too, was active and independent—and wearing Jackie Kennedy-style sheath dresses.

Though I know she didn't mean them this way, I always heard Mom's comments as an accusation, as if my being in the prime of life had nudged her from it prematurely.

Adult children caring for parents may find themselves thrust into the uncomfortable role of bad cop. Who wants to have to tell their parents that they're not safe in their homes or behind the wheel? But who wants to risk parents falling or causing a car accident? Trying to balance an older person's need for independence with his or her safety can leave an adult child feeling that nothing they do is right.

Age, pain, and dementia sometimes make people irritable and demanding, which may cause those trying to help them feel unappreciated. This in turn, can cause guilt.

"How can I get mad at her?" said one patient to me about her mother, who has Alzheimer's. "I must be a horrible person to get so frustrated with someone who can't help how she acts." This same woman developed headaches every time she saw her mother.

It can be especially uncomfortable when parents and children who haven't been close are drawn together by the parents' need for care. Several of my patients are now spending hours every week with parents and in-laws from whom they'd been distanced or even estranged. In a particularly awkward twist, one woman's mother no longer remembers that she and her daughter were never close. The newly intimate relationship that the woman's disability has necessitated seems natural to the mother—and is very painful for the daughter.

Perhaps we feel guilty because we can't completely "fix" our elders. My mother told me as much once when, near the end of her life, she sounded sad and I asked what I could do to make her happier. "Nothing," she answered, honestly. "You can't bring me back my husband, my health, my youth. . ." Even our presence is not enough, sometimes, to salve the loneliness of age. One woman told me that she traveled four hours to visit an aunt who implored her, even as she sat in front of her holding her hands: "When are you going to visit me?"

Maybe what we feel is not so much guilt, as vulnerability: Our parents' frailty feels too much like a harbinger of our own. In middle age I look and sound so much like my mother that it wasn't hard for me to imagine myself taking her place in that hospice bed—as I will one day, if I'm lucky.

Or does caring for our parents chafe because it's out of the natural order of things? There's an old proverb: "When a parent helps a child, both smile. When a child helps a parent, both weep."

Four years after my mother's death, the tears have dried and the guilt has evaporated. But I'd welcome them both back in a heartbeat if I could share one more cup of coffee with her.

Elderly Caregiving: Daughters Usually Deal with Strain of Helping Aging Parents

By Amanda Mears
Deseret News, June 14, 2010

When Amy Oglesby moved back to Salt Lake City two years ago to help care for her aging father, she knew it would be a difficult journey.

What she didn't expect was the staggering pressure and the sudden polarization she would face from family members after her dad was diagnosed with Alzheimer's.

"What's been so terribly disheartening is that instead of this disease bringing our family closer together, it's actually pushed our family apart," Oglesby said.

Oglesby said her family had always been close while she was growing up. Now, with a husband and six children of her own, Oglesby faces the daunting task of trying to salvage the relationship with her siblings while caring for her parents.

"I didn't think it was ever something we would be dealing with," Oglesby said. "So, my heartache doesn't come from the diagnosis; my heartache comes from our family's reaction to the diagnosis."

As difficult as the situation is, Oglesby is not alone. According to Laurel Kennedy, author of *The Daughter Trap* and multigenerational issues expert, women will lose an average of 11.5 years to caregiving.

"You want to be a good daughter," Kennedy said. "Most women love their parents. They want to take care of them and see them happy until it impacts their family and health."

While researching her book, Kennedy interviewed more than 200 caregiving women in order to examine the increasing pressure placed on women who take on the responsibility of caring for their elderly parents. It's a concept Kennedy said is rooted deep in society.

"The women were definitively responsible for hearth and home and family," Kennedy said. "Now you have working women, but no one ever took the responsibility [of care] off women."

Kennedy said that with 80 percent of women now working outside the home, it's important to devise a strategy that will work for everyone.

"We want to empower women and say, 'Whatever decision you make, whatever choice or model is the right one,'" Kennedy said. "There is no single best way to do it, but we are saying everyone needs to step up. If you have siblings, sit down and write a contract. If you need a mediator, get one."

A contract, Kennedy said, can be the best way to make certain individual needs are met while still providing care for loved ones.

"Talk about what's going on, if you need additional support and everyone contributing to the degree they are able," Kennedy said. "Delegate tasks. Specifically say, 'Now what's going to happen when we take our vacation? We need x number of weekends and the options are as follows: Mom can go to your care or respite care, it's your choice.'"

Although it may be hard to have an open dialogue, Kennedy said forging a new path is necessary in an age of advanced health care and prolonged retirement.

"We don't have a model because people didn't live past 80," Kennedy said.

For Oglesby, talking with siblings who aren't ready to face the facts isn't an option, so she relies on the knowledge that time will help.

"We don't have any resolve; the only thing I know is, time is a great healer, and with time things will work out," Oglesby said. "I hold to the hope that with time we will be able to heal the pain."

Maureen Henry, executive director of the Utah Commission on Aging, said early planning isn't the key for alleviating stress, but it's crucial for preventing it in the first place.

"Everyone over the age of 18 should do a life direction," Henry said. "The more health problems you have, the earlier the conversation should take place. We suggest every 10 years there should be a discussion."

Henry suggests sitting down with parents early to discuss options so that when the time comes, children aren't left without direction.

"I think one of the things that's really important is to have the discussion in a nonjudgmental way and have it in a way where the younger adult is not telling the older adult what they think the older adult needs," Henry said. "Have a listening conversation. Look at what the conditions they are facing are. Look at the reality of 'I can't give up my job to care for you; what are your ideas?'"

Oglesby said looking at the positive things of her father's diagnosis has helped her stay sane on days when she feels stretched thin.

"It's been huge to invite the grandparents into our world," Oglesby said. "My dad is able to come to all the performances and everything. We have graduations and dance recitals and piano recitals, and they haven't missed one."

Because Oglesby is not her father's sole caregiver, she said she tries to give her mother respite whenever possible. She also relies on resources such as support groups through the Alzheimer's Association, where she said she has met several people who can relate to her situation.

"Tell everybody what's happening. You'd be amazed at how many people will wrap their arms around you and tell you they know how you're feeling," Oglesby said. "I have found great connections, lots of sources of strength and information. It's people who are the power behind the help."

For women who find that the strain of caregiving is too much, Kennedy said, the first step is to alleviate the guilt associated with seeking help.

"It's OK to say 'no.' You don't need to rationalize or explain or argue," Kennedy said. "It's just, 'I'm sorry we aren't able to do that.'"

The next step, Henry said, is to look at the resources available for elderly parents.

Find programs for which the parent is eligible, and that varies dramatically person to person," Henry said. "Look at if it's short-term or long-term—if it's for rehabilitation, Medicare might cover it. If it's not covered by Medicare, look at the person's assets. Do they have lots that can support them?"

Henry also suggests looking at private pay, even if it means dipping into savings.

"That's the most frustrating for us—convincing people that it's time to use their resources," Henry said. "People want to save their money for a rainy day and it's raining."

Kennedy said another wealth of information is the Internet. The AARP (www.aarp.org), Alzheimer's Association (www.alz.org) and the National Alliance for Caregiving (www.caregiving.org) are all good places to start when looking at alternative options.

At the end of the day, Oglesby said, sometimes the only thing left to do is take a break.

"The way I deal with the stress is sometimes I just have to disconnect, and that's pretty literal for me," Oglesby said. "I'm on the phone with my mom so much, and I know that if I reach a certain overload in her problems that she has had to deal with that day, then I really do need to take a break and step back.

"I just have to know that she can get through this and tomorrow will be a better day. Tomorrow is always a better day."

Afraid to Tell Your Boss You're a Caregiver?

By Sally Abrahms
AARP the Magazine, September 1, 2011

Even though Roxanne Aune's boss is aware that her 59-year-old husband has early onset Alzheimer's, he'll never know how much it impacts her work. "I feel I can't say I'm a caregiver because a red flag will go up and my boss will think, 'Oh, there's something wrong with her husband again,'" says Aune, 57, of Minneapolis. "I can't afford to be absent, or start over again, so I don't discuss this part of my life."

Aune, an auditor at a health insurance company, believes she has suffered professionally since her husband's diagnosis last year. "I feel I get overlooked for projects," she says.

For many employees, Aune's dilemma about work versus elder care is becoming business as usual. The angst will only grow, for many reasons: Parents are living longer. Employees are working longer. More women have paid jobs, and more men are pitching in with caregiving. Smaller families mean fewer siblings to help with Mom and Dad. Federal and state budgets are slashing funds for caregiving. Families are less interested in expensive institutional care, and hospital stays are getting shorter.

The Silver Tsunami Effect

Then there are the numbers: The sheer magnitude of boomers and others who will need help in the future guarantees an elder care tsunami. According to a June 2011 report by MetLife Mature Market Institute, the percentage of age 50-plus adult children taking care of parents has tripled since 1994. The Families and Work Institute reports that 42 percent of US workers in the last five years have had elder care responsibilities and 49 percent expect to care for an older family member or friend in the next five years. And a newly released AARP study reveals that at any given time in 2009, 42.1 million US family caregivers were caring for an adult with limitations, with 61.6 million providing care at some time during the year. The estimated value of their unpaid contributions was nearly $450 billion in 2009, $75 billion more than in 2007.

Many employees are in that elder care-giving boat, yet workers with work-family conflicts are often reluctant to raise the issue with superiors. They fear they'll be viewed as not committed enough, or receive bad year-end reviews. They may also think that discussing their personal life is unprofessional or sense resentment from colleagues and the boss, who may have to pick up the slack during their absences.

Next: Challenges of Elder Care

Deborah Smith, 55, a federal employee in North Carolina, is the 24/7 long-distance caregiver to her friend Donna, who lives in Florida and has dementia and no family. Smith visits Donna every four to six weeks but avoids discussing her at work because "I fear not being promoted or selected for training that could enhance my career," she says. "I fear I may be on the chopping block if I appear too distracted."

Even when workers explain their situation, younger or parentless superiors and coworkers may not "get" it. "Instead of saying to themselves, 'I admire this person because he has the guts to take off work as a way of coping with the situation,' coworkers and managers think, 'How dare they leave, why don't they just hire someone else?'" says Sarah Bullard Steck, a Washington, D.C., social worker in private practice and former director of an employee assistance program that addressed elder care issues.

Challenges All Around

What makes elder care unusually challenging is its unpredictability. You might ask about taking off every Tuesday at 3 p.m. for your child's soccer, but you have no heads-up about when your mother is going to fall and break a hip. Experts believe there may be a bit of ageism lurking, too.

"As a society, we don't always respect and honor older adults needing care as much as we should," says Melissa Brown of Boston College's Sloan Center on Aging & Work. "Maybe we are afraid to look at our own aging."

"Many businesses don't consider elder care an issue and call me only when there's a crisis," says Linda Ziac, president of the Caregiver Resource Center, which offers corporate seminars on elder care issues. "Companies need to acknowledge the workforce is aging and has aging parents, and what not addressing their struggles costs them."

Next: Caregiving Costs

It's a hefty tab for both sides. A caregiving employee may feel forced to turn down a job promotion or relocation, radically reduce work hours, or quit altogether. Companies spend more on recruiting, hiring and training; lose productivity and experienced employees; and have higher health care costs for stressed-out workers, according to a 2006 MetLife and National Alliance for Caregiving study. US businesses lose an estimated $33.6 billion a year in productivity with employees who are caregivers full time, at an average of $2,110 per person.

Preliminary research from the Sloan Center on Aging & Work shows that people caring for older adults report more stress and depression than employees who aren't caregivers or who care for kids. The new AARP report says that 40 to 70 percent of family caregivers of older adults have clinical symptoms of depression; one-quarter to one-half meet major depression criteria.

"What people need is flexibility and support, even if they don't need help immediately," says Eliza Pavalko, an Indiana University sociology professor and expert on aging and the workplace. She and colleagues found that when companies have a family caregiving policy, employees tend to stay longer, even if they don't use the benefits, than at companies that don't.

A few decades ago, the man was typically the full-time worker and the woman handled the house, kids, parents and in-laws. "We have this ideal of the perfect worker who doesn't have any distractions from work. This doesn't fit the reality of our lives," says Pavalko.

Mary Blair-Loy, a University of California–San Diego sociologist and author of *Competing Devotions: Career and Family Among Women Executives*, agrees. "In many organizations, work is viewed as a demanding single-minded allegiance," she says. "Many organizations have an unspoken culture that devalues and stigmatizes workers that don't seem to conform to this norm."

That's what Kathleen Toomey says her former boss did. While Toomey was working as an office manager for a Boston financial company, both of her parents were diagnosed with dementia. Her brother was taking care of them, but then he had a stroke, followed by Lou Gehrig's disease.

One Friday morning at the office, she learned her father had died. She told her boss she wanted to go. His response: "Is all the work completed? Well, have a nice weekend, I'll see you on Monday!" Her boss would tell her that "my concentration was not with the company and he would always use that as an excuse for not giving me a raise," recalls Toomey, 53.

Now an administrative assistant, Toomey says her current boss couldn't be more supportive. "If I have to be at the nursing home or take my mother somewhere, there's no problem," says Toomey. "If you have a family emergency, you shouldn't have to worry, 'Will I have my job tomorrow?'"

Baby Boomers Caring for Elderly Parents—SPeCiaL Things to Do

By Ann Bettencourt
Psychology Today, December 11, 2011

Do you have a parent who is, or parents who are, getting up there in years? What are you doing about their health, their care, their finances? What are you supposed to be doing? To find answers to these questions, I went to my local library. I had hoped that experts, people with hands-on experience, and well, any ole' do-gooders could tell me how to proceed with my own aging mother. The books themselves were reassuring in general, but in my specific case, the "How To" and "What's Next" advice was not particularly helpful. Although I learned a bit from each book, no book garnered my unfettered attention. The problems and solutions explained in these books weren't specific enough to help me with my parent.

Perhaps, step-by-step specifics are less helpful in meeting your parents' needs than are global principles about helping others. Here are a few general pointers that are based on empirical research. These are not necessarily particular only to elderly care giving, but instead are broadly applicable to solving problems of everyday life.

1. **Social Support:** Everyone needs it! "Dad had been strong all his life." "Mom is a loner." However you describe your parent, he or she needs social support. A comprehensive research review conducted by Uchino, Cacioppo, and Kiecolt-Glaser (1996, *Psychological Bulletin*) suggests that people who have higher levels of social support have better cardiovascular, endocrine, and immune functioning. Moreover, much psychological research suggests that those who have greater social support are better off psychologically. One study, conducted by Ownsworth, Henderson, and Chambers, (2010, *Psycho-Oncology*) showed that caregivers who reported higher social support reported more positive psychological well-being. It seems clear that we may need to slow down and ensure that our parents receive the social support they need. In whatever way you can provide your parent social support, do so. But you cannot do everything; do what you are particularly suited toward. If you are good at finances provide this type of "instrumental support." If you are good at listening, provide this type of "emotional support." Just as important, recognize your own need for social support; gather it wherever you can—from your partner, your own children, friends, co-workers. Garnering social support from others will strengthen you and your ability to provide support for your parent.

2. **Perception:** Everyone has one! And it is common that each of us has a slightly, if not wildly, different view of a single situation. If your brother says, "Dad has a memory problem," but you do not share his perception, he is not necessarily delusional. Rather, the two of you literally see things differently. That we perceive the exact same situation in different ways is well supported by research. For example, one study (Houtjes, van Meijel, Deeg, & Beekman, *Journal of Affective Disorders*) showed that patients, caregivers, and medical staff differed significantly in their perceptions of the needs of patients, and this was particularly true when patients were depressed. In most situations, more than one person, including you, will be caring for your elderly parent. Even if those involved are from the same immediate family, it is likely that the perceptions of the elderly person's behavior and needs will differ—and sometimes significantly. What to do? Be open-minded and try your best to literally see the situation from the other's point of view. And if you still don't see what the other person sees, respect the point of view. Finally, if the perceptions of you and your family members diverge significantly, it may be necessary to obtain an expert's (perhaps more objective) opinion regarding your parent's health, care, and finances.

3. **Cooperation:** Everyone benefits from it! You know what is best for Mom!—maybe you feel it would be much easier for you to "jump in and get things done." In the long run, however, it is unlikely you will be able to "do it all." Even if you haven't talked to your sister in 10 years, as your parent's health begins to falter, it is the time to rebuild that relationship. Research suggests that sibling collaboration is important for the adequate care of elderly patients. Based on their focus group study of care giving siblings, Ingersoll-Dayton and her colleagues conclude, "As their parents age, adult siblings must find ways in which to jointly assist in their [parents'] care" (*Journal of Gerontological Social Work*). You might need to "slow down" in your efforts and find a way to cooperate with anyone who is prepared to help. Many adult children may be able make important decisions on their own, but if your parent has several of adult children (as is often the case with baby boomers), then each of you can use your individual strengths toward a cooperative effort toward caring for your parents.

4. **Learning:** Everyone has the capacity to learn! Dad is set in his ways; he cannot change. "You can't teach an old dog new tricks." Right? A variety of recent studies reveal little differences in the capacity of older and younger learners. For example, Tsvetanov and Kourtzi (*Journal of Cognitive Neuroscience*) showed that older observers were just as flexible in their learning of categories that were important for decision-making, and Bennett and colleagues (*Neurobiology of Aging*) showed that healthy older adults were equivalent to younger adults in their capacity to learn frequent and less-frequent sequences. It is almost certain that your parents have learned a lot since they were raising children, and they have the capacity to learn a lot more. Leave your past perceptions behind and consciously be aware of your parent in the present, for her or his own happiness and well-being.

Here is an easy acronym to remember these research-based principles: SPCL (Social Support, Perception, Cooperation, and Learning).

4

Redefining the Senior Years

© Randy Pench/MCT/Landov

Howard Sarasohn, 72, left; Dan Gorfain, 70, middle; and Dave Brubaker, 68, wait for their fellow cyclists along the American River bike trail in Sacramento, California. After they cycled hundreds of miles together around New Zealand in 2010, Gorfain came home and underwent a quadruple bypass three days later. And then he got back on his bike.

The Changing Perception of Age

The percentage of elderly within populations worldwide is increasing at an unprecedented pace. While some countries are the exception, the numbers of elderly entering countries' overall population is increasing. This is particularly true in the United States. The impact this drastic increase will have on the economic and psychosocial health of the country is profound, challenging, and warrants planned, thoughtful responses. While highly complex and multidimensional, the greatest salient trend lies in how seniors are identifying themselves. Indeed, they are a new breed of elderly who act quite differently than their counterparts from the previous generation. Today's elderly, for example, are finding more ways to stay physically, intellectually, and socially active.

Many elderly Americans are continuing to work after they reach retirement age. Seniors in the 2010s are now are much healthier and more active than seniors used to be, even as recently as fifteen years ago. Many seniors married and began families later in life than their own parents and grandparents did. Therefore, they must continue to work even after the retirement age because they still have family financial obligations. In addition to seniors continuing to work, there has also been an increase in what researchers refer to as encore careers, in which seniors leave their original career to pursue a second career later in life. These encore careers combine the personal interests of the individual with a social goal, and are often seen by the individual as more purposeful or meaningful work. Examples of these careers can include nursing, volunteering, substitute teaching, child care, career coaching, and even starting new entrepreneurial ventures. With age comes knowledge that many older Americans are using this to their advantage when competing in the job market with their younger counterparts. Sixty-five no longer means the end of work and a worker's lifestyle.

As life expectancy rises, people have a tendency to relegate the thought of death to a far corner of their mind and embrace actively living their lives as they get older. Many elderly, in fact, report that they experience more satisfaction in life as they age. Even though the actual life expectancy in the United States is about seventy-eight, the general public attitude is that the life expectancy is closer to ninety. Believing that they will live until ninety promotes new views of age-related goals. The quality of life into the elder years has increased exponentially. This is largely due to advances in medicine, including new drugs and treatments for diseases, and new medical technology, such as magnetic resonance imaging (MRI), that can detect potentially fatal conditions in their early stages.

Many believe that it is human nature to want to be young and healthy for as long as possible. However, not every American is taken in by the false sense of security that this is sustainable. As a result of such a large portion of the population aging at once, a considerable amount of attention is being placed on planning for life after death. Some families hold dinners and gatherings in which they discuss, in realistic terms, what will happen when the elder members pass away. These conversations usually include such topics as burial methods and what will be passed on in the will. Poor estate planning can be costly both emotionally and economically; many elderly people, therefore, want to prepare their families for life after their death while also letting their families know how they want their own death rituals handled.

Living an active and healthy lifestyle helps delay the inevitable end of life while improving its quality. As one would expect, the need for those in old age to stay physically active is paramount to them having a long and healthy life. Yet many seniors do not get enough exercise and do not feel the need to push themselves mentally after they reach a certain age. To help keep senior citizens active and mentally alert, as well as to prevent them from having to enter nursing homes, new and innovative programs are being put in place. Research shows that, in many cases, it is often the little problems or issues—such as the height of the microwave, or steepness of a staircase, or even the way a certain cabinet or door opens—in a senior's home that are responsible for many of the problems and ailments that would cause a senior citizen to be forced to enter a nursing home. In an effort to fix these small but significant problems, programs exist wherein workers will come into seniors' homes and adjust cabinets, fix stairs, and move furniture and appliances. All these efforts are aimed at increasing independence and keeping seniors out of nursing homes.

Another approach to ameliorating the need for elderly to enter skilled nursing facilities is the process of downsizing. Seniors move from their original larger family homes to smaller residencies more suited for their lifestyles. Seniors who are downsizing get rid of the clutter and less sentimental and more disposable objects in their homes and lives in order to be independent, fulfilled, and active in their old age. Downsizing and fixing up an already existing home are trends that have not gained national notoriety yet, but as the number of seniors continues to rise at an alarmingly quick rate, it is likely that the popularity of these programs will also go up.

Another reason that alternatives to expensive institutional care are needed is the sheer volume of people that are entering into senior citizenship. According to the United States Census Bureau, there were 43.1 million Americans over the age of sixty-five in 2012, and this number is expected to more than double by 2060. This drastic increase will largely be the result of the baby boomer generation, those born between 1946 and 1964. Baby boomers are a unique sociological phenomenon in the nation's history. And while they have been funding America's entitlement programs, especially Medicare and Social Security, they are now beginning to pull on these same programs for their own health and financial well-being.

The baby boomer generation first affected the nation through the expansion of school systems all over the country, which were needed to keep up with the sheer quantity of children and teenagers. They then swelled the ranks of the American workforce and provided the labor that powered the American economic machine in both productivity and ingenuity.

As they began entering old age in large numbers, baby boomers present a challenge to the stability and health of the very economy they created. Many economists worry that they will overwhelm the mainstay federal retirement programs of Medicare and Social Security. Even though many boomers are not necessarily retiring at sixty-five, the modal age Social Security kicks in, money that has been sanctioned for this program will not be enough as more and more boomers age into the programs.

Baby boomers' longevity poses another, largely unforeseen, threat to these systems. Baby boomers are expected to live longer than the generations they are replacing, and with longer life comes longer demands on the programs whose creation was principally funded by them in the first place. Seniors have greater access to a better health care system than previous generations; therefore, they are expected to live longer as well.

The baby boomers have been shaping the culture and nation since they became part of it. They are now, not surprisingly, reinventing what old age and being elderly means as they enter it. As they age, baby boomers are finding ways to cast off the stereotypical old age image that existed for their parents by keeping up a socially, mentally, and physically active lifestyle. Armed with better health and often greater wealth than previous generations, baby boomers are redefining the senior years in ways their parents could never have dreamed of. Whether it is starting a dream business, returning to school, taking up new hobbies, mastering new technologies, or risking new relationships, today's seniors are shaping and powering the culture of the elderly.

Until baby boomers emerged into the culture as the elderly, America's perspective on aging was to treat it as something that did not exist. It was, for example, considered impolite to ask someone's age in an economy where billions of dollars were being spent to simply look, but not necessarily feel, younger. Society relegated the old to the back room of life, away from the action, prejudicially believing that the elderly were done. They had lived their lives and had nothing left to offer or contribute unless it was in the will. And while there are individual exceptions to every group trend, the baby boomers are not just living longer—they are living old age younger.

Seniors in the twenty-first century are changing the way Americans view old age. Younger Americans are forced to shift their beliefs about the later years. These are years of wisdom, creativity, power, and purpose. Seniors in contemporary times are doing many things that younger adults do, and to a degree that it has ceased to be remarkable. There was a time not so long ago, that a senior running a marathon made news. Today, seniors run marathons routinely and the news is where they placed.

Learning to live healthier lifestyles with purpose and independence is quickly becoming the norm when referring to senior citizens, and will have far-reaching repercussions for future generations. These up and coming senior citizens are truly redefining what it means to enter old age and setting the stage for a whole new conceptualization of what the senior years mean to America and to the seniors themselves.

Boom: A Generation Explodes Assumptions about Aging

By Maureen Hannan
Parks and Recreation, May 12, 2013

"Yo! I'm not old!"

This is how Susan Hoskins, director of the Princeton (New Jersey) Senior Resources Center, summarizes her take on how the Baby Boomer generation is changing perceptions of aging. The prevailing attitude, she continues, goes something like this: "I've done a lot of the things I really wanted to do [rather than wait for retirement] and I don't have much money saved up for my retirement anyway. So, I'm just going to keep on working."

While Hoskins is quick to point out that profiling an entire generation of people is problematic, the question she is trying to answer is a critical one for communities. After all, every eight seconds, one of the nation's 77 million Baby Boomers—those born between the years of 1946 and 1964—turns 60. And by 2030, people 65 and older will comprise 20 to 25 percent of the US population.

As with every other chapter of life the post-World-War-II cohort has entered, their age-defying maturity challenges stereotypes and blurs boundaries. Leaders across the fields of social services, recreation, and public health have long recognized that the Boomers will transform how our society thinks about aging, retirement, health and fitness, lifelong learning, and volunteerism. Yet no one knows the exact ways in which they will ultimately do that.

Parks and recreation agencies—as well as nonprofits serving older adults—are responding to the demands of this demographic by building (or adapting) lifestyle-enhancing facilities, designing holistic programming, and promoting dynamic forms of community engagement. Regardless of whether the big drawing card in a community is a cafe-like social center or citywide teaching and learning opportunities, the characteristics of the new senior center are being defined by a set of hard-to-ignore demographic themes. (Among them, by the way, is an aversion to terms such as senior center.) Listed below are five of those themes—derived from statistics published by the American Association of Retired Persons (AARP) and numerous research organizations—that should resonate with park and recreation professionals.

Retiring Later—and with Financial Worries

The numbers bear out Susan Hoskins's observations. Only 11 percent of Boomers are planning to stop working entirely once they reach 62. With older adults working until later in life, localities can expect a change in the way residents engage in programs targeted to the 55-and-older age group. Hoskins and many of her peers around the country say their centers must extend their hours and offer assistance with career shifts, expanded skill sets, and professional "reinvention."

As for finances, fewer than half of participants in a 2011 Wells Fargo/Gallup Investor Retirement Optimism Index survey said they were confident about their ability to achieve a comfortable retirement. And with good reason: One-quarter of Boomers have no savings or investments at all, and only 9 percent meet the definition of "affluence," having pre-tax working incomes of $150,000 or more.

Space-Loving, Single—and Still Supporting Kids

Don't expect to find this rising older generation clustered together in adult community condos. Only 6 percent of Boomers plan to be living in a smaller residence five years from now. And most (76 percent) plan to live in either a same-sized or larger home. Of those who plan to remain in a home the same size, many say they hope to stay in the same residence. And despite traditional stereotypes of 50-something empty-nester couples, one-third of the Boomer generation are single (just over 25 million) and more than one-third (37 percent) have children under 18 in the household.

As older adults navigate singlehood, they are seeking places and programs supportive of single lifestyles, busy parenting schedules, and domestic partnerships (both gay and straight). As interviewees for these articles attested, older adults are flocking to "coffee-shop" settings—opportunities to connect with their peers in relaxed, unstructured environments.

Tech-Friendly, Ad-Savvy, and Eager to Experiment

Boomers are experienced consumers who also happened to have spent their working lives participating in (and, in many cases, guiding) the evolution of computers, email, and internet. Eighty-two percent use the internet, and 64 percent engage in online activities, such as instant-messaging, social media, and conducting financial transactions. And Boomers are sophisticated in their responses to advertising. Twenty-three percent of AARP members surveyed said they find ads geared toward their age group insulting, and 67 percent claim they won't buy a product if they are offended by the advertising. Finally, far from the stereotypes of older-adult brand loyalty, numerous marketing surveys show Boomers are just as likely to experiment with new products and services as much younger consumers are.

Physically Active, Youthful in Mindset

This is not a generation likely to sit by passively while aging overtakes them. The typical Boomer participates regularly in an average of 10 different physical activities.

And 11 million of them regularly bicycle. Nineteen percent identify physical health as their top priority (above even relationships with friends/family, and personal finances.) And even though the national institute of aging (NIA) reports that 80 percent of Americans 60 and older have at least one chronic health condition, Boomers' buying behaviors demonstrates their refusal to submit to the aging process.

During the next 10 years alone, according to NIA statistics, the 77-million-strong cohort can be expected to increase their wellness spending from $200 billion to $1 trillion or more.

They will, by and large, spend that money not with the mindset of old people desperate to rejuvenate—but with a youthful outlook. A recent *Los Angeles Times* survey, for example, found that Americans over age 60 feel 19 years younger than their chronological age. And boomers consistently reject terms like elderly, old, or senior—preferring descriptions like experienced and mature.

Community Minded—but on Their Own Terms

Seventy percent of Boomers AARP surveyed say they have a responsibility to make the world a better place. And this generation is volunteering at significantly higher rates than preceding generations did as they entered into their 50s. Yet according to the Corporation for National Community Service, three out of 10 boomers who volunteer for an organization choose not to volunteer the following year. Retention rates, they found, are highest among those whose volunteer activities are professional and managerial, engaging in music or other types of performance, and teaching- or mentoring-related.

The Baby Boomers are approaching—and viewing—aging differently than their parents and grandparents did. Chronological age is just a number, work does not (indeed, cannot) end at 65, health is an asset to be actively managed—and opportunities to learn and make an impact are essential. What will this largest generation in American history want and demand from their communities as it ages? From facilities, to programs, to chances to make a difference, interviews reported, traditional assumptions no longer apply.

Newer Tech on the Rise with Seniors

Laurenne Ramsdell
Foster's Daily Democrat, October 27, 2013

Although the younger population continues to lead the way when it comes to exploring technology, a generation much older than the Millennials and Gen-X have proved to be just as interested in incorporating up-and-coming gadgets into their lives.

Senior citizens across the nation are ridding their homes of landline telephones and desktop computers, turning instead to smartphones, tablets, and all-things digitized.

According to a Pew Research Center study from 2012, 53 percent of adults age 65 and older in the United States were using the Internet or email. With years prior showing little to no growth in this age category, this gain is significant.

A growing interest in using the Internet to its fullest potential has sparked the creation of programs like Silver Surfers, which provides senior citizens a crash course in technology use.

Run by a company known as Visiting Angels, which has a franchise based in Stratham, Silver Surfers is an up-and-coming program that will send technology-know-it-alls to retirement homes and individual clients to teach senior citizens how to use the Internet, smartphones and other gadgets.

According to John Spellman, owner and director of two Visiting Angels franchises, he and his staff have noticed an uptick in the number of elderly clients asking for help when it comes to using computers and other technological devices.

"We have found that there are elders in the community who are exploring social media, using iPads, emailing and even getting on Skype," said Spellman. "Nine years ago, we didn't see this kind of need at all."

Although Silver Surfers has not been fully launched yet, Spellman hopes to soon offer the knowledge of technology savvy staff members to educate senior citizens on the ways they can use today's gadgets and programs to benefit their lives.

Spellman said the idea of Silver Surfers stemmed from an incident where his company was contacted by a family member of a Visiting Angels client who shared that a memorial website had been put up online for another family member that had recently passed away. Spellman explained that the caller wanted the client to see the site, which was filled with pictures and information, but feared their elderly family member would not know how to access it.

Spellman went on to note that one of his staff members took the client to the public library, logged on to their own social media account and shared the memorial site with them.

"The woman showed interest in learning how to create this kind of account so she could see more pictures and stay up-to-date with her family," he said.

Spellman said providing senior citizens with an education on how to better utilize what the Internet has to offer is beneficial because it provides them with more conventional means for communication and obtaining information.

"Younger family members are communicating more regularly through social media sites," said Spellman. "People don't really write letters any more, let alone make phone calls. If you're not texting or emailing, you're not communicating."

Although in developmental stages, Spellman said he hopes to start getting the word out about Silver Surfers through existing clients and by making presentations available to local senior centers and retirement homes. He noted that he expects to see Visiting Angels obtain a broader group of clients by offering this technology service, as it may appeal to many senior citizens living locally.

Spellman's company is not the only business seeing an influx in the number of elderly individuals looking to explore the Internet and digital technology.

Krista Trefethen, assistant recreation director for the Dover Senior Center, said she has seen a growing number of individuals who are members of the center that are looking for information related to technology. So much so that the city has begun bringing in volunteers a couple of times a year to teach introductory computer classes to those who have a minimal background with technology.

"A lot of times we find that someone's family member buys them a computer, but they are unsure how to use it," said Trefethen. "We've also seen an increase in the number of questions coming from our members relating to tablets, Nooks, and other technology."

Although the Dover Senior Center itself does not have computers available for members to use, housed in the same building is the Dover Adult Learning Center where senior citizens are welcome to access the computer lab.

For 63-year-old Dover resident Barbara Burgess, adapting to the trending technology is something she has been preparing for since a young age.

Burgess explained that her father was an engineer who worked for General Electric and spent much of her childhood preaching that computers were the way of the future.

"And you know what, he was absolutely right," she said.

Even at the ripe age of 16, Burgess' father's words rang true as she was tasked with transposing data from a bank's handwritten punchcards to an IBM computer system.

It wasn't until Burgess, who had a home-run calligraphy business, worked with a graphic designer in the mid-1990s and discovered just some of the astounding capabilities a personal computer had to offer.

"It amazed me," she said.

By 1995, Burgess had purchased a desktop computer for her family to use at home. Soon her children were playing online computer games, and each member of the family grew fond of the device and its access to the World Wide Web.

After the loss of her husband, however, Burgess would grow a new fondness for the computer and how it helped her in the grieving process.

Connecting to an online social media chat room through AOL dedicated for widows, Burgess said she was opened up to a whole group of people who had been through a similar situation as herself. She was able to connect to people who had advice on how to grieve, and shared her personal story with those she grew close to.

"It didn't supplement my family's support, but I think it helped me get through a very hard period in my life," said Burgess.

According to the 2012 Pew study, 34 percent of senior citizen Internet users utilize social networking sites such as Facebook, while 18 percent do so routinely.

Burgess told Foster's she has continued to explore social networking sites. As a new grandmother, she has been able to keep in touch with her son in ways that have allowed her to feel closer to his five-month-old son—despite the fact that they live in another state.

Burgess said the ever-expanding world of technology is what led her to her current career, having utilized online job sites.

For the past eight years, Burgess has worked in the sales department for eCoast in Rochester. A company focused on networking and sales for thousands of technology companies, eCoast has challenged Burgess to adapt to the ever-growing technology industry.

"I remember my first week on the floor, thinking I don't know if I can do this," said Burgess.

Although she admits she was initially fearful about using unfamiliar technology as part of her job, Burgess said eCoast staff have been more than willing to train her to use software programs and new-age devices to their fullest potential.

Working in what she calls a "bees' nest of technology" has caused Burgess' personal interest in up-and-coming devices to flourish.

"My phone has become another appendage," she joked.

Not only does Burgess use her cell phone as her alarm clock, and her iPad Mini as her camera, Burgess has also eliminated televisions from her home and now streams her favorite programs on her Apple computer.

Senior citizens' interest in technology is not strictly limited to computers, however, as many have gravitated toward using up-and-coming mobile devices and tablets.

According to the Pew study, 69 percent of adults ages 65 and older own and use a mobile phone—a figure that is up from 57 percent in 2010.

For 65-year-old Kate Buckley, her interest in exploring new technology was sparked when she was introduced to the world of smartphones.

Although she was no stranger to computer technology, having worked with such devices throughout her career, using a smartphone was a whole new concept for Buckley and her husband.

Just a couple of years ago, the Buckleys' son took a job with Verizon.

"Soon he was telling us to get rid of our ancient landline and get with the times," she said.

Although she and her husband already owned cell phones, switching over to smartphones allowed the Buckleys to truly explore all of the conveniences the new devices had to offer.

"They were like bricks compared to what we have now," said Buckley when asked about the differences between her old and new cell phone.

Buckley said she has fallen in love with many of the apps made available on her smartphone, including one that has made grocery shopping more convenient than ever.

Buckley shared that she compiles a grocery list on a shopping app she downloaded to her phone. Once she is finished, she has the option of emailing the list to her husband, who happens to work near a major commercial grocery store.

"This way he can go and get what we need on his way home," she said. "It just makes our lives so much easier."

Buckley said she has also fallen in love with the Pandora app on her phone, which allows her to stream the music stations of her choice while she entertains company. When Buckley and her husband head down to Clearwater, Florida, for the winter, they use the Facetime feature on their devices to keep in touch with family members.

"This kind of technology allows us to still see them face-to-face, so to speak," she said.

Burgess and Buckley both say they will not shy away when it comes to exploring technology of the future.

"I find technology itself to be fascinating," said Burgess. "It's constantly changing, and I want to keep up with it."

Buckley is beginning to explore some of the other tech-savvy gadgets available to her.

"I think a tablet is in my future for sure," she said.

An avid reader, Buckley said she was thrilled to discover that both her local library as well as the one located near her home in Florida provide free book downloads for those who have e-reader devices like the Kindle and Nook.

According to Therese Willkomm, director of the Assistive Technology program at University of New Hampshire, the growing trend of senior citizens using today's gadgets has had an impact on the evolution of technology.

As there are many elderly individuals who now have physical and/or sensory limitations as a result of getting older, Willkomm noted that many technology companies have developed options geared toward such impairments.

She spoke of the Pebble Smartwatch, a wrist watch that syncs to a cell phone or tablet. The devices allows its user to program alarms and alerts through their phone or tablet that send a pulsing alert directly to the watch.

"Sometimes it's kind of hard to hear a phone ring or an alarm go off, but with this watch, you are alerted by the vibration," she said.

Willkomm noted that many elderly individuals may find this feature beneficial when trying to set up a medication-taking regiment, or when scheduling appointments.

Through her research, Willkomm has also come across many tablet devices that feature larger font size options for those who struggle with their sight. Such devices also offer voice recognition programs so users no longer have to type an email message, and can instead speak to the device, which will transcribe the conversation for them.

Another application Willkomm cited that senior citizens prefer is the EARs app, a program downloadable to Apple devices that amplifies sound. The app enhances the sound around its user, acting like a hearing aid. Whether it's to better understand a conversation or increasing the volume of a television show without bothering others, the EARs app offers elderly users a better chance at hearing.

It is the development of such features that Willkomm cited as strong evidence that shows the rising trend of elderly individuals integrating technology's most reputable devices into their lives is playing a significant role on the development of such technology—and will for years to come.

"These devices are adapting to accommodate all ages now, especially because senior citizens have been showing so much interest," she said.

Careers: Time for an Encore
for Baby Boomers

By Dave Carpenter
Associated Press, September 9, 2012

Here go the baby boomers again, reinventing themselves and bucking tradition as they bear down on retirement.

This time they're leading a push into so-called encore careers—paid work that combines personal meaning with social purpose—in their 50s and 60s.

As many as 9 million people ages 44 to 70 already are in such careers as the second or third acts of their working lives, according to nonprofit think tank Encore.org.

But that number is poised to multiply as many boomers and others take steps to combine making a living with making a difference. Another 31 million older workers are interested in finding encore careers, based on a 2011 survey by the nonprofit.

A mixture of longer life spans, layoffs, shifting cultural attitudes and financial realities is causing this growing urge among over-50s to seek out more purposeful work. Sometimes it's just an itch to do something more purposeful in retirements that can now last for three decades, while still pulling in needed income.

The demographics of 78 million baby boomers should ensure that this career shift accelerates, says Encore.org vice president Marci Alboher.

"This trend has the potential to be a new social norm much the way that the dream of the golden years, of a leisure-based retirement, was an aspiration for the generation before," she says.

Alboher, whose soon-to-be-released *The Encore Career Handbook* is an invaluable resource for older workers looking for purposeful career alternatives, discussed the phenomenon in an interview. Here are edited excerpts:

Q: What steps can be taken to lay the groundwork for an encore career?

A: Start by thinking about your own interests. What would you want to do if you weren't doing what you've been doing for the last 20 or 30 years? What issues matter enough that you would want to volunteer your time or talents if you knew you could make a difference? Let yourself dream a little. Identify people who have reinvented themselves in a way that's helping their community or the world. Make a coffee date with one of them and ask how they made the transition. You might find something that resonates with you. The best thing you can do to actually get started is to volunteer. Check out AARP's createthegood.org, www.volunteermatch.org and, for both work and volunteer opportunities, www.idealist.org.

Q: What fields offer the most plentiful opportunities for meaningful work?

A: Health care, education, green jobs, government, nonprofits (www.encore.org/work/top5). Health care is really the No. 1 field to look at in terms of both needs and opportunities. With an aging population and the changes that are coming in our health-care system, there are needs and opportunities for all kinds of work whether you have a medical orientation in your background or just want to help people.

Q: How useful are career coaches, and how much do they cost?

A: They can help if you're stuck and think you could benefit from working one-on-one with someone and being held accountable. But this professional help doesn't come cheap. Rates can range from $80 to $90 an hour to more than $200 an hour. There are some ways to get low-cost coaching. Some coaches offer group sessions, and many community colleges offer free or low-cost coaching or career-exploration courses (www.encore.org/colleges). Local organizations focusing on encore activities have sprouted up across the country (www.encore.org/connect/local). Or check CareerOneStop (www.careeronestop.org), a program run by the Labor Department, to see if there are any offerings in your area.

Q: Do these careers usually involve a big drop in income?

A: Not necessarily. If the work sounds altruistic in some way, most people assume they'll be making less money. For people coming from high-level jobs in the for-profit sector, they very well may be facing a cut in pay. But for people whose primary career was focused in the social-purpose arena—at a nonprofit, or in social work or education, where money is not the main motivator—many of these encore reinventions don't involve a pay cut at all.

Q: How big a barrier is age discrimination?

A: It exists. But if you feel like your age is getting in the way of what you want to do, it could be simply that you don't have the proper skills for what you're interviewing for. And that could be related to the fact you haven't brushed up your skills in the last 20 or 30 years. I always encourage people to think about what can they do to make sure that their skills are current and that they're presenting properly. And take a close look at organizations you are thinking about working with. Do you see a welcoming and diverse workplace that values people of all ages? If not, consider looking someplace else where you'll be able to thrive and your experience will be valued.

Q: How feasible is it to launch your own business with a social purpose?

A: The social entrepreneurship sector—businesses that have a social mission as well as a financial bottom line—is really growing. There's a very high interest in entrepreneurship among older workers. There are pros and cons. Being your own boss can give you more control over your life. And it can be a good fit for people who are tired of having a manager. But most people who start a business, especially one designed to do some good in the world, find that they are working harder than ever. And you do have lots of bosses, even as an entrepreneur—your clients, your funders. Before rushing to start your own thing, consider offering your skills to another encore entrepreneur and also take a look at freelancing or self-employment. Those may be ways to have more control and autonomy, while still having an impact—and keeping the risk down somewhat.

Hot Encore Jobs

A list of some "encore jobs"—those with community or social value—that are anticipated to have high need or demand in coming years for workers looking to make career shifts in their 50s or 60s, according to *The Encore Career Handbook*:

Health Care

- Nurse
- Licensed practical nurse (LPN)
- Registered nurse (RN)
- Nurse practitioner
- Nurse instructor
- Physician assistant
- Emergency medical technician (EMT)
- Home health aide
- Physical or occupational therapist
- Massage therapist
- Yoga instructor
- Patient navigator/advocate
- Community health worker
- Health or wellness coach
- Home-modification specialist

Social Services, Counseling and Coaching

- Bereavement/grief counselor
- Child-care worker
- Pastoral counselor
- Addiction counselor
- Career/vocational counselor
- Career coach
- Social worker
- Elder advocate and gerontology worker

Education

- Teacher
- Teacher assistant/aide or paraprofessional
- Substitute teacher

- After-school program support staff
- Reading tutor
- Nonprofit fundraiser/development professional
- Grant writer
- Nonprofit social-media manager
- Interim nonprofit executive director

Green Jobs

- Weatherization installer/technician
- Solar-installation trainer
- Energy auditor

Why Are Baby Boomers Leading the Entrepreneurial Movement?

By Hanah Cho
Dallas Morning News, May 20, 2013

An encore career. The second act. The new retirement.

Whatever you call it, baby boomers and seniors have been bitten by the entrepreneurship bug.

Amid economic and social changes, the 55- to 64-year-old age group has had the largest increase in entrepreneurial activity over the last decade, according to the Ewing Marion Kauffman Foundation, a nonprofit group that promotes entrepreneurship. This trend has continued in spite of the tepid economic recovery.

"It's a whole movement of starting your own business, no matter how small," said Elizabeth Isele, co-founder of the nonprofit Senior Entrepreneurship Works in Washington, D.C., and New York.

Consider Pat and Mary Sculley. They're both 65, and they built successful careers, traveled around the world and raised two children in their more than 43 years together.

They had enough of a nest egg to retire. Instead, they took some of their savings to invest in a startup health and wellness franchise operation. They opened the Exercise Coach in two locations in Dallas in recent weeks. They plan to open a third in Inwood Village in the next month. Two more are in the works.

At this point in their lives, they no longer wanted to work at a large corporation where other people are making decisions.

"We want to be in control," said Pat, who spent 23 years at Electronic Data Systems, including a stint as president of the company's operations in Japan.

Uprooted Lives

The recession uprooted lives and forced many longtime workers out of their jobs. The unemployment rate among workers 55 and up is lower than the national average, but older employees also stay jobless longer.

"There are different ways to volunteer and help nonprofits and work part-time, but if you need more income than that, you're up a creek," Isele said. She works with lawmakers and nonprofit groups to help senior entrepreneurs build businesses.

Research in 2011 by Civic Ventures, a think tank on boomers, found that 1 in 4 Americans ages 44 to 70 are interested in starting businesses or nonprofit ventures in the next five to 10 years.

Even before the financial upheaval, workplace and demographic changes were fueling an entrepreneurial boom among older workers.

For starters, baby boomers represent a huge chunk of the overall population.

The Kauffman Foundation study in 2009 predicted that the US might be on the verge of an entrepreneurship boom "not in spite of an aging population but because of it."

While overall business startup activity in the US dipped last year, the share of entrepreneurship among the baby boomer group has grown from 14.3 percent in 1996 to 23.4 percent last year, according to the Kauffman Foundation.

With baby boomers and seniors living longer and healthier, many are moving into second and third careers instead of retiring. The shift reflects a steady decline in lifetime employment at one company that was once commonplace, said Dane Stangler, director of research and policy at the Kauffman Foundation.

Plus, many older workers have the experience and wherewithal to start new businesses. Technology also makes it easier for them to venture out on their own.

"It's definitely easier to strike out on your own," Stangler said. "You can do a lot of different things, and if you're in your 50s and 60s, you have quite a lot of social capital: a large social network and a lot of experience to tap into. Those are key resources for people entering self-employment or becoming entrepreneurs."

A New Start

After traveling the globe for work, the Sculleys moved to Scottsdale, Arizona, in 2002.

Mary continued to work in human resources at big companies, while Pat got a job leading a nonprofit.

By 2011, Mary said she was ready to leave corporate life and do something else. The couple had frequently talked about starting a business together, so they looked into entrepreneurship, Mary said.

They decided to move back to Dallas and started the due diligence of finding the right business opportunity.

After considering buying an existing small business, they founded the Exercise Coach, which fit their interests in health and wellness. Unlike typical gyms, the Exercise Coach focuses on one-on-one 20-minute strength training with a coach.

Their decades of work experience combining operations and human resources, the couple says, have been invaluable as entrepreneurs.

"The fact that we've had the experience we've had in multiple countries, we're not very risk-averse," Mary said. "We're not stupid about it, but we're not that risk-averse. We trust ourselves. That's really important."

As new entrepreneurs, the couple has enjoyed the challenges of finding real estate, hiring the right people and wearing many hats. Pat said they're also having fun.

"I tried retirement," Pat said. "And I just got bored."

Living to 120 and Beyond: Americans' Views on Aging, Medical Advances, and Radical Life Extension

Pew Research, August 6, 2013

With falling birthrates and rising life expectancies, the US population is rapidly aging. By 2050, according to US Census Bureau projections, one-in-five Americans will be 65 or older, and at least 400,000 will be 100 or older.[1] Some futurists think even more radical changes are coming, including medical treatments that could slow, stop or reverse the aging process and allow humans to remain healthy and productive to the age of 120 or more. The possibility that extraordinary life spans could become ordinary life spans no longer seems far-fetched. A recent issue of *National Geographic* magazine, for example, carried a picture of a baby on its cover with the headline: "This Baby Will Live to Be 120."

Yet many Americans do not look happily on the prospect of living much longer lives. They see peril as well as promise in biomedical advances, and more think it would be a bad thing rather than a good thing for society if people lived decades longer than is possible today, according to a new survey by the Pew Research Center. Asked whether they, personally, would choose to undergo medical treatments to slow the aging process and live to be 120 or more, a majority of US adults (56 percent) say "no." But roughly two-thirds (68 percent) think that most *other* people would. And by similarly large margins, they expect that radically longer life spans would strain the country's natural resources and be available only to the wealthy.

There is, at present, no method of slowing the aging process and extending average life expectancies to 120 years or more. But research aimed at unlocking the secrets of aging is under way at universities and corporate labs, and religious leaders, bioethicists and philosophers have begun to think about the morality of radical life extension, according to two accompanying reports released by the Pew Research Center's Religion & Public Life Project in conjunction with the new survey.

The survey, conducted from March 21 to April 8, 2013, among a nationally representative sample of 2,012 adults, examines public attitudes about aging, health care, personal life satisfaction, possible medical advances (including radical life extension) and other bioethical issues. The telephone survey was carried out on cell phones and landlines, in all 50 states, with an overall margin of error for the full sample of plus or minus 2.9 percentage points.[2]

The findings suggest that the US public is not particularly worried about the gradual rise in the number of older Americans. Nearly nine-in-ten adults surveyed say that "having more elderly people in the population" is either a good thing for society (41 percent) or does not make much difference (47 percent). Just 10 percent see this trend as a bad thing.

Americans also appear to be generally optimistic as they look toward their own futures, including old age. Most say they are satisfied with the way things are going in their lives today (81 percent) and expect that 10 years from now their lives will be even better (56 percent) or about the same (28 percent). Younger adults are particularly optimistic, but even among Americans ages 65 and older, fully two-thirds expect their lives to be better (23 percent) or about the same (43 percent) in another decade. And while about a fifth of all US adults (18 percent) say they worry "a lot" and 23 percent say they worry "a little" about outliving their financial resources in retirement, more than half (57 percent) say they either do not worry "too much" about this or do not worry about it "at all."

Asked how long they would like to live, more than two-thirds (69 percent) cite an age between 79 and 100. The median ideal life span is 90 years—about 11 years longer than the current average US life expectancy, which is 78.7 years.[3]

The public also is optimistic that some scientific breakthroughs will occur in the next few decades. For example, about seven-in-ten Americans think that by the year 2050, there will be a cure for most forms of cancer (69 percent) and that artificial arms and legs will perform better than natural ones (71 percent). And, on balance, the public tends to view medical advances that prolong life as generally good (63 percent) rather than as interfering with the natural cycle of life (32 percent).

But there also is some wariness about new medical treatments. Only a quarter (24 percent) of adults say they have "a lot" of confidence that new medicines and treatments have been carefully tested before becoming available to the public. About half (54 percent) agree with the statement that "medical treatments these days are worth the costs because they allow people to live longer and better-quality lives," but 41 percent disagree, saying medical treatments these days "often create as many problems as they solve."

Views of Radical Life Extension

The survey seeks to provide a glimpse into people's initial thoughts and considerations on a subject—radically longer human life spans—that could emerge as a public issue in the future. But measuring opinion about scientific breakthroughs that may or may not come to pass is difficult. Only 7 percent of respondents say they have heard or read a lot about the possibility that new medical treatments could in the future allow people to live much longer; 38 percent say they have heard a little about this possibility, and about half (54 percent) have heard nothing about radical life extension prior to taking the survey. Since the scientific breakthroughs are uncertain and the public does not know much about this field, the wording of the survey question focuses on the result—much longer life spans—and is deliberately vague about how, exactly, this would be achieved.

At this early stage, public reaction to the idea of radical life extension is both ambivalent and skeptical. Asked about the consequences for society if new medical treatments could "slow the aging process and allow the average person to live decades longer, to at least 120 years old," about half of US adults (51 percent) say the treatments would be a bad thing for society, while 41 percent say they would be a good thing.

But most doubt that such a breakthrough will occur anytime soon. When asked about the future likelihood of "the average person" in the United States living to at least 120 years, nearly three-quarters (73 percent) say it either probably or definitely will *not* happen by the year 2050. Just a quarter of adults (25 percent) consider it likely to happen by 2050.

The public also is skeptical about the fairness of these kinds of potential medical interventions. An overwhelming majority believes that "everyone should be able to get these treatments if they want them" (79 percent). But two-thirds think that in practice, only wealthy people would have access to the treatments.

Most Americans also foresee other negative implications. About two-thirds agree that "longer life expectancies would strain our natural resources" and that "medical scientists would offer the treatment before they fully understood how it affects people's health." And about six-in-ten (58 percent) say "these treatments would be fundamentally unnatural."

Opinion is more divided over whether "our economy would be more productive because people could work longer;" 44 percent agree, while about half (53 percent) reject this idea.

Views on the likely impact of radical life extension on society vary somewhat by age, race and ethnicity. Blacks and Hispanics are more likely than whites to see radical life extension as a positive development for society. And younger adults are more inclined than those 50 and older to say that radical life extension would be a good thing for society.

But there are few differences in opinions across other social and demographic groups. Men and women are about equally likely to say that radical life extension would be a good thing for society. There are only modest differences across education and income groups, with those who have less formal education and lower incomes somewhat more inclined to say radical life extension would be a positive development for society.

Attitudes toward Aging and Medical Advances

Older adults account for a growing share of the US population. Roughly 41 million Americans are 65 and older, and they make up about 13 percent of the total US population, up from 4 percent in 1900.[4] The growth in the share of older people in the population over the past century stems from dramatic advances in public health and medical care as well as steep declines in fertility rates. The share of the population that is 65 and older is growing at a faster pace than other age groups, fueled primarily by the aging of the nation's 76 million baby boomers.

The new Pew Research survey finds that the public views this trend in American society as more positive than negative. About four-in-ten (41 percent) adults consider "having more elderly people in the population" a good thing for society.

Just 10 percent say this is a bad thing, and 47 percent say it doesn't make much difference.

The overall average life expectancy in the US at present is 78.7 years, although women tend to live longer (81.0 years) than men (76.2 years).[5] Given the option, most Americans would choose to live longer than the current average. Fully 69 percent of American adults would like to live to be 79 to 100 years old. About 14 percent say they would want a life span of 78 years or less, while just 9 percent would choose to live more than 100 years. The median ideal life span is 90 years. Younger adults, to whom old age may seem far away, are more likely than those 65 and older to give an ideal age of 78 years or less (19 percent versus 6 percent). The median ideal life span of adults under 30—at 85 years—is lower than that for older adults. Relative to whites and Hispanics, blacks are especially likely to say they would choose a longer life span (median of 94 years). But whether respondents are male or female, their median ideal life span is roughly the same. And there are no significant differences in the median ideal length of lifetime by education.

Public views of medical treatments today are largely positive, though not without reservations. About two-thirds of adults (63 percent) say "medical advances that prolong life are generally good because they allow people to live longer," while about three-in-ten (32 percent) say medical advances are bad because "they interfere with the natural cycle of life." Further, 54 percent of adults believe that "medical treatments these days are worth the costs because they allow people to live longer and better-quality lives," while 41 percent say that these treatments "often create as many problems as they solve."

Overall attitudes about medical treatments are, not surprisingly, closely related to views about the likely effect of medical treatments that would radically extend the life span of human beings. Those who see medical advances in generally positive terms are also more inclined to view radical life extension as a good thing for society, and vice versa.

Differences by Religious Group

There are mostly modest differences among religious groups in their views on medical advances in general. Majorities of all large US religious groups consider medical advances that prolong life as generally good.[6] About half or more of adults in all the major religious groups also say that medical treatments these days are worth the costs because they allow people to enjoy longer, better-quality lives. About six-in-ten white mainline Protestants (62 percent) and white (non-Hispanic) Catholics (59 percent) hold this view, compared with about half of white evangelical Protestants (50 percent) and black Protestants (52 percent). About half or more of Hispanic Catholics (53 percent) and the religiously unaffiliated (55 percent) also say that medical treatments these days are worth the costs.

However, there is a different pattern across religious groups when it comes to attitudes about the possibility of slowing the aging process and radically extending life. Black Protestants are among the most likely to say radical life extension would be a good thing for society (54 percent do so). By contrast, fewer white evangelical Protestants (34 percent) and white Catholics (31 percent) say the same.

Hispanic Catholics (44 percent) are more likely than white Catholics (31 percent) to think that much longer life spans would be a good thing for society. Among the religiously unaffiliated, 43 percent say radical life extension would be good for society, and 51 percent say it would be bad for society. About four-in-ten (41 percent) white mainline Protestants say radical life extension would be a good thing, while 52 percent say it would be a bad thing for society.

Predicting Views of Radical Life Extension

While only a minority of US adults have heard about the possibility of radical life extension, those who report having heard at least a little about it are relatively more inclined to see it in a positive light. And those who expect scientific developments to dramatically increase average life spans in the next 40 years also are more inclined to view radical life extension as good for society and to say they personally would want life-extending treatments.

The survey contains a number of null findings that may be surprising. It turns out, for example, that many standard measures of religious beliefs and practices, including belief in God and frequency of attendance at religious services, are related to views on radical life extension only weakly, if at all. Nor is there a strong relationship in the survey between the gender, education or political party identification of respondents and what they say about longer human life spans.

At least one question that deals directly with death, however, is correlated with views on radical life extension. People who oppose the death penalty are more inclined to say that longer life spans would be good for society. Beliefs about medical advances in general also are predictive of where people stand: those who think medical advances are generally good are more likely to view radical life extension in positive terms and to say that they personally would want life-extending treatments.

Perhaps most intriguing, there is an association between race and ethnicity and views about radical life extension, with blacks and Hispanics more inclined than (non-Hispanic) whites to favor radical life extension for themselves as well as for society as a whole. There may be many, overlapping reasons for these differences. Blacks and Hispanics tend to hold distinctive views on a number of questions that are correlated with views about radical life extension, such as having higher expectations that such scientific breakthroughs will come to pass by the year 2050 and being more inclined to see the growth of the elderly population as good for society. The survey cannot provide a definitive explanation for these racial and ethnic differences.

Roadmap to the Report

The rest of this report details the survey's findings on radical life extension and related attitudes toward aging, medicine, personal life, religion, and moral and social issues. The first section looks at Americans' initial thoughts about the desirability and impact of radical life extension. The second section covers views on radical life extension by religious affiliation, beliefs and practices. The third section looks at the public's views on aging in general. The fourth section explores attitudes toward medical treatments available today and the relationship of those attitudes to the public's views on radical life extension. The fifth section looks at personal life satisfaction as it relates to attitudes about longevity. The sixth section considers the morality of some social issues—including views on abortion, stem cell research and the death penalty—and how those views are related to the public's early thinking about the possibility of radically longer life spans. The seventh section provides an overview of the similarities and differences across racial and ethnic groups on views about radical life extension and beliefs about aging, medicine and personal life.

What's the Science behind Radical Life Extension? And What's the Religious Debate?

In the last 200 years, advances in medicine, nutrition and public health have substantially increased human life spans. These increases have been achieved largely by helping infants and children to live to adulthood rather than by pushing the boundaries of human aging past their known limits. Today, however, scientists at major universities, research institutions and corporate labs are investigating a number of potential ways to slow down or turn back the natural clock of human aging, including growth hormone treatments, natural or drug-induced starvation diets and genetic therapies that seek to reduce or reverse the effects of aging. So far, none of these approaches has proven to be clearly effective in humans, but together they give a sense of the possible avenues ahead.

Notes

1. See US Census Bureau, Population Division. December 2012. "Table 2. Projections of the Population by Selected Age Groups and Sex for the United States: 2015 to 2060 (NP2012-T2)."http://www.census.gov/population/ projections/data/national/2012/summarytables.html.
2. For more details on the survey methodology, see Appendix A.
3. Average life expectancy from Centers for Disease Control and Prevention. 2013. "Table 18" in "Health, United States, 2012: With Special Feature on Emergency Care," National Center for Health Statistics.http://www.cdc.gov/ nchs/data/hus/hus12.pdf#018.
4. Figures are from the US Census Bureau population estimates and Pew Research Center population projections. Also see the June 2009 Pew Research Center report "Growing Old in America: Expectations vs. Reality."
5. Average life expectancies from Centers for Disease Control and Prevention. 2013. "Table 18" in "Health, United States, 2012: With Special Feature on Emergency Care," National Center for Health Statistics.http://www.cdc.gov/ nchs/data/hus/hus12.pdf#018.

6. The religious groups that are large enough to be analyzed separately in this survey are white evangelical Protestants, white mainline Protestants, black Protestants, white (non-Hispanic) Catholics, Hispanic Catholics and the religiously unaffiliated. The survey's respondents also include members of many smaller US religious groups, and their views are reflected in the results for the overall public. But the numbers of Hispanic Protestants, Jews, Muslims, Buddhists, Hindus and other religious minorities in the survey sample are insufficient to allow them to be analyzed and reported separately.

Why Do Grandmothers Exist?
Solving an Evolutionary Mystery

By Judith Schulevitz
The New Republic, February 11, 2013

Why do grandmothers exist?

The question is not as unfeeling as it sounds.

From the point of view of the selfish gene, creatures are supposed to drop dead as soon as they lose the power to reproduce. A man can make babies his whole life, even if the sperm of his old age lacks vigor and genetic fidelity. A woman outlives her eggs by about 20 years, which almost no other female mammals do. (Only female killer and pilot whales and orcas are known to last as long after the end of their menstrual cycles.)

Besides being classed among the oddities of the animal kingdom, post-menopausal women lack obvious utility. They tend to be weak. They don't have much sex appeal. They eat food working people might make better use of. In Paraguay's Ache tribe, aging women used to listen with terror for the footsteps of the young men whose job it was to sneak up on them with an ax and brain them. Most societies don't actually murder their grannies, but that women manage to attain old age is an evolutionary mystery and requires explanation.

Are Senior Citizens Really "Greedy Geezers"?

Some people deny that women *did* live past menopause, whether in the Pleistocene era or the nineteenth century. Before modern hygiene and medicine, the argument goes, people just didn't live very long. But most scientists don't think that anymore. It *is* true that, in the olden days, fewer people reached their golden years. Children dropped dead with disturbing ease, keeping life-expectancy averages low. But humans still had the capacity to live twice as long as our hominid ancestors. Those who got to 15 had about a 60 percent chance of making it to 45, at which point odds were respectable that they'd reach old age. Many anthropologists and biologists now believe that the bodies of *Homo sapiens* were designed to last about 72 years.

So why should women stop procreating so early? In 1957, the evolutionary biologist George Williams proposed what is called the "stopping-early" hypothesis: Middle-age women need baby-free time to usher their youngest children into adulthood. In the 1980s, an American anthropologist named Kristen Hawkes and two colleagues came up with a different explanation. They had gone to northern Tanzania to study the foraging habits of the Hadza, the last known hunter-gatherers in Africa. While there, the scholars were struck by how strong the tribe's old women were and how, rather than live off the fruits of others' labor, they worked hard digging up the tribe's main starch staple, a deeply-buried tuber. "Their acquisition rates were similar to the rates of younger women," Hawkes told me, "but these old ladies were spending even more time" than their daughters gathering food, leaving camp earlier, coming back later, and bringing back more than they needed. The anthropologists also noticed that many children with grandmothers or great-aunts had faster growth rates than their counterparts.

From these slim clues, Hawkes and her colleagues developed the "grandmother hypothesis," which holds that women past childbearing age helped not just their children, but their children's children, and lengthened the human lifespan in the process. Without babies of their own to lug around, grandmothers had both time and a very good reason to be useful. When they eked out food for their daughters' children, they reduced the chance that those children would die. That gave the grandmothers a better chance of passing on their own predisposition to longevity. (In general, grandmothers appear to have helped daughters' offspring more than sons'; evolutionary theorists explain this by pointing out that a daughter's maternity affords a surer genetic connection than a son's paternity, unless you all but imprison your daughter-in-law.)

The grandmother hypothesis also explains another conundrum: Why do humans have shorter birth intervals than other primates? Chimp mothers, for instance, wait five or six years to give birth to another neonate. Women can pop out infants as soon as they've weaned previous ones. It turns out that, once humans learned the art of collaborative child-rearing, old women started spending more time with their daughters' toddlers. That freed up the young women to have more.

As the grandmother effect spread throughout the population over thousands of generations, it changed humans in another way. It made their brains bigger. As life lengthened, so did each stage of it. Children stayed children longer, which let their brains develop a more complex neural architecture.

Not everyone accepts this triumphantly feminist account of our evolutionary history. When anthropologists first heard it, most of them dismissed it as ridiculous. For one thing, it cuts man-the-hunter out of the picture. What about all the calories needed to grow our oversized brains? Didn't those have to come from the meat brought back from the hunt? Moreover, throughout recorded history, young women left their villages to move in with their men. So how would mothers have had access to their daughters' children?

The comeback to these objections is that hunter-gatherer families probably made all kinds of arrangements. In the tribes that anthropologists have been able to observe, some couples stayed in the wife's village, some moved in with her parents while starting their families, and some women left home. Patrilocality—men staying put—probably became the norm only when our ancestors settled down to farm, which made men unwilling to leave their land and wealth.

And it's not as if hunters alone brought in enough food to let the children thrive. Hawkes argues that, while meat boosted a tribe's overall nutrition, hunters couldn't be counted on to come home with a kill. When they did, the demands of status made them just as likely to share the bounty with the tribe as to hold it back for their children. The food grandmothers provided, on the other hand, was steady and reliable.

Two decades later, the grandmother hypothesis has gone from oddball conjecture to one of the dominant theories of why we live so long, breed so fast, and are so smart. The extra calories and care supplied by women in their long post-fertile period subsidized the long pre-fertile period that is childhood. And *that's* what made us fully human.

In a happy coincidence, the grandmother hypothesis comes along just as Americans enter what might be called the Age of Old Age. America's biggest generation, the baby-boomers, began retiring in 2011. This gerontocracy is expected to drain our wealth. By 2060, more than 20 percent of all Americans will be 65 or older, up from 13 percent in 2010. More than 92 million oldsters will roam the land, if roaming is within their power. People who fret about the federal budget point out that, by 2011, Social Security and Medicare were already eating up a third of it. Looming in the near future is the prospect that both programs' trust funds will vanish as the number of workers paying into the system goes down.

But are senior citizens really "greedy geezers" (a term made popular by this magazine in 1988) about to bankrupt us? The grandmother hypothesis suggests not. It suggests that we should see the coming abundance of over-65-year-olds as an opportunity, not a disaster. As gerontologist Linda Fried, dean of Columbia University's school of public health, points out, "Older adults constitute the only increasing natural resource in the entire world."

If we are going to exploit this resource in the post-industrial world, we'll have to use the social capital of the old the way the Hadza used them to dig up tubers. Mature people of both sexes have a lifetime's worth of education and experience. We'd be crazy to waste that surplus value, especially when so many people languish after retirement, mortified at no longer being needed. To show how much retirees have to offer, Fried started a program that puts them in at-risk public schools in 19 cities. Early results suggest that children read better and get sent to the principal less often in classrooms where seniors spend 15 hours a week, perhaps because they give teachers support and embarrass students inclined to act up. For their part, the volunteers do better on tests of health and happiness, probably because they like feeling useful.

As for actual grandparents, a growing body of research shows how much they help their grandchildren, even when they aren't giving them hands-on care or food. Often enough, though, they do provide those things, especially in poor families or ones with dysfunctional parents. The number of children being raised by their grandparents has been steadily rising since 2000. In 2011, there were 2.75 million such children in the United States.

But grandparents also give grandchildren more intangible gifts. In the mid-'90s, a Stanford University fellow named Luba Botcheva went home to Bulgaria to study how grandparents affected families struggling to survive the fall of communism. In the remote and very traditional region where she did her research, several generations would live under the same roof. The socialist-era factories had been shut down, and jobs were scarce. Botcheva discovered that grandparents' pensions were often the most dependable source of a household's income. In addition to paying the bills, however, grandparents buffered grandchildren against the harsh parenting that comes from acute anxiety. Children who grew up with grandparents in the home reported less depression than those without. "It was the opposite of what we expected," she said. "I called it the 'moderation effect.'" Many of the grandparents had lived through World War II, so when it came to poverty and uncertainty about the future, they had "social wisdom" to share, as Botcheva puts it, which kept tension levels down.

Unsurprisingly, grandmothers often do more for their grandchildren than grandfathers do. "Older women are the neighborhood watch and the neighborhood glue," says Fried. "They're the community purveyor of norms." When older black people in South Africa first started getting pensions from the post-apartheid government that were big enough to live on, the grandchildren who lived with grandmothers—especially the granddaughters—got taller and heavier, which observers took as a sign that they were eating better. But when it was the grandfathers who got the pensions, the grandchildren didn't grow at all. That wouldn't surprise economists who work with microfinance lending programs. They have discovered that female borrowers use their loans to improve their children's lot, whereas male borrowers, on the whole, do not.

Not that all grandparents can or want to be useful. As more people in industrialized countries postpone childbearing, parents become grandparents later and have less energy. The divorced ones may have started second or third families of their own. Global mobility puts distance between the generations. Assisted-living facilities segregate the old. Some retirement communities bar children altogether.

But children still need the nurture they once got from their mothers' mothers. So it's worth thinking, along with Fried, about institutions that would give parents and children that grandparental boost. I dream of communal houses or apartment complexes where families could live near grandparents but not right on top of them. That vision gives rise to others, some of them unlikely in our conservative United States, but realities elsewhere: publicly funded day care, better mothers' and children's aid societies, a national version of Fried's experiment of putting older people in schools. These programs would take advantage of our deepening wellspring of senior talent, which would cut costs, make old people happier, and sew up the threadbare bonds among the generations. If we want to keep enjoying the grandmother effect, we'll just have to broaden our idea of what a grandmother can be.

Something More to Say . . .

By Catherine Jackson
Therapy Today, June 13, 2013

"Hanging on in quiet desperation is the English way/The time is gone, the song is over, thought I'd something more to say."

Pink Floyd's album *Dark Side of the Moon* is, arguably, the quintessential expression of the aspirations and values of the baby boomer cohort. Escape the daily, purposeless grind, the lyrics (written by a group who were themselves baby boomers) urge; don't sit around waiting for someone else to tell you what to do; seize the moment, act for yourself, don't be eaten by the machine.

The first so-called baby boom occurred between 1946 and 1955, immediately following the end of the Second World War. This was the cohort of young people who, in their late teens and early 20s, began to foment the technicolored mix of social, sexual and (in some countries) political revolution that is widely associated with the 1960s.

From their birth to old age, this group has enjoyed far greater opportunities than any other: the National Health Service (they are the first generation to enjoy free healthcare from cradle to grave), better education (the postwar extension of secondary and university education to a far wider swathe of the population) and so greater social mobility, employment (jobs were readily available), wealth (houses were affordable in their youth and many have done well from the property boom), technological advances, and (not least) more liberal social attitudes (decriminalization of homosexuality, greater equality for women, the advent of the Pill, legalization of abortion).

But now they are in or approaching retirement age, and their numbers are causing ripples of concern: can the country afford to sustain the burden of so many aging people all at once, economically and socially? Will its health and welfare services and infrastructure be able to cope?

Last month the Mental Health Foundation published a report, *Getting on . . . with Life*, that explores how well the baby boomers are prepared for old age. The report is the fruit of its Age Well Inquiry, chaired by Baroness Lola Young, which looked in particular into the mental health, wellbeing and resilience of the baby boomer cohort, what may help them deal with the challenges of aging and what the Government should be doing to support them to maximize their own resources.

Baroness Young (born 1951), former residential social worker, lecturer in media studies and now cross-bench peer in the House of Lords, accepted the invitation to chair the inquiry because, she says, she wanted to challenge the "doom, disability and death" attitude that she finds among her friends and colleagues in response to old age. "It's as though we have so much knowledge of what can go wrong with us, it's made people much more pessimistic. To me, that knowledge is a positive thing." She in fact dislikes the label "baby boomer," partly because she detests all labels and partly because she feels it obscures "some very real differences and schisms in society at that time"—not least, the inequalities. 'Swinging London wasn't the main motif in my life in the 60s. I was brought up in a children's home and there was no love and peace in my life," she points out. There were also very few black British-born children of her age—no baby boom there.

She is clearly enjoying her older age. "Although the first 20 years of my life were miserable, I feel lucky to be doing what I am doing today and I only do what I enjoy. I am fortunate in that I am OK financially; I've got a lovely son, good friends and life is fine. And I get asked to do such interesting things. What keeps me going is knowing that I can at least contribute to the debates about some of these issues, if not change things. At its core, that is what life is about for me."

She has, she says, more freedom than ever before: "Freedom to say what I think. I'm not vulnerable any more."

The Inquiry hasn't come up with any clear answers to its questions but it has come up with a message: that baby boomers should not be regarded simply as a burden on younger generations. Just as they challenged social expectations in the 1960s, so in the 2010s they will challenge attitudes to old age and change how we care for our elders and how they care for themselves. Baby boomers, the report argues, are entering old age in a spirit of combat and adventure, not "quiet desperation."

We thought it would be interesting to talk to a small and randomly selected group of baby boomer counselors and psychotherapists about their readiness for and expectations of old age: how well do they feel their life course and choices have prepared them for the inevitability of physical and mental decline and death? Six counselors/psychotherapists agreed to be interviewed.

Life's Journey

Tim Bond (born 1949), Professor of Counseling and Professional Ethics at the University of Bristol, grammar school and university-educated child of a self-made businessman and a doctor, says he feels very fortunate. While his life has not been without its difficulties, "I have a real sense of fulfillment and achievement, particularly in close relationships, and I think that brings a sense of purpose and joy that sustains one for the future. On the mental health front, counseling when I needed it, meditation and a balance between intellectual work and physical activity all help. But in the end it's values that enable you to keep going, to endure the more difficult moments and enjoy the successes and achievements. For me, these are commitment to people, commitment to the environment, a delight in human diversity and the cultural energy of this extraordinary period we are living through, and a sustained but quiet commitment to Quaker values of peace, simplicity, honesty and equality."

Julia Buckroyd (born 1946), psychotherapist and Emeritus Professor of Counseling at the University of Hertfordshire, grew up in Scotland and went to a direct grant school for girls, followed by university, an MA and PhD, all paid for by the state or academic grants, she points out. Like Baroness Young, she believes the baby boomer label conceals important differences: "For all the stuff about the 60s, certainly where I was living in Scotland, there was not much female emancipation. I think I've struggled all my life except for the past 15 years for equality and autonomy."

She doesn't see old age as a destination—the armchair by the fireside: "Settling into old age isn't part of my life plan. My ambition is to be the person I have the potential to be, and this project will continue to the day I die. I have something to offer and I want to offer it. To me age is immaterial but it has the advantage that I feel I now have some authority; I know what I am talking about. And I don't want to go before I've told people what I've found out."

Even in rural Derbyshire, psychoanalytic psychotherapist Lennox Thomas (born in Grenada 1952; came to the UK in 1960) was aware that he was living through "probably one of the most privileged times to have been young. When I look at previous and later generations, I think we had the best of it." Although there were costs: "I lost a lot of friends who died way, way too young. One friend died through drugs, three were killed in a Mini going round the roundabout the wrong way for a laugh. Another died trying to cross the North Circular after going out clubbing. I feel fortunate: I might have been with them."

Family, friendships formed in boyhood in the church choir, his parents' Christian socialist values and insistence that their children should make their own faith choices, and psychoanalysis have all played their part in his preparedness for old age. "I began to have my own personal psychoanalysis at a pretty young age and that has been very helpful to me. It's made me what I am today, prepared me for who I am now. It's helped me to occupy the whole of myself. I have a sense of my own agency. It's taught me to be clear-minded about relationships and friendships and it's taught me a lot about me and what I want."

Michael King (born in New Zealand, 1950), Professor of Primary Care Psychiatry at University College London, faced prejudice and arrest as a young man growing up gay in a very conventional society where homosexuality wasn't legalized until 1984. "I remember seeing men arrested for so-called indecent behavior. It was not a nice climate. From my 20s, when I came to England, that was when my life began," he says.

But being gay brings many advantages that are helpful in older age, he has found. "Maybe you learn quicker to survive in a tough world. When you are on the outside of society you see the hypocrisy much more clearly. You have to survive against people's opinions, so you grow a kind of strength. I have seen death, I have lost friends to AIDS, it doesn't frighten me." Gay people, and older gay people in particular, seem to have an extra resilience. "We've done a lot of research on this and up to age 40 there are a lot of mental health problems in gay and lesbian people, two or three times as much, but in our 60s, if anything, the rates are lower.

"Gay people are very independent. There's an adaptability in gay men that is different to the typical heterosexual male with a wife doing things for him. Our relationships are more equal. It could be that we've got to the state we should have been when we were 20. As you get older, you get bolder, and not so embarrassed by things. Though I don't think you necessarily get wiser."

As Old as You Feel?

Counselor, psychosexual therapist and BACP Fellow Carol Martin-Sperry (born 1944) strongly identifies as a baby boomer. "For me, life started in 1963. Socially it was an incredibly flourishing and rich period. The 50s were all about rationing, smog, poverty, boredom, very class structured, very conventional. But I think we were quite a selfish generation. We took everything for granted and thought we had the right to everything."

Reality hit Carol Martin-Sperry around her 60th birthday, she says. "I wish I could retire but I can't because my pension is tiny, my state pension is tiny and my husband is freelance with major health problems. It hit me when I was 60—but I have no regrets, absolutely no regrets. *Carpe diem* is my philosophy: live as much as possible in the present and make the most of it. There's no point in worrying about the future."

"In my head I feel I am in my mid-30s but bits of my body keep reminding me I'm not. I think our task is to 'mind the gap' between our fantasy that we are still in our 30s and the realities of old age."

Richard House (born 1954), Senior Lecturer in Early Childhood at the University of Winchester, is an archetypal baby boomer: working-class parents, grammar school educated, followed by Oxford University and the consequent shift into the professional middle classes, although he says he still feels a deep connection to his working-class roots and has always shared his father's left-wing political convictions. House says he doesn't have a sense of being any age. "I'm nearing 60 and that just seems completely bizarre when I feel I still have the spirit, energy and passion of a 25-year-old. But my body says different. It's only when your body starts to let you down—that does begin to make you more aware of your age." The fact that he is starting to put on weight around his middle is beginning to worry him—unduly, he suspects.

And he worries too that his resilience may be waning. "I'm in a demanding job at the moment, which I'm finding very stressful, and I'm not sure whether that is because I'm older and haven't got the resources to cope with these pressures any more, or whether it's the job itself, and/or the Higher Education sector more generally that is toxic. But I'm grateful that I'm more able to process these experiences; I do feel I have a maturity that enables me to manage these things that I didn't have 20 years ago."

Tim Bond is greatly looking forward to retirement and the chance to do all the other things he wants to do in life. "So long as I am mentally agile there are several things I can move forward on the academic front. And, as I start to step back from academic life, that opens up space for other things that matter to me, such as wild-life conservation. I am looking forward to new friendships and other ways of being in the world."

He feels "well prepared" for older age, but is also conscious of the legacy his generation will be handing on to the next. "We will be creating both a social and financial burden for the young people who will be taking over the economic control of the country, and there's all the environment change, climate change that we have happily handed on. We need to think about this legacy, how we mitigate some of the harm we have done and help the next generation face these challenges but at the same time we need to hand over control."

Julia Buckroyd is positively relishing old age. "I am very powerfully driven by pur-pose and I think part of my driven-ness was having to prove myself to my parents and I don't feel that quite as much as I used to." She called a truce with herself in her 50s, after a final bout of psychotherapy. "Since then I've been so much happier, so much more content and less worried about just about everything," she says. "I went because I was sick of not being the person I thought I had the potential to be. Just the experience with that particular therapist, regular reliable contact with someone who appeared to be pleased to see me, did the job really. It has been extremely freeing."

And no, she doesn't feel her age. "I get tripped up by my physical weakening. I am not as strong as I used to be. But I am doing pretty well and I am very fortunate to have nothing of any significance wrong with me. I am much more careful about what I eat and drink and make sure I am rested in a way that I never used to. I am taking better care of myself because I want this state to continue as long as possible. I don't think I could have been that kind to myself before. One of the things I enjoy is my competence. I feel as if I know what I am doing with clients and that is a nice feeling. That could overbalance into a ridiculous conceit, but I don't think it does. I feel confident doing the work."

Resilience

So what are the qualities and ingredients of life that these baby boomers think will serve them well in old age? "Faith," says Michael King. "I have always had a strong Christian faith, not as a crutch but because I am fascinated emotionally and spiritu-ally in God and what our life means. It gives my life meaning. My partner. We've been together nearly 30 years. The fact that we can live openly together." And his job: "I like my work and living in Europe." The personal qualities that he thinks will help him through old age include his "foolish optimism," and his gregariousness: "People don't bore me. That's why I'm a psychiatrist. I love seeing people, it keeps me intellectually alert."

Lennox Thomas is looking forward to retiring at 65. "Then I will do voluntary work because it will benefit me and other people. I wouldn't want to be stuck doing nothing. I want to be doing something useful." He says his children (now in their late teens and early 20s) keep him mentally young, even though physically he does feel his age. "They keep me in touch with things and optimistic." A sense of humor and readiness to see the best in things are also going to serve him well, he believes. "I can't stand grumpy people."

For Richard House "it's the old humanistic cliché about knowing myself; being able to be myself more fully, to be real, authentic in relationship—classic Rogers stuff. I'm sure that has helped me to no end, not just in personal relationships but professional ones as well." Passion and conviction will, he believes, help him weather old age. 'It's about being passionate about life. I have a strong sense of what is wrong with the world and I'm on a crusade to set those wrongs right. It sounds grandiose and pompous and it's probably classic baby boomer stuff but that is my life journey. I don't want to be lying on my death bed knowing that I didn't do justice to what I am here for. I want to feel I have really given it my best."

For Carol Martin-Sperry, the keys to a healthy old age are self-awareness, actively taking care of her health, and acceptance of death; "it gives one a certain kind of energy," she says. She wishes she could find a group for people in their 60s to 'talk experientially about where we are now."

"Death will come to us all and we have to make the most of our relationships and friendships. I went to a workshop recently on professional retirement. The consensus was that working until you drop is a defense against fear of death and giving up work and taking up lots of activities is also a defense against death. We are all going to die. That's OK."

Death Dinners at Baby Boomers' Tables Take on Dying Taboo

By Shannon Pettypiece
Bloomberg, September 23, 2013

At a Manhattan dinner party, former Citigroup Inc. (C) executive Steffen Landauer gathered an eclectic mix of guests at his apartment off Fifth Avenue to sip pinot noir, dine on seared salmon—and talk about death.

"I think about it a lot and talk about it very little," Landauer said to the group, which included a filmmaker, a private school principal, and a professional story-teller. Not to be confused with a macabre parlor game, the evening was conceived to confront real-life issues wrapped up in death and dying that few people like to acknowledge, let alone talk about at a dinner party. Would I want a feeding tube? Does dad want to die at home? What happens to my kids if I die in an accident along with my spouse?

Those questions are getting asked more frequently. Over the past month, hundreds of Americans across the country have organized so-called death dinners, designed to lift the taboo around talking about death in hopes of heading off conflicts over finances and medical care—and avoiding unnecessary suffering at the end of life. It's a topic that is resonating as baby boomers, born from 1946 to 1964, deal with the passing of their parents, even as they come face-to-face with their own mortality.

About 70 percent of adults don't have a living will, a legal document detailing the medical interventions they'd want or not want if unable to communicate, according to the Pew Research Center. As many as 30 percent of Americans 65 and older don't have a will detailing what should happen with their assets, a Pew survey found. If those discussions don't happen ahead of an illness or death, it can leave family members conflicted over what to do.

"Family Infighting"

"Having family infighting is horrific," said Dianne Gray, president of the Elizabeth Kubler-Ross Foundation, a nonprofit focused on end-of-life issues. "No parent wants their legacy to be that at the end of their life they created a family divided."

For the generation that brought on the sexual revolution, led the anti-war movement and turned their midlife crises into a time for reinvention and self-improvement, baby boomers are trying now to have it their way right to the very end.

"The baby boomer generation got to call a lot of their own shots and make decisions and see those decisions through," said Carole Fisher, chief executive of Nathan Adelson Hospice in Nevada, who held a death dinner last month for her extended family and friends in a Southern California beach town.

"And then you talk about death and dying and realize you have no control. The only thing I can control about it is to communicate what my needs and desires are."

Taboo Topic

As the sun set over the Pacific, four generations of Fisher's family shared pizza, salad, tiramisu—and their views on what they'd like to happen at the end of their lives. Even working in hospice care, Fisher realized death was still a taboo topic around her home and she was anxious to broach the subject. Helping to lighten the mood, all 16 of her friends and relatives, from her 7-year-old granddaughter, Kaya, to her 73-year-old mother, Nan Schwartz, donned gag mustaches that Fisher passed out.

Death wasn't always such an awkward topic. A century ago, with higher rates of infant and maternal death and shorter life expectancies, people were more likely to die at home with their families rather than in hospitals behind closed doors and surrounded by doctors and nurses. It was, for better or worse, more common, natural and visible.

Today, more than half of deaths take place in hospitals and medical facilities, often after extensive interventions including the use of ventilators, feeding tubes or other life-support devices. In a culture that talks of "fighting" illness and "surviving" cancer, where doctors and patients turn to technology for answers, dying is seen as losing the battle.

"Death Denying"

"This is much more of a death-denying society than it ever has been in the past," said Don Schumacher, chief executive officer of the National Hospice and Palliative Care Organization, the largest membership group for hospice programs and workers. "We all participate in this myth that you can just keep on going. I've seen tragedy after tragedy of families that were convinced if they only did this or that, mom would recover and all would go back to normal."

American families may not be able to deny reality much longer. By 2030, 3.3 million Americans will die a year, up 32 percent from the current death rate as baby boomers age, according to the National Funeral Directors Association. With population growth and medical advances that keep people alive longer, the number of Americans older than 65 will more than double to 92 million by 2060—accounting for 1 in 5 Americans.

Aging Population

That aging population will force countless family decisions over how best to send off their loved ones with dignity. Who will make those decisions for the patient if they are incapacitated? What type of medical interventions, like feeding tubes and respirators, should be used at the end of life? When the time comes, do they want burial or cremation?

From her work in hospice, Fisher was no stranger to what could happen to a family that had failed to confront death. Yet she was anxious to broach the subject with her own family, where emotions around dying were still raw following the death of her stepson's mother from cancer several years ago and the recent loss of her brother-in-law's friend. The silly mustaches combined with wine for the grown-ups and the pink sunset over the Pacific Ocean helped ease the mood. Soon, the emotions and words were flowing.

"I want to be cremated, I don't want the box, it creeps me out," Fisher's husband Gary, 62, told the group, which included his in-laws, wife and sons from a previous marriage.

No Dispute

It was a somewhat controversial statement considering the family's Jewish faith, which forbids cremations, Fisher said. She was glad her entire family got to hear her husband's wishes so there will be no dispute when the time comes.

"Don't tube me," Fisher's mother chimed in. "If I am pooping in my pants or in diapers, I'm out of here."

"I won't stop you," Fisher's husband joked.

It was the first time Fisher's mother had told the entire family that she didn't want any interventions to prolong her life.

Then came the debate over what happens after you're dead.

"I can't believe there is nothing else," said Fisher's niece Melissa Fisher Goldman, 33. "It is so scary to think there is nothing after."

"That's why you believe in it," her father said. "People just want to believe."

"I think your soul lives on," piped up a tiny voice from the back of the patio. It was Fisher's step-granddaughter Kaya who had been listening to the conversation from her mother's lap.

No Guarantee

Having a plan and talking about it with family is no guarantee that conflicts over finances and medical care won't arise and the conversations can sometimes lead to more arguing while everyone is still alive. Yet Fisher said she feels less angst knowing her family now understands what each member wants.

"That evening really prompted more sensitive conversations, not just about death and dying, but in general," Fisher said by telephone two weeks after the dinner. "It changed people's comfort level with each other."

Talking Points

Get-togethers like Fisher's are happening largely thanks to a group of master's degree students and faculty at the University of Washington, who have started a program called "Let's Have Dinner and Talk About Death." It offers talking points, reading material on death, and how to word a death dinner invitation. Since starting last month, about 400 people have signed up to host dinners, the group said.

The idea came from Michael Hebb, a teaching fellow at the university and culinary impresario, who gained celebrity status in the Seattle and Portland, Oregon, food scenes for the underground theme-dinners he has staged since 1997. After walking away from a now-defunct group of Portland restaurants, Hebb has used food to tap into social and cultural trends, garnering him work with organizations such as the Bill & Melinda Gates Foundation and the Clinton Global Initiative.

Hebb said he chose death for his latest and largest dinner table discourse after a pair of doctors convinced him on a train ride to Seattle that Americans weren't dying the way they wanted. The topic struck a chord with Hebb, who at the age of 12 lost his father to Alzheimer's disease. His family was uncomfortable talking about the disease and Hebb regrets not having spent more time with his father before he died.

"This is a conversation that the entire country needs to be having," Hebb said.

Zucchini Pancakes

A few nights before Fisher's gathering, it was a very different conversation at Landauer's death dinner on a quiet Manhattan street a few feet from Central Park. Rather than a family looking for guidance, Landauer had brought together a group of social acquaintances to help air issues he has long been reluctant to tackle.

Despite having four children ages 1 to 23, Landauer, 54, confessed that he only recently started working on a will, to the surprise of the group given his age and large family. Now, for the first time, he and his wife are having serious conversations about who would take care of their children if both parents died.

"Two weeks of doing my will has caused us to talk about it more than in 17 years of marriage, and we aren't even really talking about it that much, we're exchanging text messages," he said.

As the group ate zucchini pancakes with caviar around the formal dining table, Laura Simms, a professional storyteller said, that at 65 she, too, lacks a will and has avoided planning for the end of her life despite having been diagnosed with cancer twice.

Baroque Music

"I often forget I'm going to die," Simms said. "I mean to make a will, I mean to clean out my closet so there isn't anything embarrassing in there. And then I just forget."

For the six New Yorkers, some of whom had met for the first time that evening, having a venue to talk about death was like releasing a pressure valve. With baroque music playing in the background, for three hours they shared stories of near death and supernatural experiences and the deaths of loved ones. They agreed that death lurks in the back of their minds, yet isn't something they were comfortable talking about before.

Simms recalled a near-death experience she had when she was mugged in Central Park, the memory of a knife pressed against her throat still fresh in her mind.

"I realized in a few seconds I could be dead and I completely relaxed," she said.

Spreading Ashes

As the server removed the dessert plates and Landauer's young daughter began stirring upstairs, many of the guests said they felt a kind of catharsis.

Since the dinner, Landauer has finished and signed his will and he says it forced him to think more concretely about what he'd like to happen to his remains. He has now made sure to include instructions in his will for his children to spread his ashes near a specific mountain in Tibet that he once visited.

"There is a power in speaking about something," Landauer said after the dinner. "That gives it a certain sense of reality that you don't have if it's just an idea in your mind."

5

How Living Longer Is Advancing Medicine and Health Care

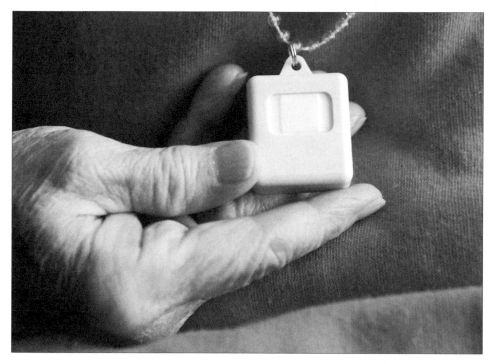

© Gary Cameron/Reuters/Landov

Inez Willis tests her medical alert device at her independent living apartment in Silver Spring, Maryland. Baby boomers wired to their iPads and smart phones are giving US health experts some new ideas about ways to cut the soaring costs of medical care in graying America.

How Science Is Extending Life

Over the last generation, there have been tremendous increases in medical advance-ments that have changed the face of medicine. As technology advanced, the op-portunities for medical advancement increased, amplifying the amount of research conducted, medical machinery developed, pharmacological agents produced, and overall understanding of biomedical sciences. These great accomplishments have all contributed to the ability of the medical field to facilitate living longer. In 1960, the average life expectancy from birth was 69.7 years, whereas in 2010, the average life expectancy had increased to 78.7 years from birth. Improved hospital settings, vaccines, health care research, increased food supply and nutrition, and medica-tions are just some of the prominent contributing factors. Medical engineering fa-cilities are constantly producing devices that allow physicians to enhance patient care. Technological advances include hearing aids, scooters, pacemakers, medical alert systems, and laboratory equipment that facilitate research studies. Health care regulations for heart disease, diabetes, and other complications have allowed re-search to focus and expand in different areas, such as Alzheimer's disease, genetic engineering, and organ transplantation.

Technological Advancements

Technology today has provided for a much higher accessibility rate in the diagnosis and treatment of diseases, as well as furthering research that directly affects health in society. The area that has provided perhaps the greatest of all contributions to medical advancements is imaging modalities. Advancements in the composition and abilities of these machines allow for the detection of tumors and abnormal physiologic changes that are not detectable by physical examination alone. With updated imaging modalities available, doctors can now use magnetic resonance im-aging (MRI) and computed tomography (CT) scans to identify a mass or abnor-mality in the body. Echocardiograms can detect deteriorating heart function, and percutaneous coronary intervention (PCI) provides the ability to see inside blood vessels so that doctors can measure and insert stents to reopen occluded vessels. The malignant activity of tumors can be measured via positron emission tomogra-phy (PET) scan, which measures the metabolic activity in areas of the body. These technological advancements allow health care professionals to identify certain con-ditions, such as cancer and heart disease, in their early stages. Treatment, therefore, has a higher rate of success because it is started before the diseases progress.

One of the largest growing medical technological advancements is electronic health records, which have provided the ability for doctors to gain quick and easy access to patients' medical records to provide the most effective care. One com-mon issue for the elderly is that patients present incorrect information regarding medicine and dosage. Such an issue provides serious complications in treatment methods, wherein a doctor may prescribe an incorrect medication or dose that may be lethal to the patient simply because the doctor was unaware of a medication the patient was taking. Electronic medical records potentially allow the doctor to communicate with pharmacies and other doctors to see any pertinent medical information the patient may have left out during the encounter, greatly aiding in diagnosis and treatment of issues, especially among the elderly.

Another technological advancement that has very recently been created is the nanoscribe system, which can build objects measuring less than one hundred nanometers. One example of its applications is to further the "lab-on-a-chip" development, a miniature system that aims to use tests run on nanometers of diagnostic samples drawn from the patients. This is an example of how health care is becoming more versatile, extending the settings that blood work and other diagnostic tests could be performed, and therefore potentially saving thousands from life-threatening situations where a patient cannot get to a hospital to run the appropriate tests. Also, the development of a three-dimensional printer has hastened the ability of engineers to prototype and test new developments including mechanical hearts, stents, and body parts.

Progressive Treatments

A common cause of death for the elderly is debilitation due to falls causing fractured hips, broken ribs, and, consequently, a sedentary lifestyle. With advancements in orthopedic surgery, joint replacements have become the common fix, replacing fractured joints with prosthetic hips or knees, thereby restoring the ability of elderly patients to pursue physical activities after experiencing a serious fall. Replacement surgeries have also greatly decreased the pain and immobility caused by severe cases of arthritis, which resulted in years of limping and pain due to shredded joint cartilage. Another emerging field used to fix torn ligaments and tendons via a near non-invasive mechanism is the injection of platelet-rich plasma (PRP), which uses the body's own growth factors to repair damaged tissues. Although it is more commonly used in sports injuries, PRP therapy may also be used on the elderly to heal ligaments torn from falls.

Another emerging area of medical advance is genetics, including medical genetics, genetic engineering, and epigenetics. Through studying DNA and environmental factors, medical professionals have been able to predict certain diseases, such as breast cancer, type 2 diabetes, and Alzheimer's disease. Amniocentesis, a process that can detect fetal genetic diseases from a mother's placenta, allows for parents who anticipate abnormalities with their child, such as Down syndrome, to prepare and accommodate for such a situation. It also gives doctors a pre-labor warning so they can prepare for the proper treatment of the baby immediately upon birth to ensure that the child can potentially lead a normal and healthy life.

Genetic testing in adults provides the opportunity to discover a potential disease in an earlier state as well as confirm a diagnosis, which may result in more effective treatment and increase longevity. Epigenetics, the study of environmental factors on

DNA, has increased the understanding of environmental effects that may be detrimental to living and should be avoided in order to live longer. Exposure to ultraviolet rays, for example, has been shown to induce thymine dimers, a genetic malformation that increases susceptibility to skin cancer. Smoking as well has been shown to induce methylation of certain genes that cause cancer, thus turning these genes "on" and promoting cancerous growth. Knowing such effects of environmental factors allows people to stay away from them and live longer, healthier lives. Through the processes of recombinant DNA and other genetic modifications, genetic engineering allows for the production of safer, more effective pharmaceuticals and vaccines, as well as the use of stem cells in the treatment of diseases including chronic lymphocytic leukemia (CLL), Parkinson's disease, and x-linked severe combined immunodeficiency (SCID). Genetic engineering has also contributed largely to the production of cells, tissues, and whole organs needed for transplantation.

Organ transplantation is an area of medicine that continues to greatly advance over time. While antirejection medications have been developed to stabilize patient acceptance of homologous organs, biomechanical engineers are progressing to produce organs and body parts using stem cell technology and, therefore, do not require an organ from a donor. The first successful homologous liver transplant was performed in 1963 by physician Thomas Starzl, and the patient passed away several days later from hospital-acquired pneumonia. In 2012, according to the American Liver Foundation, more than six-thousand liver transplants are performed yearly in the United States with a 75 percent five-year survival rate. Kidney transplants are far more frequent than liver transplants, with over 16,800 transplants performed in the United States in 2012, according to the National Kidney Foundation. In 1906, the first kidney transplants were performed from sheep, pigs, goats, and primates; today, kidney transplants are performed from human donors with a significantly higher survival rate. Heart valves are also commonly transplanted, both of bovine and, more recently, mechanical composition.

New methods of valve replacement have also significantly reduced the risk of surgical complications with innovative procedures such as transcatheter aortic valve replacement (TAVR), which replaces the valve without opening the chest wall. One of the most shocking organ transplant milestones, however, was the first heart transplant performed by surgeon Christiaan Barnard in 1967. More recently, in 2011, surgeons Billy Cohn and O. H. Frazier developed and transplanted an artificial heart that provided a continuous flow, leaving their patient without a heartbeat. Further research is being conducted to refine the device and allow for greater mobility and durability.

Further Research

Research is an integral part in the advancement of health care. It is essential for understanding diseases and risk factors, the development of new pharmacologic agents to treat disease and illness, and providing the most effective health care for patients to lead long and healthy lives. Smoking, for example, is a relatively new area of focus that has been discovered to destroy lungs and increase the risk of cancer, lung complications such as chronic obstructive pulmonary disease (COPD), and cardiovascular diseases. As recently as fifty years ago, there were commercials for cigarettes advertised by doctors that were aired on television. Only in 1963 were the first research studies suggesting that there may be adverse effects such as cardiovascular and lung diseases associated with cigarette smoke. In the twenty-first century, it is clear that smoking is detrimental to one's health, and many of the side effects are known and treatable. Moreover, the increased awareness of the detrimental effects of smoking cigarettes has lead to a drastic decrease in the number of smokers in the United States. According to the US Centers for Disease Control and Prevention, 42.4 percent of American adults smoked in 1965, whereas only 19.3 percent smoked in 2010. The decrease in the number of smokers translates into a decrease in the number of chronic and potentially fatal illnesses that result from smoking cigarettes, thus contributing to a longer and healthier life for many Americans.

Another progressive school of thought and newly researched area is the longevity of the brain. Studies have suggested that those who learned more when they were younger have a healthier brain when they are older. The theory suggests that the more one learns, the thicker the cortex of the brain will become, thus providing a greater brain reserve or cortex when it begins to deteriorate. Over time, the educational system in America has vastly improved, providing more schooling for children, increasing the amount of subjects offered, and raising the level at which they are taught. Children, for example, used to learn the alphabet in kindergarten, but today they are learning how to read full sentences and books. Extracurricular activities that promote further learning and education, such as after school music lessons and scholars programs, are increasing and gaining a wider acceptance for children. Additionally, higher education has become a standard, where many jobs require a bachelor's or master's degree. Medical professionals encourage an increase in exercising brain power as a way to prevent the early deterioration of the brain, therefore delaying or preventing the onset of dementia and Alzheimer's disease. Further research is being conducted to prove and solidify this association.

Even with the increase in education, however, there is a growing epidemic of Alzheimer's, a disease that is rising in numbers each year. According to the Alzheimer's Association, 46 percent of people with Alzheimer's disease in 2012 were eighty-five years or older, whereas 6 percent of people with Alzheimer's disease were sixty-five years or older, and only 4 percent were under sixty-five. These statistics suggest that as people live longer, their risk of developing Alzheimer's disease increases. Thus with a greater average life expectancy, the overall risk of Alzheimer's disease increases. Studies suggest that biomarkers, such as amyloid plaques and degenerating nerve cells in the brain, have been found to confirm the Alzheimer's disease state. A genetic finding associated with a higher risk for Alzheimer's disease has been prevalent among individuals with the e4 form of the gene apolipoprotein E. Research has indicated that individuals with a parent, brother, sister, or child with Alzheimer's disease are at greater risk of developing the disease, especially if more than one family member has the disease. Those with a family history of Alzheimer's disease, therefore, may be genetically tested to provide earlier detection and action taken against the disease to increase life expectancy. Previously, when one was diagnosed with Alzheimer's disease there were no treatments available. However, the advancements in understanding the disease process have provided medications that may slow the progression of the disease and support groups that make living with the disease easier. Further research is currently being conducted with the hopes that Alzheimer's disease will soon be curable.

Effects on Medicine

As medical advancements have helped increase the average life expectancy, the increase in the average life expectancy has also helped further medical advancements. Data on older patients has been collected, and the duration of time to follow up with studies has prolonged. Also, older patients tend to be more susceptible to general health problems, such as cardiovascular and renal diseases, which encourages pharmaceutical companies to create safe drugs to limit these complications and increase life expectancy. Elderly patients may also present with various complications not commonly observed in younger patients, such as Alzheimer's disease, which call into effect more research, treatment, and prevention. In essence, the increase in life expectancy has both been caused by and resulted in medical advancements that have shaped, and will continue to shape, the health care system and medical knowledge for generations to come.

We're Living Longer—and Healthier

By Alexandra Sifferlin
Time, July 29, 2013

There's no doubt that we're living longer than previous generations. Now there's encouraging news that those added years may be healthy ones as well. According to the latest tallies from the Centers for Disease Control and Prevention (CDC), in 2010 the average life expectancy rose from 78.6 years in 2009 to 78.7 in 2010. But the data has not been as definitive about whether that means people are stronger and healthier and therefore adding years to their lives, or whether medical innovations are extending lives, but leaving people sicker for longer.

Researchers from Harvard University report that there is some reason to be optimistic about our longevity. "Effectively, the period of time in which we're in poor health is being compressed until just before the end of life. So where we used to see people who are very, very sick for the final six or seven years of their life, that's now far less common. People are living to older ages and we are adding healthy years, not debilitated ones," said David Cutler, the Otto Eckstein Professor of Applied Economics at Harvard University and author of the latest study, in a statement.

The research team looked at data gathered from 90,000 people between 1991 and 2009 who responded to the Medicare Current Beneficiary Survey (MCBS), an ongoing evaluation of Medicare coverage and health outcomes. Unlike previous studies of morbidity among the elderly, which assessed people's health at different ages and then compared this data to their death rates, the scientists in the current study started with the participants' death, and then went back each successive year to measure the subjects' health at those points. That way, Cutler and his team were able to calculate at each health evaluation how far the individuals were from death, and document their health status at each of those times. To gauge how functional the participants were, the researchers studied data on whether the Medicare subscribers could cook, clean, or bathe themselves and manage their money.

The results showed that as a population, the elderly are remaining healthy into their later years. The findings do not determine what is behind this extended period of healthiness, but it's possible that the same medical innovations that some feared were keeping us alive with more debilitating conditions may also be helping us to overcome common age-related chronic conditions such as heart disease and joint disorders, so they are not as challenging to treat as they once were.

Other studies have found similar results. A Danish study earlier this month showed older people today are sharper than elderly folks in previous generations; comparing two groups of nonagenarians born a decade apart, the researchers found that those born more recently scored higher on cognitive function tests than those born earlier.

"All our studies suggest that we can change the rate of aging. When it comes to translating our findings, the question is are we going to delay everything or are we going to spend more time being sick," says Dr. Nir Barzilai, the director of the Institute for Aging Research at the Albert Einstein College of Medicine, who studies the biology of aging and longevity but was not associated with the study. Barzilai is currently studying centenarians, and says that health care costs for those living to 100 can be a third of those who don't live past their 70s. Part of the cost savings, he says, comes from the fact that centenarians require fewer medical appointments and screenings.

More awareness of how to age well by eating a healthy diet, exercising and keeping the brain active are certainly helping more people to enjoy a higher quality of life into old age. But at a certain point, says Barzilai, genetics play a role. "Now when someone breaks their hip, in a few weeks you can get them to walk again. These guys were dying before. They were in bed, getting sores, getting pneumonia," he says. The oldest old, however, likely have their genes to thank for seeing them past the chronic diseases that typically plague people past their 60s.

While encouraged by studies hinting that it's possible to extend life in a healthy way, researchers are also concerned that the trend may be short-lived, thanks to obesity. With so many children in the US suffering from obesity and adult diseases such as type 2 diabetes and high blood pressure, future generations may face a less healthy old age. Barzilai says there could be two groups of elderly—those with obesity and diabetes who continue to suffer from health problems and require high-cost medical care into their golden years, and those without those conditions who are able to live relatively disease-free, long lives. "I am very aware of the epidemic of obesity and diabetes and its potential impact on lifetime," says Barzilai. "Yes I am worried, yes it might be a challenge, but because we anticipate progress in [those areas] too, it might be okay." If anything, the current generation of elderly should serve as a model for the healthy and robust life that's possible for decades past middle-age.

Aging Baby Boomers Want to Live Active Lives, Require Innovations in Medical Treatment

By Wendy Leonard
Deseret News, April 14, 2013

The baby boomer generation is aging, and a large portion of the growing 65-and-older population isn't going quietly into a sedentary retirement.

Many are requiring joint replacement surgery, as they intend to remain active until the bitter end, according to Dr. John Edwards, an orthopedic surgeon who specializes in knee and shoulder replacement surgeries at MountainStar Healthcare's Lakeview Hospital.

"People are more active and they're more active for longer," Edwards said, "and as a result, they don't want to have pain associated with their joints."

With the population of retirement-age people in the state expected to increase by 126,700, or 51 percent, between 2010 and 2020, doctors are applying procedures such as the peripheral nerve block prior to joint replacement surgeries to reduce pain and recovery time.

Utah has the sixth fastest growth rate in the nation for people age 65 and older, according to a Utah Department of Human Services report. Doctors expect the number of surgeries to continue to climb with the aging population.

Edwards said hip, knee and shoulder joints can wear out with age, resulting in sometimes debilitating pain and the inability to move as once was possible, which can be frustrating for someone wanting to remain active.

With available medical technologies, as well as the desire of more people to be active and healthy throughout life, Edwards said many are turning to surgery to replace these aching joints.

And those seniors considering orthopedic surgery are now told that their pain level during surgery and recovery can be dulled with the help of a presurgical procedure practiced by most major hospitals and some smaller community facilities in the state, according to Lakeview anesthesiologist Dr. Tory Hinkle.

"We really use them every day," Hinkle said.

Lakeview Hospital has been ranked first in the state for the number of orthopedic surgeries it offers as well as the quality of service provided for the past three years, and it is among America's 100 Best Hospitals for orthopedic surgery, according to a Healthgrades annual report.

It is procedures like the peripheral nerve block that makes them a desirable option for the population needing surgery.

Peripheral nerve blocks, Hinkle said, can reduce the time patients spend in the hospital following a joint replacement surgery, provide a pain-free sleep during the typical post-surgery stay, and enhance their recovery process. It's not necessarily new treatment, but it has advanced over time.

"We've been doing this for years," Hinkle said. "The new part is the ultrasound technology that we are using has come a long, long way. We can see the nerves on the screen; see where the needle comes into the body. We can avoid any kind of blood vessels."

The procedure, he said, used to involve a cumbersome table and computer that provided a sometimes indecipherable image, which made correct placement of the anesthetic more difficult.

A nerve block involves numbing the nerves nearest to the surgical site with a local anesthetic to last during the most intense pain period, which typically covers the entire first 24 hours after surgery, allowing the body to focus on healing rather than the pain. It provides an alternative to general anesthesia.

"These blocks make it great on the patient," Hinkle said. "It's a lot easier, takes away a lot of stress to the body, so you don't feel that pain. . . .Also, they don't have to take as much anesthetic so they feel much better."

The nerve block also reduces the need for potentially addicting narcotic pain medications during and throughout the surgery, recovery and rehabilitation periods, which both doctors said is a tremendous advantage, given the growing number of prescription drug-related problems in Utah.

And the outcomes are also better.

"Joint replacements are very successful," Edwards said, adding that 90 percent of people are happy with the results, and the remainder likely have underlying or other medical issues that can exacerbate their joint problems. "It's still an artificial joint and is subject to wearing out, but they're lasting longer than ever with the materials being used now."

The surgeries, he said, help to take away the pain and increase levels of activity more quickly for patients.

That's exactly what Jim Dickson, of Kaysville, is hoping for following complete shoulder reconstruction at Lakeview on Wednesday.

The retired Davis High School football coach and driver's education teacher said he had been enduring problems with his rotator cuff for some time. The group of tendons and muscles in his shoulder that make it function correctly had worn down, but after a somewhat painful fall in December, he needed additional medical attention.

When arthroscopic surgery failed to fix it earlier this year, Edwards moved to reconstruct the whole joint.

A peripheral nerve block, to deaden the pain during and after surgery, Dickson said, made the process more feasible. The 63-year-old has had both knees replaced as well, but he got through those without the added pain management of a nerve block during surgery.

"It's definitely a plus" to not feel the pain," he said. Just hours out of surgery, Dickson said he felt very little discomfort and was just dealing with numbness in his hand. He hopes to get back out on the golf course as soon as possible, as it is one of his favorite pastimes.

"I'm hoping I can get out there and keep going," Dickson said.

Doctors have told him he has about six to eight months of recuperation before he can try out his swing. Only about eight weeks of that is expected to include intense physical therapy, but Dickson expects to be "good as new, if not better," he said.

Hinkle said Dickson will need pain medications for a couple days, but "the first day is the worst. You're in a lot of pain after surgery, typically."

He said patients heading under the knife for major joint replacements and other arthroscopic surgeries are encouraged to ask about the nerve block procedure. It's a more practical approach to a sometimes very painful situation, Hinkle said.

"The more education people have about these things, the better," he said. "It leads to better patient satisfaction."

Innovation in Senior Care: "Telegivers" Help More Seniors Age at Home

By Husna Haq
Christian Science Monitor, April 13, 2011

Cameras, sensors, and video chat allows caregivers to be hundreds of miles away. But some see shades of "Big Brother" in this new senior care model.

Every night at 5 when Edward and Lavinia Fitzgerald tuck into dinner in their Savannah, Ga., kitchen, they have a guest. Denise Cady chats with the Fitzgeralds about their neighbors and swaps jokes about the weather. She has known Edward and Lavinia, both octogenarians, for two years; to them, she's like a daughter. The twist? They've never seen Ms. Cady in person.

Cady is a telecaregiver who checks in on the Fitzgeralds every evening from 800 miles away in Lafayette, Indiana. She's with a senior home care company, and she joins the couple via a computer monitor set up next to the kitchen table. Thanks to two cameras and several motion detectors wired throughout the Fitzgeralds' ranch house, she can see a lot more than what's for dinner—such as if Mr. Fitzgerald has left the burner on, how long Mrs. Fitzgerald has been in the bathroom, and how many times the front door has opened and closed.

Though it may sound like "Big Brother" to some, the video-monitoring service provided by ResCare means peace of mind for Colleen Henry, who began taking care of her mother years ago after Mrs. Fitzgerald sustained a brain injury and, more recently, a broken ankle.

Future Focus: Technology Gallery

"She and my dad have required a lot more care, a lot more of my time," says Ms. Henry, who lives five miles from her parents and brings them dinner every evening. When Henry learned about ResCare's monitoring service, she thought of it as "a dream come true, and it has been…. I'm so happy to have another pair of eyes."

This year, the first of 78 million baby boomers hit retirement age, the beginning of a so-called silver tsunami that will revamp America's demographic profile. People ages 65 and older will grow from 13 percent of the US population to 20 percent by 2050, according to the US Census Bureau, a greater share of seniors than Florida currently has. Just as important, more of them want to spend their golden years at home, whether for reasons of finances, convenience, or a desire for independence.

Seniors' rising desire to "age in place" is driving innovation, as researchers, businesses, and policymakers scramble to solve new challenges and cater to a booming elderly population.

Aging Issue No Longer a Projection—It's Here

"The aging issue is no longer a demographic projection. It's here," says Joe Coughlin, director and founder of AgeLab at the Massachusetts Institute of Technology (MIT) in Cambridge. "There's a market that awaits, policy that demands to be made, and a lifestyle to be invented today—actually yesterday," he says. "Frankly we're already 20 years behind."

Professor Coughlin founded the AgeLab in 1999 to invent ways to improve seniors' health and quality of life. The lab, housed in MIT's School of Engineering, frequently looks to places like NASA for inspiration.

Among AgeLab's equipment is the Aware Car, a red Lincoln MKS wired with cameras, monitors, and sensors that evaluate a driver's behavior, to improve safety. It's a test bed for innovations. Nodding off? Cameras and infrared sensors track eyelid movements and direct the driver to pull over and rest. Sensors in the center console also track heart rate, blood pressure, and respiration, and might release a spritz of lavender, adjust the air temperature, or prompt the driver to eat a snack.

"Very soon cars are going to be taking a more active role in your safety," says Coughlin.

For the home, Coughlin's team uses the same technology that NASA does to track supplies in a space station to track Mom's medication and Dad's eyeglasses. Tiny radio frequency tags can be attached to such items, and adult children can track their location and usage on the Web.

The AgeLab's Smart Trash Can even tracks the weight and material of disposed items to alert adult kids if something is amiss.

Coughlin says the AgeLab's technologies represent the future of innovation by going beyond simply reacting to a crisis and addressing more than ailments and emergencies.

"It's no longer about detecting what's going on in somebody's house. Rather, it's about predicting and being proactive about well-being and motivating behavior to ensure overall wellness," he says. "Innovation is about where we want to be and how to get there, not simply managing where we are today."

In Tampa Bay, Fla., developer Keith Collins is designing homes and garages where seniors can park their Aware Cars. Since 2000, he has built more than 2,300 senior-friendly homes in the area. His company, New Millennial Homes, uses a concept called universal design to make homes accessible to a range of people, including seniors and those with physical handicaps.

"To build a home, you have to look at demographics and what is a person's need," says Mr. Collins, who spent time in a wheelchair after serving during the Vietnam War. Many of his clients simply want to maintain their daily routines—at home, on their own terms, he says.

His homes feature flat entries, wide doorways, low counters, and accessible front-controls on appliances for those in wheelchairs. Large, bright numbers on thermostats ensure readability, and large, low wall switches are easier to control. Some features, like rollout cabinet shelves and stove-top pot-filler faucets, now come standard in high-end homes. But with starting prices as low as $95,000, Collins's homes are anything but.

"We want to keep people in their homes longer and do it affordably," he says.

But Collins's homes aren't widely available across the country, and many AgeLab gizmos have yet to hit the market. So for folks like the Fitzgeralds, the most practical services are home-monitoring systems that repurpose existing technology.

Tracking Grandma Remotely

Take Adaptive Home. The start-up elder-care monitoring company uses sensors to track a senior's movement around his or her home. Technicians place about a dozen motion detectors around a client's home to give adult children a detailed summary of a parent's day. Sensors placed under a mat beside a bed indicate when Mom gets up in the morning. Additional sensors track when she's opened the fridge or taken various foods or medications. The sensors are programmed to feed information to a secure website for adult children to check.

The Fitzgeralds use ResCare's remote telecare service, called RestAssured, to enable their daughter to keep tabs on them. Video cameras, audio systems, and a few motion sensors placed around the Fitzgeralds' house and some 300 other homes record the residents' daily routines for telecaregivers and adult children to track remotely from a secure website. If something is amiss, caregivers and family members are alerted immediately. In fact, the cameras are so sensitive that a telecaregiver with ResCare once zoomed in on a frying pan and told her charges to cook the eggs and sausage longer because they didn't look done, says Nel Taylor, a spokeswoman for ResCare.

"[Children] feel such guilt when parents live so far away," says Ms. Taylor. "This is the first step to help people stay where they want to be and help children care for them."

But for many, there's a fine line between convenient and creepy.

"It's like Big Brother is watching you," says Nancy Schlossberg, a professor emeritus of the University of Maryland who wrote "Revitalizing Retirement: Reshaping Your Identity, Relationships, and Purpose." "It's not that I'm opposed to technology, but what worries me is whether it diminishes older people."

Too often, Dr. Schlossberg says, adult children impose decisions on their aging parents, many of whom aren't comfortable with technology to begin with. "[Seniors] have got to be part of the decision," she says, suggesting children introduce new technology in stages.

Back in Savannah at the Fitzgeralds' house, Mrs. Fitzgerald, who seems to be always laughing and in a sunny mood, insists she loves the telecare service her daughter had installed two years ago. "I love it, because it's just for me," she says. "It keeps me out of trouble."

For her daughter's part, the decision to install cameras and sensors to track her parents wasn't difficult.

"I just felt relief, that someone's going to help me," she says. Her father can go to mass in the morning or run to the grocery store, something he couldn't do before the telecare system. "I don't know what we would do without the camera system," she says. "Me and my dad have a life now."

How Health Tech Can Support the Aging Baby Boomer Population

By Alicia Torres
Venturebeat.com, April 9, 2013

Advancements in medicine and treatments have increased the life expectancy for baby boomers. Almost 87 million Americans, or one in four, will be 65 or older by 2050, according to the Organization for Economic Cooperation and Development.

Both these trends have many implications for hospitals and healthcare organizations. Over the next decade, the healthcare system will need to adapt to the influx of baby boomers, many of whom will have chronic diseases and need continued care. A recent study by the West Virginia University School of Medicine found that about 39 percent of baby boomers were obese, compared to about 29 percent of the previous generation, and approximately 16 percent had diabetes, compared to 12 percent of the previous generation.

The aging generation of baby boomers had been a concern for the healthcare industry for some years. Now, technology solutions are beginning to serve a vital role in creating the change needed to propel the healthcare industry to care for the influx of patients.

Healthcare Technology Today

Technology implementation in healthcare today is mainly driven by government incentives. In 2009, the first electronic health record (EHR) mandates were enacted by the HITECH law and included financial incentives provided by the Health and Human Services Departments.

EHR implementation has taken off over the last few years, with nearly $10 billion in EHR incentives distributed as of December 2012. One of the core reasons hospitals and healthcare providers are adopting EHRs is to improve patient safety. While there are other benefits, such as saving time and cost, the objective of EHRs is to correctly identify patients through the continuum of care, ensuring procedures and check-ups are being recorded, as well as easing medical administration.

In order for that to happen, the EHR solutions need to fit seamlessly into the healthcare practice's existing software solutions and infrastructure. Barcode technology creates a critical link between the patient and the clinician. If, for instance, a patient is unable to verbally identify himself or his medical problems, a clinician can scan a barcode wristband and have access to that patient's EHR immediately, which can inform the course of action. The clinician spends less time tracking down patient records and more time with the patient.

EHR and barcode technology implementation seamlessly links patients and clinicians; however, it is only the beginning for healthcare technology.

Connecting Patients, Clinicians and Data

In an effort to provide the best care while adapting to the influx of baby boomers, hospitals and healthcare organizations are turning to connected health. Connected health is the idea of providing healthcare services remotely, through flexible, at home care. Managing chronic diseases, maintaining health and wellness, or ensuring patients are not readmitted following hospital treatment are all issues that connected health helps to solve. Additionally, with more patients being treated in their homes, we can decrease the number of patients admitted to hospitals.

Connected health can help solve the impending issue of the influx of baby boomers into the healthcare system, and technology is at the center of it, powering interoperability and linking patients to clinicians and their data. By leveraging technology solutions, healthcare organizations can provide care to patients outside the typical medical setting, consulting at home, over the phone or via video. In using technology while caring for a patient, clinicians have immediate access to the patient's medical history, pulled from the hospital IT system, and can direct the course of treatment in real-time.

Connected health also allows clinicians to use mobile devices to deliver care or information to a patient on the spot. This is known as mobile health, or mHealth. By using tablets, mobile printers and other point-of-care solutions, clinicians can take specimen collections, issue medical or dietary information and print prescriptions. In tandem with these activities, clinicians record their course of action, medications administered, patient status and next steps. The collected information is priceless data for hospitals and healthcare organizations. In analyzing this data, new processes or improved efficiencies are discovered, all the while elevating the quality of care a patient receives.

What to Expect in the Future

As connected health begins to take off, the Internet of Things (IoT) will play a larger role in healthcare information technology. Based on the definition shared in the survey "Building Value from Visibility: 2012 Enterprise Internet of Things Adoption Outlook," 85 percent of organizations surveyed agree that Internet of Things solutions are made up of smart interconnected devices that provide more visibility into the organization's operational events.

For healthcare, this means better visibility inside hospitals and healthcare organizations, as well as outside the typical medical setting and in the home. More importantly, IoT can provide more visibility into a patient's status.

As seen at this year's Consumer Electronics Show, broader IoT adoption is in full swing. In fact, 53 percent of organizations are planning to implement an IoT solution in the next 24 months, according to "Building Value from Visibility." The healthcare industry has an even more aggressive adoption rate, with almost 60% of healthcare organizations planning to implement IoT solutions within the next two years. The gained benefits from IoT adoption that healthcare respondents noted include improved delivery process (72 percent), improved safety (66 percent), supply chain visibility (63 percent) and loss prevention (63 percent).

There are already startups developing IoT solutions for healthcare organizations specific to certain areas of inventory management and patient check-in. In the future, IoT has the ability to elevate healthcare even more, and specifically, connected health practices. Patient wristbands, medical equipment and beds encoded with sensors can track status in real-time and make hospital workflow processes more efficient. Health monitors, sensors and RFID technology at one's home can transfer data to the hospital every minute. Hospitals and healthcare organizations will be able to consistently monitor and provide care, even if clinicians are not working with a patient in-person.

We have the opportunity to change the healthcare industry and evolve with the aging population. With the right solutions and infrastructure, technology can deliver on one of the healthcare industry's biggest goals: providing the best care possible and creating a safe environment for patients.

On Beyond 100

By Stephen S. Hall
National Geographic, May 1, 2013

Our genes harbor many secrets to a long and healthy life. And now scientists are beginning to uncover them.

On a crisp January morning, with snow topping the distant Aspromonte mountains and oranges ripening on the nearby trees, Giuseppe Passarino guided his silver minivan up a curving mountain road into the hinterlands of Calabria, mainland Italy's southernmost region. As the road climbed through fruit and olive groves, Passarino, a geneticist at the University of Calabria, chatted with his colleague Maurizio Berardelli, a geriatrician. They were headed for the small village of Molochio, which had the distinction of numbering four centenarians—and four 99-year-olds—among its 2,000 inhabitants.

Soon after, they found Salvatore Caruso warming his 106-year-old bones in front of a roaring fire in his home on the outskirts of the town. Known in local dialect as "U' Raggiuneri," the Accountant, Caruso was calmly reading an article about the end of the world in an Italian version of a supermarket tabloid. A framed copy of his birth record, dated November 2, 1905, stood on the fireplace mantle.

Caruso told the researchers he was in good health, and his memory seemed prodigiously intact. He recalled the death of his father in 1913, when Salvatore was a schoolboy; how his mother and brother had nearly died during the great influenza pandemic of 1918–19; how he'd been dismissed from his army unit in 1925 after accidentally falling and breaking his leg in two places. When Berardelli leaned forward and asked Caruso how he had achieved his remarkable longevity, the centenarian said with an impish smile, *"No Bacco, no tabacco, no Venere*—No drinking, no smoking, no women." He added that he'd eaten mostly figs and beans while growing up and hardly ever any red meat.

Passarino and Berardelli heard much the same story from 103-year-old Domenico Romeo—who described his diet as "poco, ma tutto; a little bit, but of everything"—and 104-year-old Maria Rosa Caruso, who, despite failing health, regaled her visitors with a lively version of a song about the local patron saint.

On the ride back to the laboratory in Cosenza, Berardelli remarked, "They often say they prefer to eat only fruits and vegetables."

"They preferred fruit and vegetables," Passarino said drily, "because that's all they had."

Although eating sparingly may have been less a choice than an involuntary circumstance of poverty in places like early 20th-century Calabria, decades of research have suggested that a severely restricted diet is connected to long life. Lately, however, this theory has fallen on hard scientific times. Several recent studies have undermined the link between longevity and caloric restriction.

In any case, Passarino was more interested in the centenarians themselves than in what they had eaten during their lifetimes. In a field historically marred by exaggerated claims and dubious entrepreneurs hawking unproven elixirs, scientists studying longevity have begun using powerful genomic technologies, basic molecular research, and, most important, data on small, genetically isolated communities of people to gain increased insight into the maladies of old age and how they might be avoided. In Calabria, Ecuador, Hawaii, and even in the Bronx, studies are turning up molecules and chemical pathways that may ultimately help everyone reach an advanced age in good, even vibrant, health.

The quest for genetic answers has brought international scientific attention to people like Nicolas Añazco, known as "Pajarito," Little Bird in Spanish.

In many ways Little Bird is a typical teen. He plays computer games and soccer and has been known to sneak a glance at the pinup calendar that resides beside a framed picture of the Last Supper on the dining room wall of his family's four-room home in the rural uplands of Ecuador's El Oro Province. In this steep and rugged, yet oddly lush, landscape at the foot of the Andes—with a hint of Shangri-La in its exotic mix of bananas, cauliflower, and tamarillo—the young man helps his father process the sugarcane that surrounds the house.

Little Bird, 17, said he became grudgingly aware of the reason for his nickname at age six, when he looked around at his classmates: "I realized that I was going to be smaller than them." Much smaller.

Because of a recessive mutation in a single gene, Little Bird looks like an eight-year-old and is three feet nine inches tall—much shorter than his brother Ricardo, who is a year older. The mutation causes a disease of impaired growth called Laron syndrome. But it may also protect Little Bird from serious diseases that typically ravage humans as they age. And even in this area of geographical isolation and historical poverty, word of that has gotten around.

One afternoon Little Bird and three other Laron syndrome men from the region held court for an interview at the back of an appliance store, their feet dangling in child's-size shoes from their chairs. Freddy Salazar, 39 years old and three feet ten inches tall, had recently had his 1997 Chevy Forsa retrofitted with elevated pedals and a raised seat so he could see through the windshield to negotiate his town's steep hills. Victor Rivera, 23 years old and slightly taller than Salazar, was the subject of a famous photograph, shown at many scientific meetings, taken when he was four—so small that the ear of corn he was holding was a little larger than his arm. Luis Sanchez, at 43 an elder statesman among the group, threw back his head in laughter, which was joined by the others' high-pitched voices, when someone asked if they were aware of the latest scientific reports about their condition.

"We are laughing," he explained, "because we know we are immune to cancer and diabetes."

That somewhat overstates the scientific results to date but reflects a growing interest among researchers to interrogate the genomes of unusually healthy or long-lived groups of people, whose isolation, geographical or cultural, makes it easier to find genetic clues to longevity, disease resistance, and good health at an advanced age.

One such scientist is Little Bird's physician, Jaime Guevara, who was born in El Oro Province. Fascinated by the region's "little people," as they have been known since before their condition even had a name, he began to study them around 1987, and during a quarter century of epidemiological sleuthing he identified about a hundred people with the Laron mutation sprinkled through the hills of southern Ecuador.

Meche Romero Robles, a 40-year-old single mother, is also one of Guevara's patients. Just over four feet tall, Robles lives with her teenage daughter, Samantha, in a cinder-block, metal-roofed home perched on a hillside in the town of Piñas. "Look at her!" Guevara cried, giving the elder Robles an affectionate hug. "She should have diabetes. Given her body mass index, she must have diabetes. But she doesn't." Even to a nonmedical eye, Meche appeared obese. Like so many little people, however, she remained free of diabetes. "I realized this in 1994," Guevara said, "but no one would believe me."

That began to change in 2005, when Valter Longo, a cell biologist at the University of Southern California who studies aging, invited Guevara to USC to describe his research. A decade earlier Longo had begun to manipulate the genes of simple organisms like single-celled yeast, creating mutations that allowed them to live longer. The reasons for this varied. Some mutants could repair their DNA more effectively than normal cells; others demonstrated a heightened ability to minimize the damage from oxidants. Still others became better able to derail the type of DNA damage that would promote cancer in humans.

Others were studying the same processes. In 1996 Andrzej Bartke, a scientist at Southern Illinois University, tinkered with mouse genes that are involved with growth. He showed—not surprisingly—that shutting down the growth hormone pathway resulted in smaller mice. What was surprising was that they lived longer—about 40 percent longer—than normal mice.

Could similar processes be at work in humans? Could genetic anomalies protect against diseases of age? Zvi Laron, the Israeli endocrinologist who in 1966 first described the dwarfism that came to be named after him, had found dozens of people scattered through central and eastern Europe with the rare syndrome. Longo thought Guevara's patients might represent an experiment of nature—an isolated population with a condition that linked genetics to longevity.

The Ecuadorian Laron people can be traced, researchers believe, back to the late fifteenth century, when Jews traveled from the Iberian Peninsula to the New World with a very specific piece of baggage: a genetic misspelling known as the E180 mutation in the growth hormone receptor gene, which produces the molecule that receives the body's growth signals. This distinctive misspelling in the genetic code has also turned up in Israel.

"The presumption is that Sephardic Jews were desperate to leave Spain and Portugal because of the Inquisition," says Harry Ostrer, a medical geneticist at Albert Einstein College of Medicine in New York City who has collaborated with Guevara. "They went to North Africa, the Middle East, Southern Europe. Many ventured to the New World as well, but the Inquisition followed them. So it was in their interest to get out of cities like Lima and Quito, where the church maintained its strongest presence."

They settled in small towns and villages sprinkled across 75 square miles of rural Ecuador, where until the 1980s there were few roads, no phones, and no electricity. Over the centuries the mutation lurked and spread in the population, amplified by isolation and inbreeding. "Theoretically we are all from the same family," says Christian Asanza Reyes, an economist in Balsas, whose tall frame belies the mutation he and his wife passed on to two of their three children.

Guevara and Longo began to collaborate in 2006. Guevara had found a homogeneous group in one geographic location with a known genetic mutation that seemed to block the development of diabetes and cancer in individuals. Within the Laron group there were no cases of diabetes and only a single, nonlethal malignancy. In a control group of people the same age living in the same area, Guevara and Longo found that 5 percent developed diabetes and 20 percent died of cancer. Follow-up experiments conducted by Longo at USC showed that blood taken from the Ecuadorian patients seemed to protect human cells from laboratory-induced cancers. What was the magic ingredient in their blood?

"Nothing," Longo says.

Nothing? In fact, it was the absence of something—a hormone known as IGF-1, or insulin-like growth factor. The blood was protective, Longo says, because it had unusually low levels of IGF-1, which plays an important role in childhood growth but has also been implicated as an accelerant of cancers and as a powerful regulator of metabolism. Could controlling the presence of one hormone in human blood postpone the diseases of old age? It's probably not quite that simple, but the insulin–IGF-1 connection keeps popping up in longevity research.

In Calabria the hunt for hidden molecules and mechanisms that confer longevity on people like Salvatore Caruso begins in places like the Ufficio Anagrafe Stato Civile (Civil Registry Office) in the medieval village of Luzzi. The office windows here offer stunning views of snow-covered mountains to the north, but to a population geneticist the truly breathtaking sights are hidden inside the tall file cabinets ringing the room and on shelf after shelf of precious ledgers numbered by year, starting in 1866. Despite its well-earned reputation for chaos and disorganization, the Italian government, shortly after the unification of the country in 1861, ordered local officials to record the birth, marriage, and death of every citizen in each *comune*, or township.

Since 1994 scientists at the University of Calabria have combed through these records in every one of Calabria's 409 *comuni* to compile an extraordinary survey. Coupling family histories with simple physiological measurements of frailty and the latest genomic technologies, they set out to address fundamental questions about longevity. How much of it is determined by genetics? How much by the environ-ment? And how do these factors interact to promote longevity—or, conversely, to hasten the aging process? To answer all those questions, scientists must start with rock-solid demographic data.

"Here is the book from 1905," explained Marco Giordano, one of Giuseppe Pas-sarino's young colleagues, opening a tall, green ledger. He pointed to a record, in careful cursive, of the birth of Francesco D'Amato on March 3, 1905. "He died in 2007," Giordano noted, describing D'Amato as the central figure, or proband, of an extensive genealogical tree. "We can reconstruct the pedigrees of families from these records."

Cross-checking the ledger entries against meticulously detailed registry cards (pink for women, white for men) going back to the nineteenth century, Giordano, along with researchers Alberto Montesanto and Cinzia Martino, has reconstructed extensive family trees of 202 nonagenarians and centenarians in Calabria. The records document not only siblings of people who lived to 100 but also the spouses of siblings, which has allowed Passarino's group to do a kind of historical experi-ment on longevity. "We compared the ages of D'Amato's brothers and sisters to the ages of their spouses," Giordano explained. "So they had the same environment. They ate the same food. They used the same medicines. They came from the same culture. But they did not have the same genes." In a 2011 paper the Calabrian researchers reported a surprising conclusion: Although the parents and siblings of people who lived to at least 90 also lived longer than the general population, a finding in line with earlier research, the genetic factors involved seemed to benefit males more than females.

The Calabrian results on gender offer yet another hint that the genetic twists and turns that confer longevity may be unusually complex. Major European studies had previously reported that women are much likelier to live to 100, outnumbering male centenarians by a ratio of four or five to one, with the implication that some of the reasons are genetic. But by teasing out details from family trees, the Calabrian researchers discovered an intriguing paradox: The genetic component of longevity appears to be stronger in males—but women may take better advantage of external factors such as diet and medical care than men do.

In the dimly lit, chilly hallway outside Passarino's university office stand several freezers full of tubes containing centenarian blood. The DNA from this blood and other tissue samples has revealed additional information about the Calabrian group. For example, people who live into their 90s and beyond tend to possess a particular version, or allele, of a gene important to taste and digestion. This allele not only gives people a taste for bitter foods like broccoli and field greens, which are typically rich in compounds known as polyphenols that promote cellular health, but also al-lows cells in the intestine to extract nutrients more efficiently from food as it's being digested.

Passarino has also found in his centenarians a revved-up version of a gene for what is called an uncoupling protein. The protein plays a central role in metabolism—the way a person consumes energy and regulates body heat—which in turn affects the rate of aging.

"We have dissected five or six pathways that most influence longevity," says Passarino. "Most of them involve the response to stress, the metabolism of nutrients, or metabolism in general—the storage and use of energy." His group is currently examining how environmental influences—everything from childhood diet to how long a person attends school—might modify the activity of genes in a way that either promotes or curtails longevity.

Another continent, another genetic island. It was a gray day in the Bronx, and 81-year-old Jean Sisinni paced back and forth on a gray carpet in a third-floor room on Morris Park Avenue. As she walked, Sisinni struggled to recite every other letter of the alphabet ("B, D, F, H"), while the sensor on her forehead measured activity in her prefrontal cortex, and the carpet simultaneously registered the location, path, and velocity of every step.

"You're doing great!" said Roee Holtzer, a neuropsychologist at Albert Einstein College of Medicine who has been conducting studies of brain function and mobility in the elderly.

If this sounds like a scientific variation on the old joke about being able to walk and chew gum at the same time, go ahead and laugh. In a series of studies over the past several years Holtzer and neurologist Joe Verghese have shown that the amount of thinking people are able do in the executive, prefrontal part of the brain while they walk and talk predicts the risk of dementia, loss of mobility, and falls.

These experiments complement research at Einstein led by Nir Barzilai, an Israeli doctor with a mop of gray hair atop a youthful face who in 1998 began a study of three New York centenarians. The Einstein project has since grown to include more than 500 centenarians in and around New York City—all from central Europe and all Ashkenazi Jews, a historically isolated and culturally insular population. In this homogeneous group, research has again revealed a set of genes related to longevity, some of which have also turned up in Italy.

As they gathered more and more data, the Einstein researchers noticed that the Ashkenazi centenarians had exceptionally high levels of HDL, often called the good form of cholesterol, and that the children of these centenarians had even higher levels. This sent them off to analyze the DNA of about a hundred genes known to be involved in cholesterol metabolism. What they found was a variant, a distinct genetic subtype, of a gene known as *CETP* (cholesteryl ester transfer protein) that was more common in centenarians than in others.

When they investigated the centenarian version of the *CETP* gene, they confirmed earlier research showing that this particular variant protects against cardiovascular disease, and they have gone on to show that many people with this genetic subtype—not just centenarians but other Ashkenazi Jews and even non-Jewish residents of the Bronx—perform better on cognitive tasks like the "walking while talking" experiments. Two major pharmaceutical companies are now testing drugs that inhibit the amount of *CETP*, as the centenarian gene variant does.

Barzilai and his colleagues have also focused on the mitochondria of centenarians. Mitochondria are the cell's power plants, with their own DNA, their own genes, their own genetic variants—all with key metabolic responsibilities. Barzilai and his team have identified several mitochondrial proteins, which they dubbed mitochines, associated with people who live into their 90s and 100s. One of these molecules, humanin, looks especially interesting, at least in animal experiments. Barzilai says that giving a single shot of humanin to a diabetic rat normalizes its glucose levels and essentially erases diabetic symptoms in a few hours. It also prevents arteriosclerosis and Alzheimer's in mice prone to these diseases and somehow limits coronary damage when researchers induce heart attacks in the experimental animals.

Einstein's large and ambitious longevity program is part of a sea change sweeping human genetics research, where the prevailing emphasis for the past 20 years has been on the search for so-called disease genes. "Everybody is looking for genes for diabetes and obesity and things like that," says Barzilai. "I think one reason we are not finding them is because we also have protective sets of genes." Many researchers are now focused largely on the search for those protective genes, which seem to override genes associated with disease or aging.

One of the most intriguing genes is called *FOXO3*. In yet another study of an isolated, homogeneous population, University of Hawaii researchers have found variants of the gene in long-lived Japanese-American men on the island of Oahu. This gene is in the same insulin–IGF-1 pathway that has popped up both in studies of yeast and worms and in the Laron population in southern Ecuador.

Protective genes are also the target of a study at the Scripps Translational Science Institute in La Jolla, California, where physician Eric Topol and colleagues are riffling through the DNA of about a thousand people they call the wellderly. These are people over the age of 80 who have no chronic diseases, such as high blood pressure, coronary artery disease, or diabetes, and have never taken prescription drugs for them. "There must be modifying genes that explain why these individuals are protected from the deleterious genes that affect the aging process," Topol says. "The hunt is on."

The race to find the keys to longevity has even led scientists to a place that looks increasingly important in setting every individual's rate of aging: the womb. Researchers at Einstein now suspect that our pattern of aging may be set very early, perhaps before we're born.

To study this hypothesis, Francine Einstein and John Greally have been examining subtle chemical markings on the DNA of stem cells recovered from the umbilical cord blood of babies born in the Bronx and comparing differences in infants who were, for their gestational age, small, normal, or large. They have found that the pattern of DNA markings in both small and large infants is significantly different compared with that of normal-size babies. These results form part of a hot new field of biology called epigenetics, which studies how environmental influences can etch chemical modifications in DNA and thus introduce lifelong changes in the activity of genes. As Barzilai explains it, "There might be influences in the uterus that affect genetic mechanisms that somehow set your rate of aging." The fetus, in other words, may be father of the old man.

If nothing else, the plethora of new studies indicates that longevity researchers are pushing the scientific conversation to a new level. In October 2011 the Archon Genomics X Prize launched a race among research teams to sequence the DNA of a hundred centenarians (dubbing the contest "100 over 100").

But genes alone are unlikely to explain all the secrets of longevity, and experts see a cautionary tale in recent results concerning caloric restriction. Experiments on 41 different genetic models of mice, for example, have shown that restricting food intake produces wildly contradictory outcomes. About half the mouse species lived longer, but just as many lived less time on a restricted diet than they would have on a normal diet. And last August a long-running National Institute on Aging experiment on primates concluded that monkeys kept on a restricted-calorie diet for 25 years showed no longevity advantage. Passarino made the point while driving back to his laboratory after visiting the centenarians in Molochio. "It's not that there are good genes and bad genes," he said. "It's certain genes at certain times. And in the end, genes probably account for only 25 percent of longevity. It's the environment too, but that doesn't explain all of it either. And don't forget chance."

Which brought to mind Salvatore Caruso of Molochio, now 107 years old and still going strong. Because he broke his leg 88 years ago, he was unfit to serve in the Italian Army when his entire unit was recalled during World War II. "They were all sent to the Russian front," he said, "and not a single one of them came back." It's another reminder that, although molecules and mechanisms yet unfathomed may someday lead to drugs that help us reach a ripe and healthy old age, a little luck doesn't hurt either.

We're Living Longer

By Larry Kusch
Winnipeg Free Press, October 26, 2013

Report finds Manitobans' life expectancy rises

Manitobans are getting healthier—with fewer people dying before age 75—but the health gap between rich and poor continues to increase.

A study published Friday by the Manitoba Centre for Health Policy shows life expectancy rose significantly in the province between 2006 and 2011 as the incidence of diabetes, heart disease and stroke and other serious illnesses fell.

Men are expected to live until they're 77.5 years old (up from 76.6) while women are expected to live until 82.2 (up from 81.5).

Researchers analyzed more than 70 indicators of health status and health-care use, comparing them to similar reports spanning two decades.

Lead researcher Randy Fransoo termed the results of the latest provincial snapshot "stunning."

"The real surprise in this (report) is how almost universally positive the results are," he said. "Almost every one of the indicators . . . is showing improvement over time."

Particularly important is that the rate of premature mortality—the number of people who die before reaching age 75—declined. It is considered by many to be the best single indicator of population health.

Nick Diakiw, 82, had colon cancer at 68. Not only did Diakiw survive, but the former city hall commissioner began working out regularly at the Seven Oaks Wellness Centre.

"I never thought I'd live to be 82, if that's what you're asking," Diakiw said on Friday, after his aquatic exercises.

Diakiw said living longer is fine, provided his quality of life is maintained. "If you're in good health and enjoying your life, that's fine," he said.

Dean Melvie, director of operations at the Wellness Centre, said a growing number of clients are well into their 70s—and their options for exercise are expanding.

"We're seeing a great rate of participation for older adults," Melvie said. "They say 60 is the new 50, and 70 is the new 60. There's a reason for that. And I think this demographic is beginning to realize they can stay active."

However, some Manitobans are doing far better than others. The health status of northerners and those in Winnipeg's inner city either failed to improve or improved marginally compared with wealthier Manitobans.

But, Fransoo said, there's a "silver lining." The last time the MCHP took the pulse of the province, the poor were losing ground, he said. "Now at least, they're holding their own."

While there are many positive indicators in the report, several concerns remain.

The incidence of hypertension—the percentage of people diagnosed with high blood pressure each year—is down, but the prevalence (how many are living with it) keeps rising. The latter figure sits at a troubling 25.6 percent, up from 24.8 percent in 2007. People with the condition have a higher risk of heart and kidney failure and other health problems.

The report also found the incidence of diabetes is falling, but the prevalence of the disease in Manitoba is growing. Now, 10 percent of Manitobans 19 and older live with diabetes, up from 9 percent in 2007. That means the health system is keeping people with diabetes alive longer.

Dr. Jon Gerrard, Liberal MLA for River Heights, said while the decreased incidence of diabetes (to 0.85 per 100 residents from 0.91) offers a "glimmer of hope," the rate is still higher than it was a decade ago.

"There are way too many people still getting diabetes. We still have a big epidemic. We still have a long way to go in order to turn this around," he said.

The 452-page report offers a breakdown of health trends by regional health authority and by municipality. Within Winnipeg, it has subcategories for neighborhoods. For instance, the study reveals the suicide rate among residents aged 10 and older was highest from 2007 to 2011 in Point Douglas, followed by the rate downtown. It was lowest in Fort Garry.

There were significant increases in life expectancy for men in Winnipeg as well as southern and western areas of the province during the period, with no change in the Interlake or in the north. The biggest gains in life expectancy for women occurred in Winnipeg and the Southern Regional Health Authority.

6

An Aging World Population

© Eriko Sugita/Reuters/Landov

Ninety-two-year-old Toshi Uechi practices her traditional Okinawan dance with other men and women at a senior center in Naha, on the southernmost Japanese island of Okinawa. An active lifestyle and spartan diet have helped make Okinawa home to one of the highest percentages of centenarians in the world—39.5 per 100,000 residents.

The Challenges and Demands
of an Aging Population

For more than a century, one of the most significant trends in human history—the aging of the global population—has had a profound impact on every country in the world. This trend is the result of a wide range of contributing factors, including those born of the medical, engineering, economic, social, and political environments. The fact that people's lives are no longer cut short by the technological and scientific limitations of the past is in many ways cause for celebration. However, the increasing number of elderly people (sixty years of age and older) also creates a number of major social, economic, and medical challenges for nations around the globe.

In the United States, one of the world's most developed and economically powerful nations, the average life expectancy for its citizens has skyrocketed in just over a century. In 1900, according to a study by University of California-Berkeley, Americans' life expectancy rate hovered at approximately forty-eight years for women and forty-six years for men. By the end of the twentieth century, however, men were living to an average age of seventy-four and women were reaching an average age of eighty years.

This trend is not localized to so-called developed nations. In fact, the global proportion of people aged sixty and over increases by 2 percent every year, according to a 2001 United Nations study. By 2050, it is believed that one in every five persons will be sixty years of age and older, and in developed countries this number is one in every three persons. This trend is also accelerating in the twenty-first century. In 2000, there were 600 million elderly persons in the global population. By the middle of the twenty-first century, experts estimate that this figure will reach nearly 2 billion.

A wide range of factors, including modern technology, advances in medicine, and the general improvement in the quality of life for most people in developed nations, continue to foster longer life expectancy. Coupled with the extension of life expectancy is the fact that fertility rates have been on the decline—this trend began in the early twentieth century in the United States, but had accelerated a century later, particularly in less developed nations. Based on these trends, many experts conclude that the world's population will continue to age at a faster rate than growth rates in younger people. It is expected that this trend will have a major impact on the economies and societies of nations around the globe. For example, the cost of health care is typically greater for the elderly. Moreover, employers often see the elderly as a financial burden and prefer to hire younger workers, thus contributing to higher levels of unemployment for the elderly, who then must rely on government funded programs as a source of income.

One of the countries in which this trend's impact is being monitored is the world's most populous nation: China. In the late 1970s, China (led by Communist ideologue Mao Zedong, or Mao Tse-tung) introduced its own form of population control, mandating that families could only have one child. The efforts were meant to stem a perception that, unchecked, Chinese families would reproduce with such frequency that the Communist government would be unable to feed and care for them all. Ironically, the policy, which went into effect in 1979 as Zedong faded back from the government spotlight, was introduced at a period during which fertility and birth rates were already beginning a downward trend. More than thirty years later, China is seeing the long-term effects of this policy—a rapid aging of the population. In 2012, the labor pool began a sharp decline for the first time in half a century. The taxpayer to pensioner ratio, five to one that year, is expected to be two to one by 2030. China's elderly population is surging, experts argue, but there are too few younger people to care for them. Consequently, in 2013, the Communist Party voted to further relax the "one child" policy by allowing parents to have a second child if one of the parents is an only child.

The aging global population has significant implications for the societies that must care for their respective elderly populations. More elderly people, for example, require a variety of health care services. As men and women live longer thanks in part to advances in medicine, they will continue to call upon these health care services for a longer period than in previous years. For example, more and more people are living into their eighties, and the World Health Organization (WHO) estimates that 25–30 percent of people reaching this stage in life suffer from some degree of cognitive decline that will require special care.

There are also social impacts of an aging population. The high volume of elderly men and women may crowd hospitals and nursing homes, which can drain resources, resulting in deteriorating conditions and the potential for maltreatment. Researchers are only beginning to compile data on rates of abuse and neglect that can arise at overcrowded and underfunded senior care facilities. However, preliminary research has revealed that between 4 and 6 percent of elderly people worldwide have experienced some form of maltreatment. In the United States, nursing homes have seen an increase in abuse of the elderly, with 36 percent of nursing home staff reporting to have witnessed physical abuse and 40 percent of staff admitting to have committed some form of psychological abuse on their patients. The survey also found that 10 percent of nursing home staff admitted to having committed at least one act of physical abuse.

The aging global population also has a prominent impact on the economy. In the United States, where elderly health care is covered by the government's Medicare program, it is feared that resources will soon dwindle dramatically. In 2012, Medicare's "hospital fund," which supports 50 million elderly Americans' hospital care, paid out $38 billion more than it collected in taxes and insurance premiums. Experts differ on the timing, but they agree that, in light of this trend, it is likely that the hospital fund will reach insolvency in the near future.

In addition to the quantifiable impacts of the aging world population on society, there are also stigmas and negative perceptions of the elderly that become evident as older employees stay in the workforce after retirement age. Some employers, for example, express concern that older workers will be less productive due to their physical limitations. Although research on this claim is, to date, inconclusive, there remains a stigma attached to older members of the workforce, particularly as they continue to increase in number while younger workers become scarcer.

Although the aging trend has been manifest for decades, evidence of its impacts has only recently been given a greater spotlight. A question that a broad spectrum of experts—political scientists, economists, health policy analysts, medical professionals, and sociologists—have posed in recent years is a simple one: is the world prepared for the impacts of an aging population? The answer to this question, however, is far more complex.

One context in which this issue may be analyzed is that of so-called safety nets for the elderly. As they enter their sixties, elderly men and women leave the workforce and rely on their own retirement savings for income as well as government-sponsored health care, housing, and other services. World leaders are starting to pay more attention to the issue of the aging population, and they are evaluating the protections governments have in place for their respective seniors to discern if accommodating an aging population is possible. Some of the world's poorest nations have few or no pension systems and lack health care resources that address senior needs; they also have economies that cannot support physically limited seniors who choose not to retire. In Afghanistan, for example, many elderly men and women who are unable to continue as part of the labor force will resort to begging in the streets for money. Meanwhile, some of the world's most prosperous and stable economies, such as Japan and Germany, offer extensive networks and services for their growing populations of elderly men and women.

As a 2013 WHO study revealed, however, relative economic prosperity and stability is not necessarily an indication of a nation's ability to accommodate an aging population. In some cases, it is a matter of infrastructure—some governments, which are continuously evolving, may be using antiquated senior programs that are not reflective of the reality of an aging population. China, one of the world's most powerful economies, ranks thirty-eight on the WHO Global AgeWatch Index, which is lower than less developed countries like Panama (ranked thirty) in terms of social economic benefit programs for the elderly. India (seventy-three), Russia (seventy-eight), and South Africa (sixty-five) also rank relatively low on the WHO Global AgeWatch Index, behind Bolivia (forty-six), El Salvador (fifty-nine), and Kyrgyzstan (sixty-three). Russia, at seventy-eight, ranks just ahead of Laos (seventy-nine) and Cambodia (eighty), and behind Nepal (seventy-seven).

A perceived lack of preparedness for an aging population has major implications. The United States, which ranks eighth on the above-referenced WHO index, provides an interesting example of current preparedness for an increasing elderly population. In the United States, the number of elderly citizens is expected to rise by a rate of 135 percent from the start of the twentieth century through 2050. Meanwhile, the proportion of Americans aged sixty-five and under has remained relatively stable, held up by the higher-than-average fertility rates in the United States as well as an ongoing influx of immigrants. The growth of this younger population, however, has slowed, a trend which is anticipated to continue.

The impact of this trend in the United States could be significant in terms of cost. From the taxpayer side of government, the slow growth in the number of workforce-aged citizens (from ages sixteen to sixty-five) means that the tax revenues their work generates will concurrently grow at a slower rate over the next few decades. A growing number of elderly citizens, who typically rely on the government-sponsored Medicare program for their health care, will need more of the program's services. With costs far outpacing revenues, many believe that the Medicare system (and not just the aforementioned hospital fund therein) will collapse.

The larger number of elderly Americans—particularly those eighty-five and older—also poses a cost risk for the country's health care system. As Americans get older, their health care needs tend to shift. Younger Americans typically use expensive hospital services only in emergencies or for single health issues (such as a serious illness or injury), and they utilize their primary care physicians for annual checkups. For the elderly, trips to the hospital are more likely to be for multiple issues that require longer stays, more procedures, and hospice (nursing facilities designed to keep a terminally ill patient comfortable). The initiation of the 2010 Affordable Care Act has benefited seniors by expanding coverage and improving Medicare and Medicaid, including covering the charges for cancer screenings and cholesterol checks. Medicare, however, only partially reimburses hospitals for services (hospitals rely on private insurance payments from other patients to offset Medicare losses). Therefore, hospitals, in order to address the drain caused by long-term care provided to more seniors, would need to increase prices. In a nation already hampered by high health care costs, the growing number of seniors using hospital care is likely to continue weighing down the system.

Adding to this issue is the fact that Medicare does not cover all health care costs. Seniors commonly find another form of coverage to cover certain prescriptions, eye care, and other services. While some pay out of pocket or utilize private insurance, a high percentage of elderly Americans rely on Medicaid, the federal program that provides health care services to the nation's poorest citizens. Increasing demand for Medicaid, along with increasing demand for Medicare, compounds the challenges facing the United States as a result of the aging population.

Furthermore, the aging population's need for health care to treat chronic illness, such as Alzheimer's disease and osteoporosis, and multiple conditions results in greater demand for more health care workers, including doctors, nurses, home health attendants, mental health professionals, and occupational therapists. While demand for health care workers is seen as a positive development for the workforce (especially during times of economic recovery), hospitals and other institutions must have the necessary funds to pay the salaries and benefits of these new work-ers, further taxing financially challenged hospitals.

Social scientists, health care analysts, epidemiologists, economists, and world leaders are among the wide range of experts paying increased attention to the aging world population trend. Data continues to be compiled, and case studies are giving us a clearer picture of how an aging population affects society and the economy. Experts believe that the trend will not be stemmed, but with greater understanding, its impacts could be mitigated.

An Aging Population May Be What the World Needs

By Charles Kinney
Business Week, February 7, 2013

Americans just don't make babies like they used to. The US birthrate is the lowest in nearly a century, according to a study released last year by the Pew Research Center. It's half the level of the Baby Boom years after World War II. American women, on average, are likely to have fewer than two children during their lifetime, which means not enough babies are being born to maintain the current population size. Even among new arrivals, the trend is declining: The birthrate among Mexican immigrants to the US has plummeted 23 percent since 2007.

This reproductive recession is not unique to America; it's a global phenomenon. Women just about everywhere are having fewer kids and having them later in life. The world is about to get a lot older very fast.

Planetary senescence casts a shadow on the world economy's long-term prospects for growth. Already, the burden of supporting aging populations with a shrinking pool of able-bodied workers threatens the solvency of governments in advanced economies. Even so, the Baby Bust doesn't need to be a disaster. Policymakers and the public will have to adjust to changes in the way we allocate resources and define work, but an older, grayer world may turn out to be a better place.

In 1970 the average woman on the planet gave birth to 4.7 children in her lifetime. By 2011 that number had dropped to 2.5. Even in the world's most fecund region, sub-Saharan Africa, the fertility rate fell from 6.7 to 4.9 between 1980 and 2010—and births among women under 20 dropped 20 percent in the first decade of the new millennium.

In many places, populations have peaked or will soon do so. Out of 196 nations for which the World Bank had data in 2010, 71 saw fertility rates lower than two children per woman; that's up from 26 out of 187 countries in 1980. Although population levels are still rising in some of those countries, it's either because people are living longer or the country is attracting a lot of immigrants. By 2050 the United Nations estimates that 48 countries and territories out of a world total of 229 will have smaller populations than in 2010. Nations likely to shrink include China, Russia, Japan, Germany, Ukraine, Poland, and Cuba.

The combination of falling birthrates and longer life expectancies also means the world is rapidly adding wrinkles. In 1980 the median age was 23; by 2050, according to the UN, it will be 38. In 1970 about half of the world's population was younger than 20; by 2011 that figure had dropped to a little more than one-third, and the UN predicts it will be closer to one-quarter by mid-century. Meanwhile, the number of people older than 65 increased from 5 percent to 9 percent between 1970 and 2011 and will climb to 20 percent by 2050. Despite the global population being about 2 billion higher, the absolute number of young people at mid-century will be no larger than today. The global elderly will have increased from 648 million to 1.9 billion.

The secret to wealth isn't more young people, it's more productive people. Economies can continue to grow—creating demand and supplying the resources necessary to care for the infirm—if they focus on increasing the productivity of those fit and keen to work. Globally the labor supply has plenty of slack. If the rich world as a whole increased immigration from the still-expanding populations of the developing world, that alone would be a powerful dynamo for the world economy. In many developing regions, including sub-Saharan Africa and India, as much as three-quarters of all employment is in the informal sector, where productivity tends to be abysmal. By providing workers with better education and moving them into higher-output employment, countries can generate more wealth with smaller populations.

Over the long run, stabilizing global population may help alleviate fears of climate Armageddon. The richest 10 percent of the planet, which spends about 100 times a year what the poorest 10th does, is responsible for today's stress on the global environment. The big challenge in combating climate change is to ensure that a given income per person can still be delivered to everyone, but more sustainably. A smaller number of people would clearly help in that regard.

And while having fewer young people around may make the world more boring, it might also make it more peaceful, since youths commit far more than their fair share of violent crimes. Rachel Margolis and Mikko Myrskylä, in research for the National Institutes of Health, even suggest fewer kids might make for a happier planet. Their analysis of worldwide survey data from 86 countries finds that childless people are considerably happier than those with children. The gap between childless adults and parents of four kids is as big as the gap between people living in middle-income countries and those living in high-income countries.

A significantly declining global population will, of course, mean lost opportunities. Every child born might be the next Picasso or Einstein. The vast majority of people on earth are happy to be alive. But the benefits associated with stabilizing birthrates are also considerable—not least greater freedom for women and better health and opportunities for their children. The Baby Bust is nothing to fear.

In the US the young-old split will be 23 percent to 27 percent. In Europe the proportion will be 19 percent teens or younger versus 33 percent post-retirement. China is projected to become just as sclerotic: 17 percent young to 31 percent old.

Aging populations pose some real challenges, especially for industries that provide services either to the young or the old. About 5 percent of global gross domestic product is spent on education, for example; dwindling numbers of children could mean a lot of teachers will be out of work. Expenditures on the old, meanwhile, are sure to skyrocket. Pension spending in the European Union already equals about

12.5 percent of GDP. As the region's 65-plus population increases from a fifth to a third, either those payments will rise or old age will get considerably less comfortable. Supporting the aged is going to be a particular problem for developing countries, such as China, that have traditionally relied on families to look after their old and infirm. The burden on children may become unbearable without considerably expanded safety nets.

Yet the drop in birthrates is also cause for celebration. For a start, it reflects growing gender equality: Surveys suggest women usually want to have fewer children than do men. One major reason women around the world are choosing to have fewer babies is that the kids they do have are far more likely to survive and thrive. Global under-5 mortality declined by two-thirds from 1970 to 2011. Education rates, meanwhile, have been rising rapidly, especially among girls. We're close to seeing every child on the planet complete primary education. By 2050, the International Institute for Applied Systems Analysis predicts, more than four out of five adults worldwide will have completed junior, secondary, or higher education.

Global Study: World Not Ready for Aging Population

By Kristin Gelineau
Associated Press, September 30, 2013

The world is aging so fast that most countries are not prepared to support their swelling numbers of elderly people, according to a global study being issued Tuesday by the United Nations and an elder rights group.

The report ranks the social and economic well-being of elders in 91 countries, with Sweden coming out on top and Afghanistan at the bottom. It reflects what advocates for the old have been warning, with increasing urgency, for years: Nations are simply not working quickly enough to cope with a population graying faster than ever before. By the year 2050, for the first time in history, seniors older than 60 will outnumber children younger than 15.

Truong Tien Thao, who runs a small tea shop on the sidewalk near his home in Hanoi, Vietnam, is 65 and acutely aware that he, like millions of others, is plunging into old age without a safety net. He wishes he could retire, but he and his 61-year-old wife depend on the $50 a month they earn from the shop. And so every day, Thao rises early to open the stall at 6 a.m. and works until 2 p.m., when his wife takes over until closing.

"People at my age should have a rest, but I still have to work to make our ends meet," he says, while waiting for customers at the shop, which sells green tea, cigarettes and chewing gum. "My wife and I have no pension, no health insurance. I'm scared of thinking of being sick—I don't know how I can pay for the medical care."

Thao's story reflects a key point in the report, which was released early to The Associated Press: Aging is an issue across the world. Perhaps surprisingly, the report shows that the fastest aging countries are developing ones, such as Jordan, Laos, Mongolia, Nicaragua and Vietnam, where the number of older people will more than triple by 2050. All ranked in the bottom half of the index.

The Global AgeWatch Index (www.globalagewatch.org) was created by elder advocacy group HelpAge International and the U.N. Population Fund in part to address a lack of international data on the extent and impact of global aging. The index, released on the U.N.'s International Day of Older Persons, compiles data from the U.N., World Health Organization, World Bank and other global agencies, and analyzes income, health, education, employment and age-friendly environment in each country.

The index was welcomed by elder rights advocates, who have long complained that a lack of data has thwarted their attempts to raise the issue on government agendas.

"Unless you measure something, it doesn't really exist in the minds of decision-makers," said John Beard, Director of Aging and Life Course for the World Health Organization. "One of the challenges for population aging is that we don't even collect the data, let alone start to analyze it. . . . For example, we've been talking about how people are living longer, but I can't tell you people are living longer and sicker, or longer in good health."

The report fits into an increasingly complex picture of aging and what it means to the world. On the one hand, the fact that people are living longer is a testament to advances in health care and nutrition, and advocates emphasize that the elderly should be seen not as a burden but as a resource. On the other, many countries still lack a basic social protection floor that provides income, health care and housing for their senior citizens.

Afghanistan, for example, offers no pension to those not in the government. Life expectancy is 59 years for men and 61 for women, compared to a global average of 68 for men and 72 for women, according to U.N. data.

That leaves Abdul Wasay struggling to survive. At 75, the former cook and black-smith spends most of his day trying to sell toothbrushes and toothpaste on a busy street corner in Kabul's main market. The job nets him just $6 a day—barely enough to support his wife. He can only afford to buy meat twice a month; the family relies mainly on potatoes and curried vegetables.

"It's difficult because my knees are weak and I can't really stand for a long time," he says. "But what can I do? It's even harder in winter, but I can't afford treatment."

Although government hospitals are free, Wasay complains that they provide little treatment and hardly any medicine. He wants to stop working in three years, but is not sure his children can support him. He says many older people cannot find work because they are not strong enough to do day labor, and some resort to begging.

"You have to keep working no matter how old you are—no one is rich enough to stop," he says. "Life is very difficult."

Many governments have resisted tackling the issue partly because it is viewed as hugely complicated, negative and costly—which is not necessarily true, says Silvia Stefanoni, chief executive of HelpAge International. Japan and Germany, she says, have among the highest proportions of elders in the world, but also boast steady economies.

"There's no evidence that an aging population is a population that is economically damaged," she says.

Prosperity in itself does not guarantee protection for the old. The world's rising economic powers—the so-called BRICS nations of Brazil, Russia, India, China and South Africa—rank lower in the index than some poorer countries such as Uruguay and Panama.

However, the report found, wealthy nations are in general better prepared for aging than poorer ones. Sweden, where the pension system is now 100 years old, makes the top of the list because of its social support, education and health coverage, followed by Norway, Germany, the Netherlands and Canada. The United States comes in eighth.

Sweden's health system earns praise from Marianne Blomberg, an 80-year-old Stockholm resident.

"The health care system, for me, has worked extraordinarily well," she says. "I suffer from atrial fibrillation and from the minute I call emergency until I am discharged, it is absolutely amazing. I can't complain about anything—even the food is good."

Still, even in an elder-friendly country like Sweden, aging is not without its challenges. The Swedish government has suggested people continue working beyond 65, a prospect Blomberg cautiously welcomes but warns should not be a requirement. Blomberg also criticized the nation's finance minister, Anders Borg, for cutting taxes sharply for working Swedes but only marginally for retirees.

"I go to lectures and museums and the theater and those kinds of things, but I probably have to stop that soon because it gets terribly expensive," she says. "If you want to be active like me, it is hard. But to sit home and stare at the walls doesn't cost anything."

Aging Population More at Risk from Environmental Threats

By Gary Haq
The Conversation, October 28, 2013

The global population is aging. This is happening at a time when the rate and scale of human-induced environmental change is exceeding critical ecological limits, raising concerns over the consequences for society.

Our understanding of the interaction between an aging demographic and a changing environment is in its infancy. We've heard much about the impact an aging population will have on government spending on health, social services and pensions and the need for people to work longer before retiring. Yet one area that is not sufficiently addressed by the sustainable development agenda is the vulnerability of older people to environmental change.

Although comprehensive data is not always available regarding the age breakdown of deaths from flooding, heat waves, cold snaps, air pollution and storm events, there is increasing evidence to suggest most fatalities occur in vulnerable older people. This is particularly important in developing countries that lack the appropriate policies and frameworks to address the needs of an aging population. HelpAge International has highlighted the problem, especially in how to meet the needs of older people during natural disasters and emergencies.

Environmental threats include long-term exposure to toxic pollutants in air, water or food as well as sudden natural or human-induced shocks, such as heat waves, flooding and storms. The 2003 heat wave across Europe resulted in an estimated 14,800 deaths in France, of which 70 percent were people aged over 75. When floods, snowfall and bush fires disrupt services, the knock-on effects on everyday life are felt mainly by older people.

Older people are a diverse group and some are physically, financially and emotionally less able to cope than others. This is due to a number of factors such as ill health, income, geographic location, family support and friend networks, quality of public health infrastructure and access to relevant local information.

As people grow older their biological strength declines and they are susceptible to age-related chronic diseases, reduced mobility and strength, and loss of sight and hearing. These difficulties are further compounded by loss of income, and loss of a spouse, friends or family. All these factors will determine to what extent an individual's way of life is disrupted by environmental threats that force them to cope to avoid a decline in their wellbeing.

Research by the Stockholm Environment Institute at the University of York together with Simon Fraser University's Gerontology Research Centre in Vancouver, Canada, highlights the need to raise awareness of the effects of a changing global environment on older people.

Researchers undertook an international pilot survey of older people's attitudes in Australia, Canada, Sweden, USA and UK. The survey, while not completely representative of over 55s in these countries, gives an indication of the attitudes of a sample of older people.

The respondents were concerned about the environment, the threat of climate change, and energy and water security. They were pessimistic about the planet that their grandchildren and future generations will inherit, and believe environmental problems will have grown significantly by 2050. But respondents expressed limited concern on how climate change will impact their own lives, surprising given their vulnerabilities.

The report calls for policies to encourage older people to reduce their personal contribution to environmental change by promoting greener behavior, especially with regard to home energy use and transport. This could be helped by providing appropriate infrastructure, such as more energy efficient homes, and incentives to allow them to lead greener lifestyles. A 2010 SEI report presented the case for better engagement of older people on climate change.

So more needs to be done to ensure people reach later life with sufficient reserves to cope with present and future environmental threats. This will include ensuring they have access to local support networks, health care, information, coping skills and savings.

In addition, older people should be encouraged to take part in environmental volunteering. Their knowledge of the local environment, its unique elements or weak points, would mean they could use them to play a key role in developing local environmental protection strategies.

Our social and economic policies need to be shaped by a shared understanding of the aging of our society and environmental change. We can adapt to each of these separately, but that risks seeking solutions in one area that might have adverse effects on the other. Policies therefore need to be "age proofed" so that they can support older people through their lives, minimize the negative impact of environmental change, and harness the contribution older people can make to addressing a changing world.

Women Living Longer Worldwide

By Alexandra Sifferlin
Time, September 13, 2013

Fewer women are dying of childbirth-related health issues, but a World Health Organization (WHO) report says more can be done to improve women's health by addressing more than reproductive concerns.

The WHO found that globally, a woman's life expectancy at age 50—meaning the number of additional years she can expect to live based on current mortality trends for her country—has increased by an average of 2.3 years, with women in Brazil and Japan enjoying the greatest gains of four years or more and those in the US gaining just under the worldwide average at 2.2 years.

Most of the gains can be traced to improvements in reproductive health efforts that raise maternal and infant survival following childbirth, and lower deaths from preventable infectious and communicable diseases such as AIDS. And there is evidence that in lower income countries, mortality patterns are shifting to gradually resemble those of higher income nations, as health care services start to make inroads in controlling communicable diseases.

But the WHO says the gap between women living in high- and low-resource countries remains wide. Most healthcare services for women in developing nations focus on reproductive health, and the report predicted that overall, deaths from chronic conditions such as heart disease and diabetes, as well as from cancer, will increase—by eight million for heart disease, to make up 38 percent of total deaths among women by 2050, and by 3.6 million for cancer, to account for 17 percent of total deaths. Applying some of the lessons learned by developed nations could curb this rising tide, say the WHO report authors, as these diseases creep into the developing world. Adding strategies for preventing and managing heart disease such as screening for high blood pressure or elevated cholesterol levels could avoid some heart-related deaths, while monitoring for the first signs of tumors with mammograms and pap smears, as well as vaccinating against human papillomavirus (HPV), which contributes to cervical cancer, could also protect more women from late-stage cancers, which are more likely to result in death.

Even with such efforts in place, the WHO experts say public health officials shouldn't expect to see immediate benefits in the form of longer-lived women. The data also showed that in middle-income countries where more women are starting to die of chronic diseases typical of better-off nations, the women are dying earlier than their wealthier counterparts. That suggests that their health may be more vulnerable, due to factors such as stress, untreated conditions including hypertension, and poorer nutrition, that could make heart disease and cancer more deadly at earlier ages. "The trends described in this paper highlight the urgency of adapting health systems to better meet the changing health-care needs of women in low- and middle-income countries, primarily by improving the capacity to prevent and manage noncommunicable diseases," the report authors write.

There is evidence that such programs do work. In developed countries, drops in blood pressure, cholesterol and obesity—all risk factors for heart disease—had contributed to a decline in heart-related deaths among women, and rates of breast, stomach, colon and cervical cancers have also declined, helping more women to live longer. But tobacco use among women hasn't changed enough to push lung cancer rates down in developed countries, which may contribute to smaller gains in longevity in countries like the US.

Major Study Finds That Overall Population Health in US Has Improved, but Has Not Kept Pace with Other Wealthy Nations

Journal of the American Medical Association, September 10, 2013

In a major study that includes data on the status of population health from 34 countries from 1990–2010, overall population health improved in the US during this period, including an increase in life expectancy; however, illness and chronic disability now account for nearly half of the health burden and improvements in the US have not kept pace with advances in population health in other wealthy nations, according to a study published online by *JAMA*. The study is being published online in connection with an event at the White House and the National Press Club regarding the state and trends of health in the US. Dr. Murray and *JAMA* Editor-in-Chief Howard Bauchner, M.D., will be among the speakers at the National Press Club.

"The United States spends the most per capita on health care across all countries, lacks universal health coverage, and lags behind other high-income countries for life expectancy and many other health outcome measures. High costs with mediocre population health outcomes at the national level are compounded by marked disparities across communities, socioeconomic groups, and race and ethnicity groups," according to background information in the article. "With increasing focus on population health outcomes that can be achieved through better public health, multisectoral action, and medical care, it is critical to determine which diseases, injuries, and risk factors are related to the greatest losses of health and how these risk factors and health outcomes are changing over time."

Christopher J. L. Murray, M.D., D.Phil., of the Institute for Health Metrics and Evaluation, University of Washington, Seattle, and the US Burden of Disease Collaborators, conducted a study to identify the leading diseases, injuries, and risk factors associated with the burden of disease in the United States and how these health burdens have changed over the last 2 decades, and compared these outcomes with those of 34 Organization for Economic Co-operation and Development (OECD) countries. The researchers used the systematic analysis of descriptive epidemiology of 291 diseases and injuries, 1,160 sequelae of these diseases and injuries, and 67 risk factors or clusters of risk factors from 1990 to 2010 for 187 countries developed for the Global Burden of Disease 2010 Study.

Years of life lost (YLLs) due to premature mortality were computed by multiplying the number of deaths at each age by a reference life expectancy at that age.

Years lived with disability (YLDs) were calculated by multiplying prevalence by the disability weight (based on population-based surveys) for each sequela; disability in this study refers to any short- or long-term loss of health. Disability-adjusted life-years (DALYs) were estimated as the sum of YLDs and YLLs. Healthy life expectancy (HALE) was used to summarize overall population health, accounting for both length of life and levels of ill health experienced at different ages.

The researchers found that US life expectancy for both sexes combined increased from 75.2 years in 1990 to 78.2 years in 2010; during the same period, healthy life expectancy increased from 65.8 years to 68.1 years. In 2010, diseases and injuries with the largest number of years of life lost due to premature death were ischemic heart disease, lung cancer, stroke, chronic obstructive pulmonary disease, and road injury (which includes bicycle, motorcycle, motor vehicle, and pedestrian injury). Age-standardized YLL rates increased for Alzheimer disease, drug use disorders, chronic kidney disease, kidney cancer, and falls.

In 2010, diseases with the largest number of years lived with disability were low back pain, major depressive disorder, other musculoskeletal disorders, neck pain, and anxiety disorders. "As the US population has aged, years lived with disability have comprised a larger share of disability-adjusted life-years than have YLLs. The leading risk factors related to disability-adjusted life-years were dietary risks, tobacco smoking, high body mass index, high blood pressure, high fasting plasma glucose, physical inactivity, and alcohol use," the authors write. With an increase in life expectancy and the number of years lived with disability for the average American, "individuals in the United States are living longer but are not necessarily in good health."

Morbidity and chronic disability now account for nearly half of the health burden in the United States. "Mental and behavioral disorders, musculoskeletal disorders, vision and hearing loss, anemias, and neurological disorders all contribute to the increases in chronic disability. Research and development has been much more successful at finding solutions for cardiovascular diseases and some cancers and their associated risk factors than for these leading causes of disability," the researchers note. "The progressive and likely irreversible shift in the disease burden profile to these causes also has implications for the type of resources needed in the US health system."

In the last two decades, improvements in population health in the United States did not keep pace with advances in population health in other wealthy nations. "Among 34 OECD countries between 1990 and 2010, the US rank for the age-standardized death rate changed from 18th to 27th, for the age-standardized YLL rate from 23rd to 28th, for the age-standardized years lived with disability rate from 5th to 6th, for life expectancy at birth from 20th to 27th, and for healthy life expectancy from 14th to 26th."

"Regular assessments of the local burden of disease and matching information on health expenditures for the same disease and injury categories could allow for a more direct assessment of how changes in health spending have affected or, indeed, not affected changes in the burden of disease and may provide insights into where the US health care system could most effectively invest its resources to obtain maximum benefits for the nation's population health. In many cases, the best investments for improving population health would likely be public health programs and multisectoral action to address risks such as physical inactivity, diet, ambient particulate pollution, and alcohol and tobacco consumption," the authors conclude.

How Growth of Elderly Population in US Compares with Other Countries

By Francesca Colombo
PBS.org, May 24, 2013

Editor's Note: This article is part of a series in which the PBS NewsHour and the Organization for Economic Co-operation and Development, or OECD, explore how health care and health policy in OECD's 34 member countries compare with the United States. Below, Francesca Colombo, an OECD expert on the economic impact of aging, examines the rapid growth of the elderly population in many nations—and what might be done to help alleviate some of the looming costs.

As populations age and require expensive health care, we must find cost-effective ways to deliver it.

By 2050, more than 32 million Americans will be over the age of 80, and the share of the 80-plus generation will have doubled to 7.4 percent. Across the 34 OECD countries, the share of people over the age of 80 is projected to grow even faster, from 4 percent today to almost 10 percent in the same time period.

While more and more elderly people will still enjoy active, healthy lives and contribute to society, many are likely to have at least one chronic condition. Today, three out of four Americans aged 65 years and older have to cope with health concerns such as cardiovascular disease, diabetes, cancer or chronic respiratory diseases.

The biggest impact will be on their families. Across OECD countries, more than one in 10 adults over the age of 50 takes care of aging family members. Almost two-thirds are women, and their work is usually not paid.

These family caregivers are the backbone of any care system for elderly. In the US, the economic value of their service is estimated at $350 billion a year. However, family caregivers who spend at least 20 hours per week taking care of a relative are less likely to have a paid job and hence are more likely to be poor when they retire. They also run a high risk of developing mental health problems because of the stress of caring.

Counseling, the possibility of taking a break and flexible work arrangements would help the families, employers looking for skilled and reliable workers and tax-payers who would otherwise have to finance professional health care services.

The growing number of elderly will also affect health and social care services. Expensive medical services such as diagnostic procedures, treatment of chronic conditions and hospitalization, combined with the cost of care services, will further strain both government and family budgets.

The OECD estimates that the public cost of providing care to the old and frail will more than double—to 3 percent of GDP in 2050—driven largely by the cost of recruiting qualified personal. It is difficult to recruit workers to care for people with disabilities or chronic illnesses and even harder to keep them. In the US, more than two-thirds of home-health aides stay less than two years, and 70 percent of certified nursing assistants change jobs every year. The direct cost of this turnover is huge—some $2,500 per worker. With the demand for care workers set to double by 2050, pressure on wages will rise, leading to even higher costs.

To address this challenge, countries should take a three-prong approach: They should invest more in improving the quality of care and preventing the need for care. Regular exercise, combined with sufficient calcium and reducing hazards in the home can mean fewer broken bones. Among people over 65, falls—many of them preventable—are the most frequent cause of injury and hospital admissions due to trauma. The medical costs of falls in the US represent an estimated $30 billion annually.

A second strategy would be to encourage people who suffer from disabilities to continue to live in their homes, with a higher quality of life and lower costs for the health care system. Across OECD countries, only one-third of dependent elderly people live in residential care homes but they account for almost two-thirds of the costs.

And lastly, staying active as long as possible is important, but when health fails, social systems should have a responsibility to pick up the extra costs. Because the pensions of even those in the middle class might not be sufficient to cover costs for care, sharing the burden is important. In addition to public systems, most OECD countries provide help for elderly in need of care; developing a private market with simple insurance products is also important as cost pressures continue to rise.

Do Other Countries Take Better Care of the Elderly?

By Miriam Goodman
Examiner, November 9, 2011

Sometimes we hear a story repeated so many times that we never doubt that it is true and it becomes a "well-known fact." However, we also know that there are many myths that become truths and most of us never stop to wonder if perhaps they were once true but that they no longer apply.

One such "myth" is that Asian countries take better care of their elderly than we do. I am sure I am not the only one who has heard that Japanese families embrace their elder members, bringing them into their homes and caring for them as they age. Sounds nice, but is it really true?

According to a recent article in Reuters, aging Japanese citizens are a new social problem. Almost 5 million older people live alone in Japan and with the growing number of aging people, more and more live alone and unfortunately are dying alone. Often their bodies go undiscovered for days.

Local authorities in Japan are getting together with agencies such as the post office to check in on seniors, adding to their social contact and possibly enhancing their lives. In the Shinagawa ward of Tokyo, at least 25 elderly people died alone last year. Now postmen will make sure nothing is amiss when they visit the homes of the elderly. They can contact a welfare officer if they think something is wrong.

Social welfare and public health officials say that a deep social Japanese reluctance to interfere in the lives of others means that some people go for days without talking to anyone. Also, there is a gradual shifting away from "traditional" ideas about community bonds resulting in increasing isolation instead.

A Japanese realtor hopes to help some elderly people by promoting the idea of house sharing between single mothers and seniors. They see this as a win-win for seniors who might have extra room in their homes and mothers looking for affordable housing. The CEO of the realty firm, Hiroshi Kuwayama, said that he realizes that "younger single mothers are more flexible but it takes time for the elderly to accept the concept of house sharing." Still, he hopes it will work.

Another Japanese firm, this one delivering daily meals to seniors, has trained delivery personnel in basic first aid skills and tells them to check to see if the customers are okay. While they are not doctors, they are often the first to find a body or a customer who is ill.

A social commentator, Tomoko Inukai, said that a "flaw in Japanese society is that we don't look each other in the eye when we see people in the streets. We need to rethink the Japanese fear of interacting with others."

Are Americans so different? I don't think so. Let's each decide to look out for elderly neighbors and friends this holiday season. That's the true spirit of holidays.

Bank on It: Is This Volunteer Program the Solution to China's Elder-Care Crisis?

By Benjamin Shobert
Slate, November 5, 2013

We have become so accustomed to thinking about China as an almost unstoppable economic juggernaut that we have overlooked one of the most basic ways China's ascent could be arrested: the speed with which it will grow old. In 2012, 10 percent of China's population was 60 or older; by 2050, the percentage will triple. In absolute numbers, that's an increase from 128 million to 431 million. Globally, this will make China the country with the largest elderly population by far. Estimates are that by 2040 China will have more dementia patients than exist in the rest of the developed world—this in a country in which the very word in Mandarin for *dementia* is stigmatized. China needs solutions to its aging problem, and fast.

The majority of China's elderly are geographically separated from their children. Families have been split apart, as young adults have moved away from their rural homes to urban areas in search of employment. In addition, while China's one-child policy was designed to stop a particular demographic concern (overpopulation), it turned out to create another, what the Chinese call their "4:2:1" problem. The "4:2:1" refers to the painful reality across China that every one adult child today has two parents and four grandparents to care for, because filial piety remains a widespread and deeply held Confucian value. Traditionally, multiple generations would cohabitate, allowing the young to take care of the old. But the combined pressures created by the urban-rural geographic separation and the 4:2:1 problem make it nearly impossible for them to honor traditional values and family expectations.

Most Chinese expect their government to come up with a solution. After all, of what benefit is the country's economic growth if it does not provide better health care for all and support for the elderly in particular? The choking smog that wraps its fingers around China's cities and the contaminated food and water supplies are constant reminders of the sacrifices the average Chinese family has been asked to make at the altar of economic progress. Today, many across China are far from certain the sacrifice is going to be worth the price. This realization has driven China's central government to make massive investments in its health care system, at the same time it is pursuing innovative ideas to deal with the country's aging. One such innovation being tested around the country: volunteer banks.

The idea is simple enough. As an adult worker, you agree to get a basic level of training on senior care from a government agency. In turn, you volunteer in the homes of the elderly as you are able, providing companionship and basic care services such as cleaning, shopping, cooking, counseling, and personal hygiene. The government records the number of hours you work over your lifetime, until you reach retirement age and begin to need care yourself. At that point, you are able to debit against the total number of hours you volunteered for your own care needs.

The concept appears to have been first tested by social entrepreneur Feng Kexiong in Chongqing. Feng had a little red book, but instead of Maoist poetry, his held the number of hours volunteers worked with the elderly. The idea was that the program could grow in size over time until volunteers would be able to debit from their accumulated hours when needed.

For Feng's idea to scale, the Chinese government had to get involved. The plan required systems to give caregivers background checks, collect and investigate complaints from the elderly, and ensure no one is abused. The bank of hours itself had to go into a database of some kind, and an exchange mechanism put in place that allows for credits to be collected and debits to be deducted. However, when measured against other, much more costly programs—such as building new housing for the elderly or providing caregivers—the cost of administering and maintaining a volunteer bank is small.

Policymakers in China understand all too well that the majority of solutions they will be able to pursue are probably not going to create commercial opportunities. Yes, the pharmaceutical industry will benefit as new drugs are consumed by an increasingly older Chinese population. Equally, the wealthy and upper middle class across China will find they can access a growing set of retirement housing products that will bear striking similarity to options available in the United States and Europe. But the sheer size of China's aging population, coupled to the fact that most of the country's elderly are poor and live in rural areas, means it must find solutions that blend private engagement with public oversight.

Would something similar work in the United States? The demographic burdens in both countries are severe, but America is growing old well after it grew rich. The same cannot be said of China. As a consequence, China not only needs innovative solutions to its aging problem—it needs those solutions to be extremely cost-effective. And what's more cost-effective than volunteers?

America's accumulated wealth and cultural approach to giving back make a similar approach such as China's volunteer banks a bit more difficult to pull off. We want to believe that the combined efforts of personal savings and government-led health care and pension programs such as Medicare and Social Security will be adequate to address our needs during retirement. Yet as every passing debt ceiling crisis illustrates, portions of America's electorate are deeply divided over the sustainability of entitlements. It seems all but inevitable that changes to both programs will come, which in turn will force people to rethink what they need from family and community. Volunteering has deep roots in America, yet the idea that a new program coordinated by the federal government could get through Washington anytime soon seems frustratingly quaint.

That China will get old is a demographic certainty. That it will get rich is not certain at all. The country will get old years before it solves basic questions about its national health care and pension systems. Because of these concerns, China is more willing than the United States to try innovative community-centered ideas such as the volunteer bank simply because the country has no other choice. Yet if China's embrace of an idea such Feng's volunteer bank proves successful, it may touch on a simple truth: Government can be a powerful force in shaping how society responds to crises like aging, even if it does nothing more than organize and oversee a community's collective efforts. America's spirit of volunteering is certainly strong and vibrant enough to respond to this challenge. But whether our political system is capable of similar innovative thinking seems uncertain.

Asia's New Aging Rich Break Family Ties for Gilded Retirement

By Rina Chandran
Bloomberg.com, November 20, 2013

After P. S. Ramachandran turned 80, he and his wife decided it was time to stop living alone. Rather than take the traditional path of moving in with their son, the Ramachandrans chose an option once rare in India: a retirement community.

"We wanted to be independent," said Ramachandran, now 85, a former government official who moved to the Brindavan Senior Citizen Foundation's retirement village overlooking the Nilgiri hills near Coimbatore city in southern India. "We have company and everything we need here, and activities to keep us busy as long as we're physically able."

Rising wealth from the region's rapid growth in recent decades is changing the way many Asians grow old, breaking up the traditional family unit as children move to the cities or go abroad in search of better-paid jobs. The change is a new source of business for companies from India's Tata Housing Development Co., Malaysia Pacific Corp. and Singapore's ECON Healthcare Group, which are constructing retirement villages for the wealthy that offer cafes, tennis courts and yoga.

The developers are following companies from adult-diaper makers to holiday operators that have swooped in on Asia's silver economy, catering to the region's growing cohorts of over-60s. Excluding Japan, the market will be worth about $2 trillion by 2017—more than the current Indian economy—according to Singapore-based market researcher Ageing Asia Pte.

Filial Piety

"Filial piety is still big in Asia, but it has less of a role now," said Janice Chia, founder and managing director at Ageing Asia. "My grandparents were satisfied with staying home, watching a bit of TV, walking in the park and looking after the grandkids. But my parents want to travel, keep their minds active and don't necessarily want to live with their children."

While populations in emerging Asia are still among the youngest in the world, in India the proportion of people above the age of 60 will more than double to 18 percent by 2050, from about 8 percent in 2010, according to United Nations data. In Southeast Asia the ratio will rise to 22 percent from 8 percent, while in China it will increase to a third from 12 percent.

The numbers make these markets compelling, Chia said. India is forecast to have about 118 million people aged over 60 years by 2017, more than double the number in Japan, while China's senior population will number 217 million, according to Ageing Asia's estimates based on US Census Bureau data. Indonesia's senior population may reach 24 million by 2017.

More Wealth

An increasing number of those retirees will be wealthy. The Asia-Pacific region will see a 75 percent increase in millionaires over the next five years to 11.5 million in 2018, with China alone seeing an 88 percent rise, according to Credit Suisse AG.

"So far, Asian economies have largely been reaping the benefits of the demographic dividend and governments have not really had to think about the aging population," said Dylan Eades, a Melbourne-based economist at Australia and New Zealand Bank Ltd. "There's quite a significant economic opportunity for private companies in marketing to wealthier retirees."

At the Brindavan complex, where the Ramachandrans live, options include one-, two-, or three-bedroom villas on a 20-year lease, which can be extended, according to the company's website. The residents have access to a maid service and an on-site nurse, with daily visits from a doctor.

Heated Pool

Malaysia Pacific's Platinum Residence in Iskandar, a special economic zone in Johor state, touts its jogging tracks, heated indoor pool and close proximity to an 18-hole golf course. Max India Ltd.'s Antara Senior Living retirement village in the Northern Indian hill town of Dehradun promises "holistic living" with a temple, a spa and an herb garden.

"We're not looking to change attitudes of people who still live in large joint families," said Tara Singh Vachani, chief executive officer at Antara. "We're here to provide options for those who already live independently and are able to afford the price point of more than $200,000. Even if less than 1 percent of the population over the age of 60 meets our criteria, that's still a fairly large market."

Most of the demand in India is from people in the mid- to high-income segments in cities, who are able to pay 6 million rupees ($95,000) to 10 million rupees, said Ashutosh Limaye, Mumbai-based head of research and real estate intelligence services at Jones Lang LaSalle Inc. A growing market is non-resident Indians who have spent their working lives abroad and want to come home for a comfortable retirement, he said.

Sociological Shift

Advertisements for the 180 units of Tata Housing's first senior-living community, Riva Residences in Bangalore, generated more than 4,000 inquiries in the first month, said Chief Executive Officer Brotin Banerjee. The potential demand in

India is for more than 300,000 units, with only about 3,000 currently available, he said.

Governments that once left elder care to families are beginning to react to the change, from subsidizing land for developers to laws that protect the elderly.

In China, where urbanization and the one-child policy led to more seniors living alone, the government last year passed a law banning "ill-treatment and abandonment" of the elderly.

For the vast majority, private retirement homes will remain out of reach, keeping the responsibility for care-giving in the home and reinforcing the traditional family model. A fifth of Asia's population lives in extreme poverty, earning less than $1.25 a day, according to the Asian Development Bank.

Those opting for private retirement communities "will always only be a small percentage," said Ageing Asia's Chia.

In an online poll by the ADB, 48 percent of respondents said children should take care of their parents, while 38 percent said it should be the government. Only 14 percent said the elderly should look after themselves.

Marigold Hotel

Some governments are courting retirees from wealthier nations, touting exotic locales and cheaper living costs, a trend popularized by John Madden's 2011 film The Best Exotic Marigold Hotel, which chronicled the lives of British pensioners who move to a retirement hotel in Jaipur, India.

Thailand offers renewable one-year visas to older expatriates, while Sri Lanka's My Dream Home visa for expats over 55 highlights safety and kindness to foreigners, alongside opportunities for snorkeling and fishing.

Malaysia's My Second Home Program gives expats over the age of 50 a 10-year multiple-entry visa that can be renewed every 10 years, and grants tax exemptions.

"From a practical perspective, it makes perfect sense for some Singaporean retirees who can live far more comfortably in Johor Baru or Iskandar in Malaysia," said Theresa W. Devasahayam, a researcher at the Institute of Southeast Asian Studies in Singapore. "But it's also unfortunate because there is a sense that you're being pushed out of your own country because you can't afford to retire here anymore."

For others, it's the children who move abroad, such as Tara Chandramouli, a property and business adviser to the Australian government, who is based in Melbourne. Her parents Seethalakshmy Nagarajan, 78, and Ramnath, 83, live in Ananya Shelters Ltd.'s retirement village in Southern India.

"They're doing things that they perhaps didn't do in their younger days because of the pressure of raising a family," said Chandramouli, who visits them three or four times a year. "My kids don't think this is unusual, they think it's the norm."

Aging in Ghana: Is it Indeed a Blessing or What?

By Alhaji Alhasan Abdulai
GhanaWeb, November 18, 2013

In Africa, old age goes with wisdom and a store of knowledge. However, in Ghana and other parts of the world, aging is becoming problematic in the areas of recognition and honor in public and even at home. By law, at 60, all persons in public service must give way to the young ones.

The retired officials are often hounded out first by colleagues who wish to know when their colleague would leave the system. Whether they will leave or not, the retirees are prepared for retirement. After spending their pension entitlements, they are then faced with aging blues, lack of adequate medical care, perhaps with no good home care and good companionship.

Ghana is known worldwide as a leading hospitable nation. Almost all manner of persons in Ghana and abroad are treated with lots of honor. While in time past, courtesy and honor given to the aged is fast fading off. Even though the aged are old men and women who bear their own names, the generic names for them at home and in the public places are "old man" and "old lady." In not a distant past, the honor done the aged included the younger persons giving up their seats on public transport and public places, but this is largely not the case today.

The guiltiest of these are some tro-tro drivers and mates and some traders. Heads of departments, ministers and the heads of state or presidents (however young and without their knowledge) are often called old men and women.

Ordinarily, there is nothing wrong with an aging person being addressed as such. However, the tag is given to the older persons in a derogatory manner that often makes them sad. Some of the older persons who are on pension but have to work often regret venturing out to town to transact business or visit friends and relatives.

The time has come for the government to turn attention on the myriads of problems confronting the aged. The young must be sensitized to know how to treat older persons at home and in the public places by being courteous to them. The ministry of Gender, Children and Social Protection under Nana Oye Lithur is capable of dealing with issues of aging in Ghana.

Older persons after serving the nation deserve to be given all the necessary assistance towards their health and happiness.

Officialdom is aware of this and are said to be preparing to do something about it.

Currently, a policy of aging is being prepared by government to deal with the problems facing the aging population.

Mr. Moses Asaga, former Minister of Employment and Social Welfare, once said government would present a bill to Parliament on the National Ageing Policy this year to legalize the establishment of the National Council on Ageing.

The policy when passed into law would ensure the implementation of recommendations and coordination of government activities related to the elderly in a more organized approach.

As a follow up, the Ministry would develop and implement a pilot social pension scheme for the older persons without formal social security in 2013 and would be done side by side with the strengthening of existing social security schemes to provide income security for older persons. But the problem is that internationally, as in Ghana, the number of the aging is growing rapidly.

Information from the Ghana Statistical Service showed that life expectancy at birth had increased to 60.7 years for males and 61.8 years for females and that life expectancy at the age of 60 had been estimated at 17.03 for males and 19.49 years for females.

Persons in the country were expected to live up to 77.03 years, and the 2010 Census results indicated that the population of persons 60 years and above had increased to 1,643,978 representing 6.7 percent of the total population.

Unlike most other population groups such as children and the youth, there is relatively little interest shown about the situation of older people. The absence of comprehensive information means that aging is poorly understood and, as a result, adequate resources are not allocated to meet the needs of the older population. The absence of an agreed definition of "older person" to achieve consistency with international conceptual understanding exacerbates the problem as comparative analysis is difficult even where data exists.

Available data, however, indicates that the number of persons over 60 will increase from about 600 million in 2000 to almost 2 billion in 2050 and the proportion of persons defined as older is projected to increase globally from 10 percent in 1998 to 15 percent in 2025. The increase will be greatest and most rapid in developing countries where the older population is expected to quadruple during the next 50 years. In Africa, the proportion is expected to double by 2050. In sub-Saharan Africa, where the struggle with the HIV/AIDS pandemic and with economic and social hardship continues, the percentage is expected to reach half the level. Such a demographic transformation has profound consequences for every aspect of individual, community, national and international life.

It is evident that population aging will become a major issue in developing countries, which are projected to age swiftly in the first half of the twenty-first century. The proportion of older persons is expected to rise from 8 to 19 percent. The fastest growing group of the older population is the oldest old, that is, those who are 80-years-old or more. In 2000, the oldest old numbered 70 million and their numbers are projected to increase to more than five times that over the next 50 years. Another major demographic difference relates to gender. Older women outnumber older men. The gender dimension of aging must be a priority for global and national policy action.

There are also rural and urban demographic differences in aging. Currently, an overwhelming proportion of older persons in developed countries live in areas classified as urban while the majority of older persons in developing countries live in rural areas. This trend is expected to continue in the future.

In Ghana, the situation is not very different. Available statistics from the population census of 2000 and other surveys on population indicate that the majority of people in Ghana (64 percent) live and work in rural areas where the greater proportion of older persons also reside.

Available data indicate that older persons aged 65 years and above constitute 5 percent of the Ghanaian population (GSS, 2002). This figure is among the highest in Africa. Most of these elderly persons reside in rural areas. There is also evidence to show that the aged in Ghana has been increasing over the years. The 2000 Population and Housing Census Report indicate that the proportion of the elderly (65 years and above) formed 5.3 percent of the population, an increase from 4.0 percent in 1984. The percentage increase of the aged population between 1960 and 1970 was 12.5 percent. This decreased to 11.1 percent between 1970 and 1984. However, between 1984 and 2000 the figure increased to 32 percent. The aging of the population is also reflected in the increase of the median age from 18.1 years in 1984 to 19.4 years in 2000. It is established that the aging of Ghana's population has been precipitated by rapid fertility decline and improvements in public health services, personal hygiene, sanitation and nutrition.

Another important issue of demographic concern is that the proportion of the elderly population in Ghana as a developing country is growing much more rapidly than those in the developed countries. In the developed countries, the demographic transition process leading to an aging population took place over the span of about a century (Angel and Angel, 1997; 1982; Olson, 1994), giving ample time to prepare and cope with the increased numbers of elderly persons. In addition, the process of industrialization after the Second World War was enhanced by the "Baby Boom" in these countries, which made it possible for them to utilize effectively the large youthful population that entered the labor market at the time.

In Africa, this process of demographic transition is occurring in a few decades (Mbamaonyeukwu, 2001). Though the transition provided large numbers of youth, it was not accompanied by the needed process of industrialization to absorb the youth. As a result, Africa is not able to effectively utilize its window of opportunity, which is the youth, for development to benefit the aged.

Regional demographic dynamics in Ghana follow similar trends. In all the ten regions of the country, older persons aged 65 years and above have been increasing. Most regions, however, have a greater proportion of surviving females above 65 years than males. The age structure of districts are also characteristic of the population experiencing rapid growth, with some districts as high as 8.8 percent with larger proportions of older persons aged 65 years and older accounting for 4.1 percent.

Aging and the Development Challenge

In the recent past, older persons were accorded a high-ranking place in the traditional Ghanaian society, but in the process of social change resulting from urbanization, migration and other global issues, traditional norms have been affected in several ways. These social transformations as well as poor infrastructure development in the rural areas have affected the patterns of social interactions and relationships in families and communities and consequently how they relate to older persons. Thus migration in all forms create social distance and, with it, social disengagement and a systematic reduction in certain forms of interactions with families. The situation of migrant workers and aging is also of great concern.

Older persons in Ghana are showing gradually signs of loneliness, poverty and neglect. The impact of this social neglect is, however, felt the most among older women (Apt, 1996), who are overburdened with widowhood rites and responsibilities, social and cultural discrimination (e.g., witchcraft) and in recent times the care of HIV/AIDS orphans and people living with AIDS. Thus not only are older people at risk of contracting HIV but they are the main providers of care in some cases to those affected by AIDS and for orphaned children.

The issue of aging is important and a matter of concern to all who would definitely grow old. Therefore as we give support to children and youth, there is the need for the government, with the help of parliament and the civil society bodies in Ghana, to expedite action to offer the needed assistance to aging.

Bibliography

❖

Binstock, Robert H, Linda K. George, Stephen J. Cutler, Jon Hendricks, and James H. Schulz. *Handbook of Aging and the Social Sciences*. 7th ed. Amsterdam: Academic, 2011. Print.

Blieszner, Rosemary, and Victoria H. Bedford. *Handbook of Families and Aging*. 2nd ed. Santa Barbara: Praeger, 2012.

Coughlin, Joseph F, and Lisa A. D'Ambrosio. *Aging America and Transportation: Personal Choices and Public Policy*. New York: Springer, 2012. Print.

Crisis of Caregiving: Social Welfare Policy in the United States. S.l.: Macmillan, 2013. Print.

Cruikshank, Margaret. *Learning to Be Old: Gender, Culture, and Aging*. 3rd ed. Lanham: Rowman, 2013. Print.

David, Steven, Douglas Kimmel, and Tara Rose, eds. *Lesbian, Gay, Bisexual, and Transgender Aging: Research and Clinical Perspectives*. New York: Columbia UP, 2006. Print.

Durrett, Charles. *The Senior Cohousing Handbook: A Community Approach to Independent Living*. 2nd ed. Gabriola Island: New Society, 2013. Print.

Glasgow, Nina, E H. Berry, and Edmund J. V. Oh, eds. *Rural Aging in 21st Century America*. Dordrecht: Springer, 2013. Print.

Loue, Sana, Martha Sajatovic, and Siran M. Koroukian, eds. *Encyclopedia of Aging and Public Health*. New York: Springer, 2008. Print.

Mehrotra, Chandra M., and Lisa S. Wagner. *Aging and Diversity*. 2nd ed. Abingdon: Routledge, 2009. Print.

Morgan, Leslie A, Suzanne Kunkel, and Leslie A. Morgan. *Aging, Society, and the Life Course*. 4th ed. New York: Springer, 2011. Print.

Pobee, Kojo. *Cut Through the Noise: Nursing Home Care in the Baby Boomer Era*. Charleston: Advantage, 2013. Print.

Robine, Jean-Marie, Carol Jagger, and Eileen M. Crimmins. *Annual Review of Gerontology and Geriatrics: Volume 33, 2013*. New York: Springer, 2013. Print.

Rowles, Graham D, and Miriam Bernard. *Environmental Gerontology: Making Meaningful Places in Old Age*. New York: Springer, 2013. Print.

Schulz, James H, and Robert H. Binstock. *Aging Nation: The Economics and Politics of Growing Older in America*. Westport: Praeger, 2006. Print.

Sullivan, Dennis B. *Senior and Boomers Guide to Health Care Reform and Avoiding Nursing Home Poverty*. Conshohocken: Infinity, 2013. Print.

Wilmoth, Janet M, and Kenneth F. Ferraro. *Gerontology: Perspectives and Issues*. 4th ed. New York: Springer, 2013. Print.

Websites

❖

AARP
http://www.aarp.org

Formerly the American Association of Retired Persons, AARP offers an abundance of services and support, including health insurance and savings plans, insurance plans, discounts on goods and travel for members, online job resources, and online tools to research and plan for caregiving. With an estimated 38 million members, it is one of the largest American membership organizations.

American Society on Aging
http://www.asaging.org/

With a stated focus on a diverse aging society, this organization and its website offers information through several media, including web seminars, videos, and blogs, and covers topics pertinent to multicultural, religious, and LGBT communities.

Gerontological Society of America (GSA)
http://www.geron.org/

The Gerontological Society of America is a leading supporter of gerontological research and one of the leading advocates for aging education in America, with strategic focus on the growing demands of the aging Baby Boomer population.

International Association of Gerontology and Geriatrics (IAGG)
http://www.iagg.info/

The IAGG is the global body dedicated to research in aging and the promotion of aging education. The website contains a wealth of literature, including clinical papers, training documentation from courses on aging, and scientific lectures on gerontology and senior health.

Medicare.gov
http://www.medicare.gov/

This is the official government portal for Medicare, the federal health program that provides access to health insurance for certain residents aged sixty-five and older. As of 2013, approximately 50 million Americans were provided health insurance through Medicare. It remains a controversial program, particularly in regard to cost and sustainability.

National Council on Aging (NCOA)
http://www.ncoa.org/

This nonprofit advocacy group works toward improving the lifestyles, employment, health, and independence of older Americans and offers numerous online services and resources, including mortgage counseling, benefits counseling, employment programs, and health-awareness materials.

National Institute on Aging (NIA)
http://www.nia.nih.gov/

Funded through the National Institutes of Health (NIH), the NIA aims to be a leading body in aging research and training and remains the primary designated government agency on Alzheimer research.

Retirement Research Foundation
http://www.rrf.org/

This foundation, which is dedicated to improving quality of life for older Americans, is a leading provider of grants and funding to benefit senior citizens and offers a wealth of age-related resources on their website.

Index

❖